Rejection and Emancipation

Edited by
Michael Butler and Malcolm Pender

Rejection and Emancipation examines developments in writing in German-speaking Switzerland within the context of Swiss social, political and cultural evolution since 1945. The discussion pays tribute to the achievements and international stature of the two founding fathers of contemporary Swiss letters, Max Frisch and Friedrich Dürrenmatt, and goes on to focus principally on ten representative writers who have followed in their footsteps. Less well known outside Switzerland, these writers bear witness in differing ways and from different generational perspectives to a thriving literary culture in a society whose traditions are being profoundly challenged by rapid political and economic change in Europe. Against this background the Swiss confederation celebrates in 1991 the 700th anniversary of its foundation. *Rejection and Emancipation* seeks to set such change and celebration in clearer focus.

Michael Butler is Professor of Modern German Literature, University of Birmingham.
Malcolm Pender is Reader in German Studies, University of Strathclyde.

Rejection and Emancipation
*Writing in German-speaking Switzerland
1945–1991*

Edited by
Michael Butler and Malcolm Pender

OSWALD WOLFF BOOKS
BERG
New York / Oxford
Distributed exclusively in the US and Canada by
St Martin's Press, New York

First published in 1991 by
Berg Publishers Limited
Editorial offices:
165 Taber Avenue, Providence, RI 02906, USA
150 Cowley Road, Oxford, OX4 1JJ, UK

British Library Cataloguing in Publication Data
Rejection and emancipation: Writing in
German-speaking Switzerland, 1945–1991.
  I. Butler, Michael   II. Pender, Malcolm
  830.09

  ISBN 0–85496–748–6

Library of Congress Cataloging-in-Publication Data
Rejection and Emancipation: writing in German-speaking
  Switzerland, 1945–1991 / edited by Michael Butler and
  Malcolm Pender.
    p.   cm.
  "Oswald Wolff books."
  Includes bibliographical references.
  ISBN 0–85496–748–6
  1. Swiss literature (German)—20th century—History and criticism.
  I. Butler, Michael.   II. Pender, Malcolm.
  PT3868.R44   1991
  830.9'9494'09045—dc20   91–9185
                                                                       CIP

Printed in Great Britain by Billing & Sons Ltd, Worcester

Contents

Acknowledgements   vii

Introduction   1

I   The Context

1. The Political and Economic Development of
   Switzerland 1945–1991
   Clive H. Church   7

2. Trends in Writing in German-speaking
   Switzerland since 1945
   Malcolm Pender   24

II   Challenge and Example

3. Max Frisch and Friedrich Dürrenmatt
   Michael Butler   41

III   New Directions

4. Otto F. Walter: Literature and the Strategies of
   Revolt
   Ian Hilton   59

5. Peter Bichsel: 'In Geschichten leben'
   Ronald Speirs   74

6. Adolf Muschg: Glimpses of Freedom
   H. Morgan Waidson   93

7. Hugo Loetscher: The Committed Intellect
   Hans Seelig   106

8. Kurt Marti: 'Chaos in die Ordnung bringen'
   Michael Butler   119

IV   Widening Perspectives

9. E. Y. Meyer: The Construction of History
   through Literature
   Wilfried van der Will   141

10. Christoph Geiser: The 'literarische Ich' as
    Vantage-point
    Malcolm Pender   156

Contents

11. Margrit Schriber: Women and Fiction in
    Switzerland
    Mary E. Stewart   171

12. Hermann Burger: 'Die allmähliche Verfertigung
    des Todes beim Schreiben'
    John J. White   184

13. Gertrud Leutenegger: A Feminist Synthesis
    Elizabeth Boa   202

V   Continuity and Change

14. The Fourth Generation after Frisch and
    Dürrenmatt
    Malcolm Pender   225

Afterword   240

Notes on Contributors   242

Select Bibliography   244

Index   252

Acknowledgments

The editors would like to thank the following for their support: the British Academy, the University of Birmingham and the University of Strathclyde for research grants which enabled preliminary work to be carried out; Pro Helvetia, the Swiss Council for the Arts, for a generous subsidy towards the costs of publication; and the Luchterhand Verlag for permission to quote copyright poems by Kurt Marti from the following sources: 'machtverhältnis', 'opposition in der schweiz', 'weihnacht', 'heilsmaschinen', 'früelig', 'wie geits?', 'rosa loui', 'liebesgedicht' from *Schon wieder heute*; 'grosser gott klein', 'die passion des wortes GOTT' from *abendlied*; 'schwarze frühling', 'mailid' from *Mein barfüßig Lob*; and 'heil vetia 4' from *Der Vorsprung Leben*.

Michael Butler
Malcolm Pender

Introduction

In 1991 Switzerland celebrates the past and looks uncertainly towards the future. On the one hand, the 700th anniversary of the Treaty of Everlasting Alliance is cause for justified pride, an opportunity to recall the historical role of Switzerland in Europe and to be grateful for the durability of her unique democratic institutions. It is a moment, too, to reflect on the extraordinary success of her economy which, since the Second World War, has transformed a relatively poor country into one of the richest nations in the world. On the other hand, rapid and far-reaching change in Europe is affecting Switzerland in many, deeply unsettling ways. The creation of the Single European Market in 1992, for example, will have enormous implications for the Swiss economy; the upheavals in Europe which involve major changes in the relationships between the power blocs will raise fundamental questions about the cherished principle of Swiss neutrality; and the environmental costs of industrialised society are nowhere more starkly apparent than in this landlocked country, limited both in area and natural resources. All these pressures are combining to alter Swiss perceptions of their identity and institutions – especially of the army and of government itself. As the political, economic and ideological barriers of post-war Europe are rapidly dismantled, the future role of Switzerland is not easy to discern.

Since 1945 the literature of German-speaking Switzerland has acquired a status which it has rarely if ever before enjoyed. This is of course due in large measure to Max Frisch and Friedrich Dürrenmatt who came to prominence in the immediate post-war period and who, despite their differences in age, temperament and literary development, came to be considered as the founding fathers of Swiss letters. Yet, essential as their contribution has been, they could not have established on their own the thriving literary culture which exists today. The writers who followed their example have contributed their own distinctive emphases. It therefore seems an appropriate moment after the deaths of Dürrenmatt and Frisch within months of each other, which together with the wider changes noted above mark the end of a historical era, to look more closely at some of these other writers and to present an overview of the literature which has developed in German-speaking Switzerland since 1945.

The historical and political ethos of a country inevitably interacts with its literary culture, and the last forty-five years have seen a considerable shift in the role of the writer within Switzerland. In particular, the intense pressure on the writer to affirm Swiss identity, the country's institutions and social structures, which dominated the period during and immediately after the Second World War, gradually diminished, and the inward-looking obsession with Switzerland as a positive literary theme ceased to engage the younger generation of writers. Instead, as increased cultural interchange in an era of rapidly expanding communications had an emancipatory effect, both formally and thematically, these writers began to challenge the national myths nurtured by a profoundly conservative society. The restrictions inherent in the concept of the 'Kleinstaat', long regarded as a unique feature of Swiss culture, came to be perceived as no longer a specifically Swiss problem, but as a paradigm for a general sense of limitation in contemporary European society. Indeed, the legend of Swiss 'innocence', of exemplary democracy, was finally vitiated by the political disturbances of 1968 and 1980, which shook Switzerland as profoundly as similar events affected her European neighbours. Literature reflected these developments, and changing attitudes were best summed up in 1980 by Adolf Muschg when he compared contemporary writing with that of earlier decades: 'Die Gemeinplätze stimmen alle nicht, oder nicht mehr.' The fact that the writing of German-speaking Switzerland enjoys such a high reputation today testifies to the general validity of its themes and models, however 'Swiss' their colouring.

The thematic diversity of this writing in German-speaking Switzerland can be characterised by focusing principally on twelve writers whose work, set in the context of social, political and cultural evolution in Switzerland since 1945, both reflects individual achievement and represents broader lines of development. Obviously, we are very aware that any selection attempting to cover almost half a century will be to some extent arbitrary and reflect subjective criteria. We do not feature, for example, such gifted and varied writers as Silvio Blatter, Erika Burkart, Jürg Federspiel, Walter Matthias Diggelmann, Erica Pedretti, Niklaus Meienberg, Gerhard Meier, Herbert Meier, Paul Nizon, Hansjörg Schneider, Gerold Späth, Jörg Steiner, Werner Schmidli, Walter Vogt or Urs Widmer. Nevertheless, we feel that the writers chosen for discussion from the extraordinary richness of contemporary literature in German-speaking Switzerland provide a representative cross-section which gives an accurate picture of the present situation and how it came about.

With the exception of Kurt Marti, these authors are primarily writers of prose. Prose fiction, indeed, has always constituted the central strength of the literary tradition in Switzerland, as exemplified in the nineteenth century by Gotthelf, Keller and C. F. Meyer, and in the first half of the twentieth by Robert Walser, Meinrad Inglin and Jakob Schaffner. Paradoxically, the fact that Frisch and Dürrenmatt achieved fame initially as dramatists serves only to confirm them as exceptions to the rule. And indeed, from the perspective of the 1990s it is clear that their reputation too will eventually rest upon their narrative fiction, and in the case of Dürrenmatt, perhaps also on his multifaceted philosophical essays.

It is one of the paradoxes of post-war Swiss culture that her writers are predominantly, and often fiercely, critical of a social and political system whose success in terms of stability and the creation of wealth is unparalleled in Europe. First, this phenomenon is traced in its political and economic dimension since the Second World War, and then the complex response of writers over the same period is outlined. As a framework for the ensuing discussion of individual authors, we have found it convenient to employ the generational model which has become a commonplace of specialist studies. The discussion of the writers thus opens with an analysis of the manner in which the work of Frisch and Dürrenmatt first challenged received thinking and traditional attitudes in post-war Switzerland, and a review of their later work demonstrates the extent of their contribution to the development of literature in German-speaking Switzerland.

Five writers who came to the fore in the 1960s, the so-called 'second generation', are then shown to extend the thematic range of imaginative writing by creating fresh perspectives from which to examine Swiss society. The break from the constrictions of national mythology, set in train by Frisch and Dürrenmatt, is taken a decisive stage further: the macrocosm of 'Switzerland' is displaced as a theme by the depiction of specific localities and the examination of microcosmic social structures. The later work of O. F. Walter, Peter Bichsel, Adolf Muschg, Hugo Loetscher and Kurt Marti continues to display a consistent belief in literature as a medium for social criticism. Despite great variations in temperament and emphasis, all five exemplify the writer as a socially committed individual.

The 'third generation' is presented in the work of five writers born during or immediately after the Second World War, who experience in their formative years the sceptical, questioning spirit of their older colleagues, and who are consequently more dispassionate in their attitude towards revered national myths. In particular, Gertrud Leutenegger and Margrit Schriber reflect the growing importance of feminist perspectives and begin to establish a major role for the woman writer, hitherto an isolated figure in German-speaking Switzerland. Together with E. Y. Meyer, Christoph Geiser and Hermann Burger, they depict Switzerland in an increasingly differentiated fashion: the stresses of the workplace, illness deriving from social pressures, the enormous human cost of a materialistic consumer society – these are all typical themes which reverse the comfortable notion of the 'Sonderfall Schweiz' and present contemporary Switzerland not as a utopian haven of peace and stability worthy of imitation, but as a negative model for the rest of Europe.

Finally, the work of some of the writers of the 'fourth generation' is reviewed. Here, too, Switzerland or specific Swiss localities are treated as paradigms for wider European contexts. Born in the 1950s, these writers begin to publish for the most part in the 1980s. Free from many of the inhibitions of their older colleagues, they prove more radical in their attitudes. They seek little compromise with established forms of expression, and their work reflects various aspects of the theme of 'Verweigerung', that is to say, they identify and articulate individualistic behaviour patterns which are resistant to social and political manipulation, and which question the premises of society itself. Nevertheless, their concern for the individual, for ways of living which are tolerable and humane, provides a dimension of continuity and shows clearly how indebted they are to their older colleagues, and in particular, to the challenge and example first set so magnificently by Max Frisch and Friedrich Dürrenmatt.

I

The Context

1

The Political and Economic Development of Switzerland 1945–1991

Clive H. Church

Post-war Switzerland is often regarded as a kind of unchanging, unproblematical 'bourgeois Eldorado'. Historically speaking, this image is no more than a half-truth. Indeed, since 1945 Switzerland has undergone a virtual social and economic revolution. Yet, at the same time, political change has been far more subtle because of the stability of the country's institutions and the continuing influence of the political attitudes generated in response to fascism and the Second World War. Partly because of this contrast there have been more divisions and problems than is often appreciated. Thus although the country has become very middle-class, affluence has also promoted some alienation and self-questioning. This dialectic between socioeconomic change and political continuity evolved in five main, and overlapping, phases. During the war years the Swiss turned in on themselves and sought to develop their social unity through progressive reforms which were to be widely imitated in post-war Western Europe. Thereafter things began to change. From the late 1940s to the late 1960s came the boom years and the great transformation. Yet even before this had reached its peak, the beginnings of scepticism about the new society emerged, from the early 1960s to the mid-1970s. In a fourth phase this was given a new and more social orientation under the impact of the oil crisis of 1973. Finally, from the early 1980s onward there has been a period of economic revival and changing political fortunes as the old order has sought to adapt to the challenges of new problems and forces, notably environmentalism and the growing pace of European integration.

Clive H. Church

The 'Igelstellung', 1937–1950

Although Switzerland during the Second World War is often seen as a land flowing with milk and honey, the late 1930s and especially the war years were actually a period of real strain and menace. To resist such pressures the Swiss had to look to their own resources: cultural, diplomatic, military, economic and political. And to concert their resistance they developed the concept of 'geistige Landesverteidigung'. Thus on the cultural level the country defended its independence first by making Romansch a national language, sending a clear message to Mussolini who claimed that the language made this area of Switzerland, like the Ticino, part of the Italian sphere of influence. Then, more informally and spontaneously, the German-speaking Swiss moved to differentiate themselves from Nazi Germany by emphasising their *Schwyzertütsch* dialects. At the same time Pro Helvetia, the Swiss Council for the Arts, was created to develop the image of Switzerland abroad in line with the first national cultural policy of December 1938. The rising sense of the importance of Swiss history and culture was deliberately reinforced by the National Exhibition, held in Zurich in 1939.

Diplomatically, the country returned from differential to absolute neutrality in 1938 following the breakdown of collective security through the League of Nations. The army was also reformed and in 1939, on the eve of hostilities, entrusted to the leadership of the Vaudois Henri Guisan. It was General Guisan who based resistance on the concept of the mountain 'fortress', backed by the Wahlen Plan to ensure that there were adequate economic and food resources to resist encirclement. Efforts were also made to develop morale amongst soldiers and civilians through the Army's 'Heer im Haus' department. Hence, although some elements in Swiss society feared (or perhaps even welcomed the possibility) that they might have to adapt to the fascist New Order, majority opinion refused to do so. However, their resistance did not wholly spare them. On several occasions invasion appeared to be a real possibility, and Hitler did declare that Switzerland would be the number one enemy of the New Germany. So there were two general mobilisations, involving some 400,000 men, and eighty partial mobilisations. The economy was further constrained by Axis pressures, by severe limits on access to outside markets and resources, and by the presence of numbers of refugees and prisoners of war.

Yet in the end, despite the many compromises forced on an isolated country, the policy of the 'Igelstellung' succeeded. Understandably, this fact encouraged Swiss belief in the value of their institutions and political culture. The Americans and Russians, however, took a much more sceptical view. The latter were highly critical of the way in which the Swiss were seen to have facilitated the German war effort. Thus the Swiss were accused of self-censorship, of connivance in antisemitic policies, and of a restrictive attitude towards refugees. Equally, they were attacked for aiding, and profiting from, the German war effort and of going too far in managing the proceeds of the Nazi looting of Europe's gold and treasures. But as Churchill realised, such criticisms, though not without foundation, overlooked the exigencies of the Swiss situation.

As well as encouraging a refusal to tolerate outside interference, the crisis also made the Swiss more conscious of their own national cohesion. This process had, of course, begun before the war with the signing of the 1937 Labour Peace between unions and employers in engineering and metallurgy. The practice spread rapidly and was underwritten by the government, which showed itself more willing to consult its 'social partners' than in the past. The war also promoted a series of social changes, linked to the rising number of votes cast for the Socialist Party (SPS) and its 'New Switzerland' policy. As the largest party, it entered government in 1943, forcing the conservatives to listen to calls for pension and family protection programmes. However, the growing gap between wages and prices, coupled with Russian successes in the war which encouraged the Left, meant that social harmony and unity were far from complete.

Hence, with the end of hostilities there were both increasing labour unrest and calls for a purge of fascist sympathisers and profiteers. Left-wing parties, including the new Communist Labour Party (PdA), continued to gain ground, and there were demands in 1946 for a complete revision of the Constitution. This was not acted on, any more than Initiatives for the socialisation of the economy and the right to work. Nevertheless, prices and rents were controlled, the principle of old-age pensions accepted, and diplomatic relations with the USSR restored. Then, with the 'economic articles' of 1947, not merely was the government given extra powers of economic management, reflecting the enhanced role it had had to play during the war years, but the principle of consultation with employers and unions was constitutionally enshrined.

The boom years, 1945–1970

The combination of social radicalism and international isolation was to be short-lived. By the later 1940s the mood was already changing because, since the war, the Swiss economy has boomed. Growth rates have been markedly above those of most European countries, despite a lack of indigenous food, raw materials and energy, which has meant a persistent trade deficit. Real GNP rose from Sfr. 34.6 billion in 1948 to 52.4 billion in 1957, and then, after a slight hiccup, it again rose consistently, at an annual average of almost 5 per cent, reaching 83 billion by 1968, and ultimately 106 by 1974. During this period the inflation rate often fell, and averaged not much more than 3 per cent in the 1960s. So, despite a period of mild overheating in the mid-1960s, most indices pointed consistently upwards.

This was due to a combination of factors. To begin with, exports prospered, often taking up to 90 per cent of major firms' output. The range of products sold and the percentage of value added all increased. The value of exports rose from Sfr. 4 billion in 1950 to 22 billion by 1970. This was both cause and effect of Swiss participation in the expanding, EEC-dominated, West European economy. Exports rose more than imports as a proportion of GNP, and by the late 1960s the trade deficit was falling. However, apart from the early sixties, the current account stayed in the black. Earnings from the manufacturing sector, notably chemicals and engineering, were supplemented by the rising yields from tourism, foreign investments and other invisibles produced by the expanding service sector.

The competitiveness that this demonstrates was linked to other factors, such as the very high investment rate, which rose from 13.6 per cent of GNP in 1949 to 33 per cent at its peak in 1964. Government spending remained both stable and low, at never more than some 10 per cent of GNP for most of the period. Bank deposits rose from Sfr. 27 billion in 1950 to 470 billion by 1970 as well, aiding the banks to become a major, if debatable, element in Swiss life. With wages and money supply being kept under tight control there were considerable gains in productivity. These also derived from structural changes in the economy. There was a major shift from agriculture to manufacturing and services. The labour force in agriculture fell from 415,000 in 1941 to 231,000 by 1970. Over the same period the numbers employed rose from 861,000 to 1.44 million in manufacturing, and from 716,000 to 1.32 million in services. This super-boom was sufficiently unexpected to be regarded as another sign of the country's uniqueness, the much envied 'Sonderfall Schweiz'.

Economic growth also had a dramatic impact on social conditions and structures. Incomes rose continuously, with average real wages going up 250 per cent between the end of the war and the early 1970s, compared to 66 per cent in the preceding thirty years. Real GNP per capita likewise rose from Sfr. 7,460 in 1949 to Sfr. 16,360 in 1973. This put the country on the way to one of the highest standards of living in the world. Alongside striking private affluence, matched by improved welfare benefits and well organised trade unions, the country also enjoyed growing levels of public investment with a new network of motorways, a nuclear power programme, television services and better educational provision. This reflected the changes in social structures. Society became increasingly mobile. People ceased to be tied to their places of origin, and changed jobs and location more frequently. The fall in agricultural employment led to the population becoming increasingly concentrated in the towns and suburbs of the *Mittelland*, as the latter took 30 per cent of new industrial jobs and 65 per cent of those in the tertiary sector. But if the population was redistributed, it did not diminish; indeed it continued to rise, from 4.5 to 6.2 million by the early 1970s.

The shift away from agriculture into services also helped to make the Swiss much less of a class society. There was a marked fall in the number of self-employed, both on the land and in commerce and industry. Firms grew in size and were increasingly run by managers. So, with the proportion of qualified workers amongst the native population rising in comparison to the semi- and unskilled, white-collar salaried status became the norm. However, this did not prevent growing disparities in wealth and income. Swiss society became a matter of complex stratification in which differences and conflicts were changed rather than abolished. If basic standards of living were high, contrasts between élites and popular strata remained, not simply because of economic factors, but increasingly because of contacts, influence and privileged access to culture. The Swiss élite was distinguished by its business and social networks, its domination of political office and the higher ranks of the army, and its ability to exploit the limited opportunities offered in higher education. At the same time, the position of other classes was reinforced by the development of a new underclass, as increasing numbers of *Gastarbeiter* arrived to take up the less pleasant jobs in industry and the lower ranges of the service sector.

Prosperity also had emollient effects on politics, both externally and internally. Abroad the country regained its confidence and international esteem, playing a fuller role in international affairs, participating in the affairs of UN agencies and providing good offices in the Korean and other wars. Its neutrality was recognised by the USSR, although this did not prevent the Swiss from taking up a forcefully anti-Communist line at the time both of the Hungarian Rising in 1956 and the Prague Spring in 1968. The Cold War, indeed, served to encourage prevailing political attitudes at home while helping to end the country's international isolation. In Europe, however, Switzerland hesitated to join the Council of Europe because of its supranational ambitions, only joining in 1963 when these proved illusory. Economic and political reservations about supranationality also led her to take a leading part in setting up the European Free Trade Association in 1959–60, as an alternative form of European integration, more acceptable to Swiss traditions. However, the subsequent British decision to apply for membership of the EEC led to EFTA developing a new identity as a focus for the economic interests of the smaller powers. EFTA thus facilitated the signing of the 1972 Free Trade Agreement with the European Community which gave Swiss industrial products free access to the Community market. Even so, the fact that this was approved very easily by referendum rather reflected the lack of interest then accorded to foreign affairs.

This sprang from a certain depoliticisation at home. With full and well-paid employment and regular consultation of trade unions, there was a certain embourgeoisement of the working classes. So old social divisions became less acute, and generally politics seemed to be less important. Equally, more and more people were represented in government, either through corporatist management and consultation, or by the way that the Socialists were brought into the main stream of politics. After 1959 they gained permanent and proportional representation in the Federal Council with the adoption of the famous *Zauberformel*. As a result turnout at *Abstimmungen*, or popular votes, began to fall, from an average of well over 50 per cent in the early 1950s to under 40 per cent ten years later. Increasingly, Initiatives were rejected and most laws passed without challenge. When challenges did take place, voters were prone to reject any increase in Federal powers, taxes and restrictions. On the other hand, there were very large majorities for moves to expand roads and educational subsidies.

Turnout at general elections also fell, from at least 70 per cent in the later 1940s to 57 per cent by 1971. Political parties had to react to such declining interest. Following the failure of several of its campaigns, the Socialist Party changed tack, and at Winterthur in 1959 it dropped its Marxist tenets in favour of a social democratic programme, as the West German SPD did at the same time in Bad Godesberg. Two years previously the Catholics began to evolve towards a more open and ecumenical stance which was to lead them to become the Christian People's Party (CVP) by 1970. Equally, the Farmers' Party found it necessary to widen its appeal and turned itself into the People's Party (SVP) in 1971. Yet, for whatever reason, the balance of votes and parliamentary seats hardly changed. The Catholics lost only 0.1 per cent of their vote in twenty years and the traditional Swiss party of government, the Freisinnigen or Radical Democrats (FDP), lost only 0.8 per cent of theirs. Prosperity had clearly reinforced the wartime preference for compromise, so that the emerging *Konkordanzdemokratie* enjoyed wide support. With calls for political change fading, corporatist management of the economy and the inward-looking political ideas of the war years remained largely unchallenged.

The beginnings of self-doubt, 1960–1975

During the 1960s, although patterns of growth and consensus continued unabated, questions were asked about the nature and direction of the new Switzerland. The ability of government to provide the quality of management demanded by the enlarged scale of things was thus called into question, for example, by the 1964 Mirage scandal in which the Federal Council was shown to have lost control of its military budget in a way which existing forms of parliamentary scrutiny had been unable to check. The government was therefore forced to define its aims and objectives more carefully by issuing general policy lines at the beginning of each parliament, and was finally given more economic powers with the Cartel Law and the so-called Conjunctural Articles of 1964. Calls for revision of the Constitution were finally acted on, reflecting growing criticism of the way in which women and minorities were treated. Much of this was symbolised by the strong protest vote for the Communists and, especially in 1967, for the 'Landesring der Unabhängigen', a radical centrist group founded by Duttweiler of MIGROS, the well-known cooperative grocery and leisure chain, to challenge large Federal and commercial interests. The emergence of modern pressure groups like the Swiss Consumers Association was also symbolic of such trends.

Questions were also asked about the conservative ethos of Swiss society. Building on criticisms by Max Frisch in the 1950s, Max Imboden and others in the 1960s began to talk about a 'helvetisches Malaise' and the problem of 'Unbehagen im Kleinstaat'. Politically, effective concern about nuclear weapons and nuclear power began to emerge amongst intellectuals such as Otto F. Walter, Kurt Marti and the theologian Karl Barth. In foreign affairs, criticism focused on the illicit export of arms by the Bührle company to be used against the Biafran rebels during the Nigerian Civil War. A popular Initiative in 1972 came close to banning all arms exports. The government, faced with hostility both to Switzerland and the Red Cross in Nigeria, felt it necessary to act in parallel with UN sanctions on Rhodesia and subscribe to the European Convention on Human Rights. This was part of a drive to make foreign policy more open and active in support of world needs which led, in 1969, to the first reassessment of non-membership of the UN. Debate about foreign policy after the publication of the Bonjour Report (1970) on the handling of Swiss neutrality during the Second World War encouraged such rethinking.

These trends were to be encouraged by the effects of 1968, which galvanised new groups into social and political activity of a new and challenging kind, often known as the 'New Left'. The growing unease of intellectually aware circles was clearly reinforced by manifestations of populist *Basisdemokratie*. Hence in 1969 the Olten Group seceded from the Swiss Writers Union in protest against its support for Ministry of Defence demands for continuing resistance to foreign ideas in order to defend traditional Swiss values. The easy victory of the proposal for female suffrage in the referendum of 1971 also points to the development of a more liberal ethos.

Fuelled both by the economic difficulties of the 1960s and by reactions to the Vietnam War and the ill-fated Prague Spring, the questioning of the sixties also provided the basis for new political groups. Such groups differed from the extra-parliamentary opposition (APO) in West Germany because, as well as taking part in direct action, they also made full use of the possibilities of conventional politics. Thus the main exponent of this trend, the Progressive Organisations (POCH), established a clear niche for itself in Swiss politics in the 1970s. The targets of referenda began to widen to include environmental and other challenges to the prevailing *bürgerlich* order.

Such movements drew on the younger and more educated strata of society, notably teachers and independent professionals. In some big cities student radicals linked up with discontented apprentices to create an alternative youth movement. This began with the occupation of the old Globus building in Zurich in June 1968, and spread in the early 1970s to Biel (Bienne), Lausanne, Geneva and Lugano, providing the basis for a youth culture. Although this appeared to offer peer-group solidarity to those who felt that normal society did not provide the kind of personal relationships which they sought, it worried the establishment, who often violently over-reacted in dealing with the problem.

One significant aspect of the growing radicalism was that it gave a further, and politically coloured, boost to the use of dialect in German-speaking Switzerland. Paradoxically, this tendency encouraged another force which drew support from the prevailing radicalism: Jurassian separatism. The treatment of the French minority in Bern had been on the political agenda since 1947, but although its identity and language rights were reinforced in the 1950s, more radical elements, grouped in the Rassemblement Jurassien (RJ), began to push for separation. They often used violent means, especially after secession was defeated at a cantonal referendum in 1959. Although by 1967 the Bernese largely conceded the principle of separation and devised a process to permit an amicable divorce, the RJ refused to cooperate. They continued their campaign with the occupation of embassies in 1972 and 1973, but this failed to stop the referenda on the creation of a new canton going ahead in the later 1970s.

If this development shows the very clear limits to violence and change in Switzerland, it was still the case that there was enough to concern many conservatives, already worried by the way in which economic growth had eroded traditional Swiss values. If terrorism on behalf of language interests and what they saw as socialist destabilisation worried them, it was the way that modernisation was introducing a large number of foreign workers which was their real *bête noire*. For right-wing traditionalists, *Gastarbeiter* were having unacceptable effects on Swiss society. By the late 1960s their numbers were approaching a million, and this apparently inexorable growth was seen as a threat to the religious and cultural balance of the country and to its political system. The National Action, founded in 1961, and led by the charismatic James Schwarzenbach, had long argued that immigrants from other parts of Europe did not share Swiss democratic sympathies.

This line of argument attracted many *rentiers* and small businessmen, often with relatively low levels of education, who found themselves threatened by the growing scale of the cartelised economy of the times. Hence, foreigners, like women and the young, served as convenient scapegoats. In September 1970 the Schwarzenbach Initiative against *Überfremdung* drew nearly three-quarters of the electorate out to vote in the ensuing referendum, the best turnout since 1947. The Initiative carried seven cantons and attracted 558,000 votes, only 97,000 less than those rejecting it. Then in the general election of 1971, despite divisions, the Far Right parties gained 17 per cent of the vote with the Republicans winning seven seats in the Nationalrat and the National Action four. Many people saw the phenomenon as essentially racialist and as the major threat to the Swiss system.

Economic crisis and the shift to the Left, 1973–1983

If the Swiss were less affected by the post-1973 oil crisis than most, they were far from escaping it. So, while economic growth continued unchecked into the 1970s, it was then twice to fall, in 1975–6 and again in 1978–81, during the second oil shock. Because the country was heavily dependent on imported oil, the abrupt rise in prices brought about a marked deterioration in trading conditions. As a result there was one of the largest declines in Gross Domestic Product amongst the OECD countries, with a fall of 7.7 per cent in 1975 alone and a further 1.25 per cent in 1976. Although there was then something of a recovery, by 1978 the growth in GDP was down to 0.37 per cent and was to fall absolutely in 1981–2. Equally, per capita GDP did not recover its levels of 1974 until 1980, and it too was to fall in 1982–3.

This sudden reversal in economic fortunes had implications both for inflation and employment. From 2 to 3 per cent in the late 1960s the former went up to 6 to 7 per cent in the early 1970s and reached over 9 per cent in 1973–4. However, the government's decision in 1973 to float the franc helped to squeeze inflation out for a while. And, if interest rates also remained low, this did not stop a 15 per cent drop in industrial production and the disappearance of 7 per cent of all jobs. The watch industry in particular lost heavily, the work force declining by nearly half to 45,000 by 1980. Generally, the number of unemployed rose from a few hundred in the early 1970s to over 20,000. Only the fact that large numbers of *Gastarbeiter* contracts were not renewed helped to keep unemployment down to no more than 1 per cent. Even so, employment fell by a further 3 per cent in the early 1980s, with women being particularly affected.

The decline in foreign workers, brought about by government

ceilings and economic trends, was one of the most striking social phenomena of the times. Their numbers fell from a peak of 1,065 million in 1974 to under 900,000 in 1978–80. This began to relieve pressure in the major urban agglomerations to which jobs and housing began to return. This strengthening of the Golden Triangle of Basle, Bern, and Zurich renewed disparities. The recession also tended to lessen social mobility and to reinforce social divisions. However, the real social divide continued to be that between poorly paid non-Swiss and the native population as a whole. The latter were, for example, over-represented in the service sector, where real wages held up better than in manufacturing. So, although there was a revival in trade unionism and industrial disputes, the Labour Peace remained untroubled.

The social problems of the late 1970s were the problems of a still prosperous, middle-class society. With marriage rates falling by a third in the decade and divorces rising, the country experienced a sharp fall in the birth rate. Yet this did not lead to expanding prospects for the young, whose alienation from what was seen as an unexciting and unfriendly consumer society continued. As a result, levels of conscientious objection shot up, reaching a peak of 788 cases in 1984. This caused a major shock to the establishment since the obligation of military service is central to national identity and political culture.

In 1980 the youth problem exploded into violence on the streets of Zurich and other major cities, triggered by the contrast between the millions being spent on the renovation of the Zurich Opera House and the poor facilities available in the 'Autonome Jugend-Zentrum' catering for the alternative and rock cultures of the city's youth. The authorities and police again responded heavy-handedly, partly because of the fear that drugs were involved (as they increasingly were at this time); so the disturbances continued spasmodically for a couple of years. The level of violence involved provoked much agonised debate about the alienation of the young and the threat this presented to society.

Although the essentials of Swiss democracy remained intact, the youth violence was part of a wave of political experiments, encouraged in part by the revival of the Left. The Far Right parties saw their parliamentary strength halved and subsequent Initiatives against foreigners were roundly trounced, while the Socialists were the great victors of the 1975 elections and POCH made its national debut four years later. The SPS became increasingly radical under the leadership of intellectuals like Jean Ziegler, and this led to a series of abortive attacks on the institutions of capitalism, including an Initiative demanding controls on the banks (after revelations of fraud in the Schweizerische Kreditanstalt's Chiasso branch), proposals for co-determination in the work place, and the 'Être Solidaire' Initiative for better treatment of *Gastarbeiter*.

Nonetheless, the recession did help to weaken the resistance of conservatism to some long desired reforms. Environmental legislation, an equal rights amendment for women, reform of the marriage law, price controls and a reinforcement of the economic powers of government, together with major developments in pensions and unemployment insurance, were all carried. There was also intense discussion of a total revision of the Constitution, following publication of an official draft in 1977 after several years of consultation. Against this strengthening of central government activity there was also an attempt to revive federalism, both to prevent the undermining of the cantons and to ensure that the Federal Council was not used as a dumping ground for the duties and costs that local authorities disliked.

However, this did not go far enough for some. The 1970s thus saw the emergence of the 'New Politics' of decentralised, grassroots populism, involving new values and new styles of political activity. Although there were occasional examples of terrorism, the new approaches were essentially pacific. The use made of Initiatives shot up, at both cantonal and national level. In 1978 there were fourteen *Abstimmungen*, whereas there had only been one in 1967. And by the end of the decade Green candidates were beginning to gain election to parliaments. This reflected the fact that there was a growing distance between such 'New Politics', with its preference for *Bürgerinitiativen*, and established public opinion and political élites. When it came to the contentious issue of nuclear power, for example, ordinary citizens were increasingly willing to take direct action, as at Kaiseraugst in April 1975 when plans to build a new power station in a crowded and archaeologically sensitive area were effectively halted.

Present and future problems, 1981 to 1991 and beyond

By the 1980s the wheel had turned almost full circle. Full prosperity again encouraged opposition to political change, especially that promoted by the SPS, and the country moved back towards the Right. The growth rate began to creep up above 4 per cent a year with exports showing renewed strength, and manufacturing output, especially in chemicals, surged. Even in the watch industry things began to improve, with successful consolidation of many firms and the launching of the long-needed new product, the 'Swatch' watch, which combined fashion with quartz technology in amusing new ways. This restored the Swiss market share in Europe and began to sell well in the Far East. As a result, unemployment fell back to its earlier levels and the number of foreign workers began to rise once more. Despite the surge in growth, inflation was controlled, dropping from over 6 per cent to below 3 per cent. Hence, even though wage rises were still modest, there were rising levels of income and GDP per capita.

The mainstream Right, in the shape of the FDP and the Liberal Party (LPS), thus did well in the elections of 1979 and 1983, the former emerging as the largest party in both national and cantonal parliaments. As a result, attitudes to youth unrest, sexual morality, and refugees became harsher, while an increasing stress on free-market policies was visible in economic and social matters such as banking and training levies. Such tendencies towards deregulation went along with an increasingly vigorous defence of the army and its budget. In March 1986, when the longstanding question of entry to the UN was finally put to the electorate, the government suffered one of its most humiliating defeats ever, failing even to carry Geneva. At the same time the Far Right began to revive, encouraged by the rising numbers of Tamils seeking political asylum in the country. However, it was not able to push government as far as it wanted on controlling either the number of foreigners or the right of asylum. But left-wing attempts to help foreigners were rebuffed, which added to the SPS's growing problems with factionalism and voter resistance to radicalism.

That the Socialists' difficulties did not really reinforce the position of the Right, but led to a period of uncertain transition, was due in part to the rising tide of environmentalism, which conflicted with ideas of deregulation. Environmental concern had surfaced in the later 1960s, but became increasingly prominent in the 1980s because of the renewed pace of economic growth and the problems this caused. This tendency was reinforced by the effects of such disasters as the damage caused to Swiss forests by acid rain. Such issues were increasingly quoted as the major problem of the day in opinion polls, and the Swiss reacted accordingly. The result was a stream of legislation, so that the Swiss now have some of the strictest norms in Europe.

Some felt that this was still too little, which has led to the emergence of an increasingly important Green lobby, represented by Alternative and New Left groups and, increasingly, by the

Grüne Partei der Schweiz (GPS). Mainstream parties like the Socialists were also affected, and even the National Action suffered an ecologically inspired split. Consequently, the *bürgerlich* parties decided that it was wiser to give up the idea of a new nuclear power station at Kaiseraugst. However, expectations of a Red/Green coalition in 1987 proved exaggerated, reflecting a certain ambiguity in Swiss responses. For while environmental Initiatives for protecting the Rothenturm marshes and upgrading the rail network were passed, others – of equal importance – failed. Nor did the public always rush to change its lifestyle in ecological ways. Some even began to campaign against environmentalism, encouraging the emergence of the AutoPartei which sought to defend the interests of car users.

This helped to restrict the influence of the Far Right, which became increasingly extreme and xenophobic in its attitude to asylum-seekers. With their numbers rising to over 30,000 a year by 1990 and their claims to being genuine political refugees cast in doubt, the Tamils, in particular, became a major issue. Local authorities were hostile because they could hardly cope with the influx. Yet progressive opposition was critical of what they saw as harsh and restrictive government policy. This was one of the factors in the opposition to the FDP's Elisabeth Kopp, the first woman minister in Swiss history. She was forced to resign early in 1989 after warning her husband about a pending enquiry into his firm's role in laundering money from drug dealings.

Although Kopp was acquitted on a technicality in February 1990, the 'Koppgate' scandal was to have significant political effects, which went beyond causing her party some embarrassment. The affair also focused attention both on attitudes to money from drugs in Switzerland, notably in banking circles, and on authoritarian tendencies in government. The growing power of central government and its apparent willingness to turn a blind eye both to the activities of the well-connected and to evidence produced by its own police forces, while keeping secret and unverified files on one-sixth of the native population, caused massive resentment and criticism. Reforms in the police system have been put in hand, the files largely opened to public inspection and new laws passed against recycling money with a criminal origin. This new suspicion of the State amongst ordinary citizens was also one reason why, in late 1989, after a vitriolic campaign involving Max Frisch, other leading intellectuals and MPs, nearly 36 per cent of those voting in the referendum backed a call to abolish the army. A connected motive for this astonishing vote was provided by the revolutionary events in Eastern Europe. These seemed to remove the need for massive defences, symbolised by the purchase of F18 fighters, the costs of which were said to be rising as uncontrollably as those of the Mirages had once done.

Another foreign policy issue which raised an equal number of questions about Swiss identity and interests was how to react to the success of the European Community in developing European integration. The changing shape of Europe has thus become a major issue in Switzerland, partly because the creation of the Single European Market in 1992 promises to undermine Swiss prosperity by threatening nonmembers with marginalisation. The increasing dynamism of the Community has also cast doubt on the value of other European institutions in which Switzerland has sought to forward its interests. So when, in January 1989, Jacques Delors offered the EFTA countries a more structured partnership in the running of the so-called 'European Economic Area' there was some enthusiasm in Switzerland. However, the terms available from Brussels do not seem to offer much hope of the EFTA countries gaining the share in EEA decision-making which their sovereignty requires. Given that the political costs of strengthening EFTA and adapting to Community leadership and policies may be higher than public opinion is willing to pay, as the re-emergence of pressure groups on behalf of a free and neutral Switzerland suggest, the question of membership will have to be faced. By the end of the 1980s the idea of membership was being ruled out much less emphatically than was once the case, and 1990 saw moves to launch an Initiative to commit the government to seeking entry, so that the matter can be fully and openly debated. However, even if this might offer greater gains for no more cost than an EEA agreement, especially as it would offer a helpful counter to some of the disadvantages accruing from a united Germany, it is not clear that public opinion is yet ready for this.

Nonetheless, here, as elsewhere, the Swiss are having to re-examine their insistence on preserving the fiercely independent way of life which has guided their long history. They will have to balance possible economic and political losses involved in staying out of the mainstream of European integration against the ideological and emotional satisfaction of maintaining the status quo, which some observers believe already makes the country a virtual satellite of the Community. Equally, thought will have to be given to reshaping political institutions to take account of 'Koppgate' and the rapid changes in Europe. Responses to these dilemmas often cut across conventional lines of political cleavage, so the outcome of current debates is doubly hard to predict.

If the political problems can be solved, the Swiss can look forward to continuing economic growth. They should be able to weather most difficulties caused by 1992, especially if they secure entry to the EEA or the Community itself. Many of the key multinationals have already established firm bridgeheads inside the Community. Equally, competitiveness has been maintained and the prevailing 2 per cent plus growth rate seems likely to continue. Labour shortages are far more of a threat to expansion than unemployment. The success of the economy may cause a slight deterioration in terms of trade and on current account, but inflation and interest rates are likely to remain low. The assumption must be that the competent, somewhat corporatist, strategy of the past will continue.

Yet if the Switzerland of the 1990s is likely to be economically stable, it still has to deal with the effects of growth. If the ecological threat to the forests has stabilised, there are still major problems over energy policy, toxic waste and the development of transport facilities. Equally, the rising number of foreigners, now numbering 1,023 million in a population of 6.7 million, may be necessary for economic reasons, but still gives cause for concern, especially when combined with the emergence of neo-Nazi groups such as the Patriotic Front, attacks on asylum seekers and even the first racialist murders ever known in the country. Nonetheless, the country remains remorselessly peaceful in comparison to most. Old religious tensions, for example, are clearly declining. However, they may be being replaced by language divisions as growth brings further pressure on Romansch and creates regional imbalances which affect relations between the Suisse Romande and the dominant *Mundart* of Zurich and the rest of the 'Golden Triangle'. Language difficulties remain, as the August 1989 government report on 'Quadrilingualism' showed. Nevertheless, against the odds, the Swiss have been able to preserve their political culture and their system of direct democracy and federalism, even though the social and economic foundations which gave rise to them have been transformed. Some critics now talk of 'the comfort that chloroforms' and the need for 'Swissnost', and it is true that the Swiss face difficult questions about their future orientations and the wisdom of preserving special features (which even Ministers call 'helvetianisms') in a rapidly changing world. Their response is likely to be cautious and pragmatic. Major upheavals or wholesale abandoning of those things which help to define Swiss identity are unlikely. After all, despite persistent irritations and criticisms, the evidence of the post-war years suggests that the system remains flexible enough to enable it to absorb most pressures. In the future, as in the past, there will not be stasis but subtle adjustment.

2
Trends in Writing in German-speaking Switzerland since 1945
Malcolm Pender

In 1914, when the prestige of Germany stood high, Carl Spitteler, at great cost to his reputation there, proclaimed the political independence of the German-Swiss within the context of German culture. Exactly thirty years later in 1944, when Switzerland stood politically at its farthest point from Germany, Karl Schmid stressed the necessity for the German-Swiss of a cultural link to their larger neighbour.[1] A year later the end of the Second World War permitted a gradual normalisation of the complex dialectic in German-speaking Switzerland between political and cultural dimensions. But the re-establishment of German-Swiss 'Doppelbürgertum', dual membership of a state and a culture which are not co-extensive with one another, occurred in radically altered conditions. On the one hand, the political changes in German-speaking Europe resulting from the war further fragmented a culture which had never been effectively centralised, and this promoted individual development in its constituent parts, such as German-speaking Switzerland. On the other hand, nuclear weapons and the political evolution of Western industrialised society challenged Swiss notions of neutrality and non-involvement. These changes have inevitably coloured German-Swiss literature and its relationship to Swiss society over the forty-five years since 1945.

The resumption of interchange with Germany after the war took place in conjunction with a complex interplay of forces within German-speaking Switzerland itself, between a dominant conservatism powerfully strengthened by the emergence of Switzerland intact from the war, and a more critical spirit of enquiry which was initially fostered by the opening of frontiers. These two attitudes are reflected in literary developments over the following years, as some examples show. In 1953 in Bern Eugen Gomringer published *Konstellationen*, a pioneering text in concrete poetry, and in 1954 Max Frisch published *Stiller*, the most important novel in post-war German-Swiss literature, one of the features of which was a trenchant critique of Swiss society. On the other hand, in 1955 Meinrad Inglin brought out a revised version of his *Schweizerspiegel* (first published in 1938), which was the classic Swiss novel on the positive virtues of the Swiss state, and in the same year Kurt Guggenheim published *Alles in allem*, a conservative and affirmative chronicle of Switzerland's major city, Zurich, which Frisch had particularly mocked in his novel. In 1964, one anthology of recent Swiss writing praised in its foreword the wholesomeness of Swiss literature in terms reminiscent of thirty years before, whilst a second claimed that the progressive nature of contemporary Swiss literature was marked by the fact that it now had no distinctively Swiss characteristics at all.[2] In 1966, when the second generation of writers after Frisch and Dürrenmatt was beginning to establish itself with searching examinations of Swiss society, Emil Staiger, the doyen of the conservative Swiss academics and critics, made a sweeping condemnation of aspects of modern literature and unleashed a controversy, the so-called 'Zürcher Literaturstreit', which involved the entire German-speaking world.[3] In 1970 the more radically and politically orientated *Gruppe Olten* broke away from the Swiss Writers Union, and thus in a sense formalised progressive and conservative attitudes in the writing profession. It is nonetheless tenable to suggest, twenty years after 1970, that these divergent attitudes are probably closer to one another than they were in the late 1940s and early 1950s.

Convergence between social attitudes and the views advanced by literature is less apparent. In 1959 O. F. Walter's *Der Stumme*, which presents a confrontation indicative of wider change between the older and younger generations, was published, yet in the same year conservative Swiss male voters rejected female suffrage. 1962 saw both the enormous success of Friedrich Dürrenmatt's *Die Physiker* and the refusal of the same electorate to endorse a proposal to ban nuclear weapons in Switzerland. The Swiss manifestations of the 1968 student movement did not initiate social change and this failure was reflected in the dark tone of much writing of the 1970s. In 1980 the brutal reaction of the authorities and the hostility of the population at large to the youth protest in Zurich and other cities left the writer Reto Hänny, for example, feeling 'fremd und fern wie in Grönland'.[4] In 1986 the electorate, strongly supporting a traditional perception of national identity, rejected Swiss membership of the United Nations, and a year later the young writer Dante Andrea Franzetti claimed that 'die Frage nach nationaler Identität zunehmend absurd (erscheint)'.[5] In 1989 the reaction to Frisch's *Schweiz ohne Armee? Ein Palaver* contained elements of hysterical xenophobia not dissimilar to those which greeted Otto Marchi's *Schweizer Geschichte für Ketzer* in 1971.[6] It is thus probably true to say that general public attitudes are evolving more slowly than those of writers, and that these attitudes, despite the influence of environmentalist groups and others, remain broadly conservative, while literature reflects progressive views more exclusively than was the case forty years ago.

This increasing polarisation helps to highlight the situation of the writer in German-speaking Switzerland in two ways. On the one hand, the sheer success and continuity of Swiss society over the last 150 years, and especially since 1945, render his or her task more difficult and the writer's position more marginal than is the case with his or her counterpart in Germany. Hermann Burger's satirical short story '*Die Leser auf der Stör*' (1970), for example, portrays a situation where the affluent citizen purchases books, but hires other people to read them – a prosperous society views the writer as a cultural ornament. Over a decade later, when public financial support of literature has paradoxically grown enormously, Niklaus Meienberg claims that the subversive thrust of contemporary literature is deflected by the fact 'daß die Subversion von jenen, welche subversiert werden sollen, gelobt wird'; and in 1981 Adolf Muschg, commenting on the esteem extended to the writer in another culture, recalls de Gaulle's remark on Sartre 'Lui aussi, c'est la France', and asks: 'Wäre ein solches Wort in der Schweiz möglich?'[7]

On the other hand, from the point of view of the writer, the myths sustaining German-Swiss society seemed by 1964 so divorced from social reality that Walter Matthias Diggelmann, for example, was able to ask, in response to claims that writers were misrepresenting Switzerland, 'wer eigentlich die Schweiz zur bloßen Fiktion gemacht habe, täglich zu machen versuche'.[8] For Max Frisch the task of the Swiss writer during the War had been to present to the warring nations 'das Vorhandensein einer andern Welt'.[9] Arguably, the task of the Swiss writer now was to present another world to his countrymen. This function is discussed in Kurt Marti's *Die Schweiz und ihre Schriftsteller – Die Schriftsteller und ihre Schweiz* (1966) and in Max Frisch's collection of speeches *Öffentlichkeit als Partner* (1967), and further exemplified by Hugo Loetscher in the satirical chapter 'Die Entdeckung der Schweiz' in his novel *Der Immune* (1975), where Switzerland is viewed from the perspective of the outside world. The rediscovery of Robert Walser, Friedrich Glauser and Albin Zollinger and the publication of anthologies and collections, culminating in Charles Linsmayer's thirty-volume *Frühling der Gegenwart 1890–1950* (1979–1983), added a historical dimension to a perception of the oppositional role of the writer in society and helped to undermine a traditional view which, reinforced by the encirclement of Switzerland in the war years, expected the German-Swiss writer to be affirmative of the Swiss body politic.

These changing relationships were adumbrated in the first major work in German-Swiss literature after 1945, Max Frisch's *Tagebuch 1946–1949* (1950). The entries chart the growth of Frisch's awareness, not simply in relation to the political characteristics of Switzerland, but also in relation to the dilemma of a Swiss who shared a language and a culture with a country whose recent descent into barbarity had almost destroyed both. The *Tagebuch* is important in three ways. Firstly, as a compendium of attitudes to Switzerland by a critical writer, it acts as a precursor to, for example, Peter Bichsel's *Des Schweizers Schweiz* (1967, 1969 in book form) and Kurt Marti's *Zum Beispiel Bern 1972* (1973). Secondly, as an autobiographical record, the writer of which perceived his 'Schreibrecht' to be anchored 'niemals in seiner Person, nur in seiner Zeitgenossenschaft',[10] the *Tagebuch* anticipated several texts written in the 1970s claiming similar relevance, such as Fritz Zorn's *Mars* (1977) and Lukas Hartmann's *Gebrochenes Eis* (1980). Thirdly, as a text which was formally open-ended, which did not set out to prove a thesis, but which sought to explore, the *Tagebuch* represented a style of writing and an attitude to literature which was to be assumed by others.

Max Frisch's *Stiller* is also important, both in its own right as a major novel in German of the 1950s and in the development of contemporary German-Swiss writing. It marks both an inversion of the large novel affirmative of Switzerland and also contains wider implications, since the Swiss hero is assimilated at the close, not to play a role in the ordered life of the community, but to exhaust himself in the sterile world of *Reproduktion* where mass-produced artefacts and manufactured images debilitate all response. Direct comparisons can be drawn to E. Y. Meyer's *Die Rückfahrt* (1977), which presents prosperous Switzerland as a negative model for other countries, and to Beat Sterchi's *Blösch* (1983), in which the hero, a Spanish 'Fremdarbeiter', can only reassert his humanity by leaving a Switzerland desecrated by industrialised farming and mechanised food production. *Stiller* reverses expectations in a second way: the security offered by the country has become a prison in which the prisoner-hero is observed with detachment, and this is the precursor of a narrative stance towards Switzerland assumed by later writers such as Urs Widmer in *Schweizer Geschichten* (1975), Adolf Muschg in *Besuch in der Schweiz* (1978), and above all, by Sterchi in *Blösch*. A third reversal of expectation is provided by Anatol Stiller's *ferme vaudoise*. Traditionally the literary symbol of Swiss reliability and solidity, the house in Frisch's novel is a counterfeit construction representing the inauthentic images of themselves held both by the hero and by Switzerland. The house in Peter Bichsel's stories *Eigentlich möchte Frau Blum den Milchmann kennenlernen* (1964) and in his novel *Die Jahreszeiten* (1967) characterises the insubstantiality and insecurity of the lives of its occupants, and the houses in Adolf Muschg's *Gegenzauber* (1967) and Hermann Burger's *Schilten* (1976) have similar functions; the work of Christoph Geiser demonstrates the debilitating restrictions of the apparently solid *großbürgerlich* house; Gerhard Meier's Baur and Bindschädler trilogy (*Toteninsel* (1979), *Borodino* (1982) and *Die Ballade vom Schneien* (1985)) stresses repeatedly the impermanence of human habitation; in the work of Franz Böni houses are scenes of strife and unremitting noise; and, significantly, the restricted space of the house is a notable theme in women's writing in the mid-1970s and 1980s, for example in the work of Elisabeth Meylan, Margrit Schriber and Maja Beutler.[11]

The prose writing of Friedrich Dürrenmatt in the early 1950s – *Der Richter und sein Henker* (1952), *Die Stadt. Prosa I-IV* (1952), *Der Verdacht* (1953) – did not at the time establish the same influence as Frisch's *Tagebuch* and *Stiller*. Nevertheless, it has been argued, perhaps too schematically, that two strands in German-Swiss narrative prose in the 1970s owe much to Dürrenmatt and Frisch respectively: the first, characterised by a grotesque exaggeration of reality, is represented by Walter Vogt, Hermann Burger, Gerold Späth, Franz Hohler, E. Y. Meyer and Urs Widmer; the second, characterised by social criticism and psychological realism, is represented by Adolf Muschg, W. M. Diggelmann, O. F. Walter, Werner Schmidli and Christoph Geiser.[12] If that analysis arguably overestimates the literary influence of Dürrenmatt, it is indisputable that he has never been perceived as having the moral authority of a 'Vater-Figur' for younger writers or as being a 'Motor und Anreger' of literary life in German-speaking Switzerland in the manner of Frisch.[13]

The ethos and particular circumstances of Switzerland as a political entity no longer offered such a strong focus of interest to new writers after the mid-1950s, partly because it was difficult to develop the theme beyond the point reached by *Stiller*, partly because circumstances were changing. Two aspects of the writing of the younger generation who came forward at the end of the 1950s and the beginning of the 1960s highlight this. Firstly, a very specific locality circumscribes the actions of their protagonists, as in O. F. Walter's *Der Stumme*, Jörg Steiner's *Strafarbeit* (1962) and Hugo Loetscher's *Die Kranzflechterin* (1964). The locality, traditionally perceived as offering communal protective security, has become the setting for the specific limitations to the individual life. An overarching concept such as Switzerland is no longer relevant: 'Schweizer bin ich etwa in dritter Linie', was O. F. Walter's famous formulation of the change in perception.[14] These novels point forward to the much darker depictions in the 1970s of the debilitating effects of locality, such as E. Y. Meyer's *In Trubschachen* (1973) and Burger's *Schilten*. Secondly, the novels of this generation broaden the social range of their protagonists to include, for example, a worker, an inmate of a borstal, a social dropout, and in this they are the forerunners of the novels of the 1970s and 1980s which display a broad social spectrum.

A gradual widening of historical perception in respect of the immediate past was set in train by the publication, from the late 1950s onwards, of a series of studies and official reports on the role of Switzerland in the Second World War.[15] In the sphere of fiction, David Wechsler's *Ein Haus zu wohnen* (1961) dealt in part with antisemitism in the army during the war, but the most notable attempt at a Swiss 'Vergangenheitsbewältigung' was Diggelmann's highly controversial *Die Hinterlassenschaft* (1965) which sought to link a fictional portrayal of the official policy towards refugees during the war with a thinly disguised reportage of the notorious persecution in 1956 of Switzerland's leading Marxist, Konrad Farner. Other aspects of Switzerland during the war years were treated by Heinrich Wiesner's *Schauplätze* (1969), Frisch's *Dienstbüchlein* (1974) and Niklaus Meienberg's 'Reportage' *Die Erschiessung des Ernst S* (1974).

One of the German-Swiss publications most noted in the 1960s outside Switzerland was Peter Bichsel's *Eigentlich möchte Frau Blum den Milchmann kennenlernen*. This volume of *Kurzprosa* had in fact had immediate predecessors, Kurt Marti's *Dorfgeschichten* (1960), Jürg Federspiel's *Orangen und Tode* (1961) and Raffael Ganz's *Orangentraum* (1961), yet it was Bichsel who became known abroad, possibly because he was awarded the prize of the West German *Gruppe 47*. Several reasons have been advanced for the popularity of *Kurzprosa* as a means of expression for German-Swiss writers at this time and subsequently:[16] the restricted form is an appropriate vehicle for the literary concerns of those who employ it; experiment with form is a feature of the uncertainty of a transitional period such as the 1960s; *Kurzprosa* represents part of a search for a form suited to express a fragmented reality; and interest in previous practitioners of the genre revived, especially in Robert Walser, whose stature as a great master of *Kurzprosa* began to be properly appreciated for the first time in the 1950s and 1960s.

It is perhaps significant that the manifestations in Switzerland of the 1968 student movement are commonly referred to as the 'Globus-Krawall', a designation which, relating to a Zurich department store, both circumscribes and neutralises the phenomenon. Certainly, the much more limited demonstrations in Switzerland created nothing like the social repercussions which occurred, for example, in West Germany and France. Nonetheless, the political failure of the movement and the ability of the existing power structures to withstand change decisively influenced the literature of the 1970s, for writing now challenged the validity of traditional views of Switzerland which, strongly nurtured by politicians, presented a well-defined area of unchanging stability. In the post-1968 climate, Switzerland was increasingly perceived by its writers as a repressive capitalist society intolerant of modes of life other than its own. Accordingly, the tone of much writing is sombre, but its focus, in contrast to more subjective trends in West Germany, remains broadly on the social framework of the life of the individual.

In the early 1970s a wide variety of attitudes relating to the general intellectual climate is apparent, both in the work of established figures and in that of writers publishing for the first time, such as Werner Schmidli, Gerold Späth, Urs Widmer and E. Y. Meyer – the so-called third generation after Frisch and Dürrenmatt. On the one hand, specific aspects of Switzerland are subject to reappraisal or examination: its history (Max Frisch's *Wilhelm Tell für die Schule* (1971), Otto Marchi's *Schweizer Geschichte für Ketzer*), its school system (Heinrich Wiesner's *Notennot* (1973)), its army (Max Frisch's *Dienstbüchlein* (1974)). On the other hand, a series of novels portrays the pressures on the individual in contemporary Switzerland: O. F. Walter's *Die ersten Unruhen* (1972) is set again in the invented town of Jammers, changed drastically in the name of progress and technological advance; E. Y. Meyer's *In Trubschachen* records the relentless constrictions of life in the apparently idyllic Swiss countryside; Adolf Muschg's *Albissers Grund* (1974) depicts the failure of a middle-class teacher and army officer to reject the values of the social system; and Werner Schmidli's *Fundplätze* (1974) charts a similar failure at a lower social level.

It is worth recording, however, that the darker tone of much writing in the 1970s contrasts with an upsurge in literary life. 1968 saw the establishment by Christoph Geiser and Werner Schmidli of *drehpunkt*, a literary journal which promoted new writing and became a forum for literary and social debate. The impact of small publishing houses such as Zytglogge in Bern, Lenos in Basle and Limmat in Zurich widened the range of material already being published in Switzerland and the Federal Republic, and the growth of public subvention, however dubious many of its aspects, certainly encouraged writers. In 1979, for example, the Solothurner Literaturtage were initiated with official support as an annual gathering of predominantly German-Swiss writers and critics, a formal affirmation that a vigorous literary climate existed in Switzerland.

If, in the 1960s, there was some attempt to come to terms with Switzerland's relationship to Nazi Germany, from the 1970s onwards the scope of the critical reassessment of the past widened. Firstly, the legacy of ideas and literature is assessed. For example, in 'Die Rede der Pflicht', at a key point in E. Y. Meyer's *In Trubschachen*, the perverted application of Kantian philosophy to underpin the work ethic is excoriated, through the example of Switzerland, as a debilitating feature of life in modern society. In Otto Marchi's *Rückfälle* (1978), the vision in Keller's *Der grüne Heinrich* of the potential for human community in democratic society contrasts with the soulless dictates of economics which actually govern the life of the hero in modern Switzerland. Lukas Hartmann's *Pestalozzis Berg* (1976, revised edition 1988) suggests that the teachings of the great man, impeded in their realisation by his own society, have been misrepresented in their spirit by present-day society.

Secondly, periods in the more immediate past are presented from an individual viewpoint but with some claim to representative status: Herbert Wiesner's *Der Riese am Tisch* (1978) describes a childhood in the 1930s dominated by an overbearing father with a drinking problem, a theme taken up at a different social level in O. F. Walter's *Zeit des Fasans* (1988); in Hansjörg Schneider's *Lieber Leo* (1980) a generation, born in the late 1930s and reared in the restrictive attitudes of the 1940s and 1950s in Switzerland, is incapable of establishing inner stability in the changing society of the 1970s; Christoph Geiser's *Grünsee* (1978) and *Brachland* (1980) depict in representative fashion childhood and adolescence in a certain class in the 1950s and 1960s; Dante Andrea Franzetti's *Cosimo und*

Hamlet (1987) portrays, at a point in time closer to the subject of its recollection, the problems of assimilation and xenophobia associated with an immigrant childhood in urban Switzerland in the 1970s and early 1980s.

Thirdly, the past is, in more general fashion, viewed as a repository of alternatives to the technologically based consumerism which has sundered all continuity with former modes of life: in E. Y. Meyer's *Die Rückfahrt* the young hero, seeking to re-establish the link to his own past after temporarily losing his memory in a car accident, discovers the importance of history in coming to terms with contemporary life; and in O. F. Walter's *Das Staunen der Schlafwandler am Ende der Nacht* (1983) the brief vision of the possibilities contained in a past mode of life influences crucially a decision taken by the hero in the present.

Fourthly, non-fictional forms contribute to the creation of a historical dimension by revealing submerged aspects of social reality in the past. Laure Wyss's collection of *Frauen-Protokolle aus der Schweiz* (1974) records the experience of a number of women from differing backgrounds in a society which kept all women disenfranchised at Federal level until 1971. Rosalia Wenger's *Rosalia G – Ein Leben* (1978) depicts a life of deprivation and hardship which was a common female lot in the earlier part of the century. In addition to these records, there are the investigations into recent Swiss history by Niklaus Meienberg, one of the more recent of which, *Die Welt als Wille und Wahn* (1987), deals with the Germanophile attitudes of the Swiss General Ulrich Wille during the First World War.

This increase in historical and social awareness is accompanied by a twofold perception of the fragility of the individual.[17] Firstly, the individual is seen to be exposed to social forces inimical to his definition and development. The attitude of the central figure towards survival in Hugo Loetscher's *Der Immune* (1975) and its sequel *Die Papiere des Immunen* (1986) is representative: he is a person 'der sich soweit gegen die Ansprüche dieser Gesellschaft immunisieren möchte, um ihr nicht total zu erliegen'.[18] In differing ways and with differing degrees of success, the central figures of Gertrud Leutenegger's *Vorabend* (1975) and Hermann Burger's *Schilten* seek to protect and define their individuality against the environment which threatens constantly to diminish or engulf them. In Gerhard Meier's *Der schnurgerade Kanal* (1977) the diary, the individual's record of himself, is written in the *man* form – also used by the narrator in *In Trubschachen* to express a problematic identity – and registers, as does the 'Bericht' in *Schilten*, an incapacity to find a mode of expression for the personality of the writer. In Gerold Späth's *Commedia* (1980), all attempt to define personal contours is thwarted by normative social pressures which, far from creating human bonds, isolate and debilitate.

A second assault on the individual is made by the forces of death and disease, taboo subjects in a world dominated by notions of perfectibility. One mode of writing, personal testimony in the face of approaching death, made its appearance with Fritz Zorn's *Mars* (1977). The sensational success of *Mars* derived from the claim by the author that there was a direct causal link between his terminal cancer and the life-denying social attitudes of his wealthy *groß-bürgerlich* background. Two further records by sufferers from terminal cancer, Walter Matthias Diggelmann's *Schatten. Tagebuch einer Krankheit* (1979) and Peter Noll's *Diktate über Sterben und Tod* (1984), reflect more a determination to come to terms with the inevitable in a dignified fashion. A second mode of writing seeks to distance the experience of death, illness and physical incapacity by means of a more literary framework. The title story of Thomas Hürlimann's *Die Tessinerin* (1981) depicts the lingering death of a woman, doubly estranged by her origins elsewhere and by her approaching end, and *Das Gartenhaus* (1989) shows the stratagems devised by those coping with the loss of a loved one. Maja Beutler's *Fuß fassen* (1980) and Erica Pedretti's *Valerie oder Das unerzogene Auge* (1986) deal with the problems of women trying to cope with cancer in an environment which has simply not created a place for illness, least of all for cancer. And Claudia Storz's *Jessica mit Konstruktionsfehlern* (1977) describes the social embarrassments encountered by a woman with a physical disability.

It is certainly not without significance that women writers should contribute to the theme of social stigmatisation associated with illness and incapacity, deprived as they were until twenty years ago of a political role in an almost exemplary patriarchal society. Indeed, in a curious simultaneity with female enfranchisement at Federal level, the 1970s witnessed the arrival of Margrit Baur, Eveline Hasler and others. Again in a remarkable parallel, Gertrud Leutenegger's presentation of the political woman in *Vorabend* appeared in 1975, the same year as Verena Stefan's *Häutungen*, the enormously successful feminist cult book in West Germany. Franziska Greising's *Kammerstille* (1983) addresses the theme of restricted space, and her chillingly realist depiction of female victimisation in rural Switzerland, together with Margrit von Dach's *Geschichten vom Fräulein* (1982), a witty demolition of reader expectations, act as markers to show the thematic and formal range of women's writing at the beginning of the 1980s. By the end of the decade, after the arrival of writers of short stories such as Helen Meier and Ilma Rakusa, women's writing had begun to make a major contribution to German-Swiss literature.

The workplace, where so much of the average life is spent, features as the setting for a series of novels and stories in the 1970s and 1980s. In Silvio Blatter's collection of short stories *Schaltfehler* (1972) and in his 'Erzählung' *Genormte Tage, verschüttete Zeit* (1976), the repetitiveness which characterises factory work extends to life outside, and the individual's awareness that his inauthentic life is shared by thousands of others creates no sense of solidarity. The novels of Emil Zopfi, *Jede Minute kostet 33 Franken* (1977) and *Computer für tausendundeine Nächte* (1980) present similar restrictions on the individual in relation to the operation of modern technology, whereas Urs Karpf's novels *Der Technokrat* (1977) and *Die Versteinerung* (1981) deal with the shrinking possibilities of the manufacturing and commercial world. The writing of Franz Böni and Beat Sterchi's *Blösch* portray most tellingly the relentless assault on the energies and sensibilities of the individual by the nature of modern work. In the bleak and inhospitable landscapes of Böni's world, the protagonists are shown to be mercilessly incorporated into the mechanical processes which they serve (*Schlatt*, 1979), move from one place of soulless drudgery to the next (*Die Wanderarbeiter*, 1981), or are exploited in unskilled work on the margins of industrial society (*Die Alpen*, 1983). In *Blösch* the same relentless economic pressures which industrialise farming also degrade workers in the slaughterhouse to serve machines which ruthlessly maximise throughput. The horror of the work processes described by Böni and Sterchi constitutes an indictment of the unexamined belief in the value of the work ethic and the profit motive.

The resistance to political change in the course of the decade which was ushered in by the suppression of the 1980 demonstrations in Zurich again contrasts with the richness and liveliness of the literary scene over the next ten years. If Frisch, after *Blaubart* (1982), fell silent until *Schweiz ohne Armee? Ein Palaver*, Dürrenmatt reasserted his creative vitality during the period, coming forward with, amongst other work, *Stoffe I-III* (1981), *Justiz* (1985), *Der Auftrag* (1986) and the short novel *Durcheinandertal* (1989). Additionally, Dürrenmatt's early prose *Die Stadt. Prosa I-IV* (1952) underwent a reassessment with the publication of *Stoffe I-III*, and the motifs of labyrinths and caves in both collections are seen to link with similar motifs in the work of writers such as Burger, Späth and Martin R. Dean.[19] The reputation of the second generation continued to grow, as evidenced by the invitations extended for example to Muschg, Bichsel, Nizon and Loetscher to deliver prestigious 'Poetik-Vorlesungen' in Frankfurt and Munich.[20] The third generation also continued to publish, and a fourth generation came forward at the end of the 1970s and the beginning of the 1980s, for example, Martin R. Dean, Rahel Hutmacher, Marcel Konrad and Matthias Zschokke. A measure of the distance travelled in twenty years is obtained by comparing the debate of 1965–66 on the absence in contemporary writing of the theme of Switzerland with the so-called 'Realismus-Debatte' of 1983 in which the focus was wider, and the discussion questioned the validity of definitions of literary realism in capitalist society of the late twentieth century.[21]

Two further aspects of contemporary German-Swiss writing in relation to its social background should be mentioned. Firstly, the refusal to accept the interpretations of the political status quo – highlighted in the 1980 demonstrations – finds its counterpart in the literary theme of 'Verweigerung':[22] the work of E. Y. Meyer, Hermann Burger, Gerold Späth, Gerhard Meier, Hanna Johansen and others seeks to identify and give articulation to that within the individual which, aware of the disjunction between experience and ideology, resists political and social manipulation. Secondly, the challenge to reader expectation seeks to promote a revision of social perception: the depicted fragility of the traditionally solid Swiss house has been mentioned; Switzerland is presented as an example, not in the traditional sense of 'ein Vorbild Europas', but in the sense of a warning of what is to come elsewhere in advanced societies, in novels such as *Die Rückfahrt*, *Blösch* and Gertrud Leutenegger's *Kontinent* (1985); the idyll traditionally associated with the Swiss countryside is destroyed in novels such as Walter Kauer's *Spätholz* (1976); titles such as Urs Widmer's *Schweizer Geschichten* (1976) or Franz Böni's *Die Alpen* create expectations of affirmation which they do not fulfil. By setting itself at odds with a political ideology which obscures and distorts reality, literature thus becomes 'ein Instrument für die Erforschung unserer Wirklichkeit'.[23]

If the perceived social role of the writer in German-speaking Switzerland has undergone change since 1945, it is no less true that writing has taken itself much less for granted as a reliable means of communication over the same period. Certainly, this is not a development confined to Switzerland, but it is particularly worthwhile recording its presence in a literature with a strong realist tradition. It has been suggested that, if the first major theme of post-war Swiss literature is 'die Reflexion auf Umwelt und

Öffentlichkeit', the second 'besteht im Reflektieren auf das schriftstellerische Metier, auf das Wie, auf Form und Sprache'.[24] Both writing about the problems of writing and experimentation with form had already appeared in the 1960s and established themselves more firmly in the subsequent two decades. The first is exemplified by Peter Bichsel's *Die Jahreszeiten* (1967), by Christoph Geiser's *Grünsee* (1978), or by Matthias Zschokke's *Max* (1982). The second mode can be exemplified by Paul Nizon's *Canto* (1963), Clemens Mettler's *Glasberg* (1968), Christoph Mangold's *Konzert für Papagei und Schifferklavier* (1969), the work of Jürg Laederach from *Einfall der Dämmerung* (1974) to *69 Arten den Blues zu spielen* (1984), the writings of Felix Philipp Ingold and Margrit von Dach, and Marcel Konrad's *Erzählzeit* (1984).

Attempts to categorise individual works and individual authors can at best result in approximations, and general statements are notoriously prone to reflect subjective reactions. Within the framework of these qualifications, it seems to me that the thoughts and impressions generated in the reader by contemporary writing in German-speaking Switzerland stand at odds in two ways with the same reader's experience of the smooth functioning of Swiss society and the ubiquitous evidence of a very high material standard of living. Firstly, this writing acts as a reminder of how little prosperity and the satisfaction of consumer wishes contribute to the fulfilment of human needs, of how inadequate the myths of Western industrialised society are. Secondly, this writing records the impact of the forces of modern life on a localised society and expresses the resulting sense of dislocation: 'Der Grundzug, der Grundton eines Fremdwerdens im Vertrauten, eines Heimatloswerdens im eigenen Ursprung, eines Verlustes von Identität kann als strukturelles Merkmal deutschsprachiger Dichtung in der Schweiz heute gelten'.[25] If it is true that the author in German-speaking Switzerland still writes today within the political and cultural dialectic mentioned at the beginning of this review,[26] it certainly seems to the outside observer that the dominant concern of writing over the last four decades has moved from political affirmation in the 1940s to defence of the individual in the 1980s. O. F. Walter, going back in the German-Swiss literary tradition to a figure whom he considers to have offered at a certain historical point possibilities of personal emancipation, wonders if the modern writer can do the same: 'Was die Mythen Gotthelfs den Berner Bauern offrierten an Selbstfindungsmöglichkeit – kann die Literatur diese Dienstleistung der Gesellschaft, wie wir sie heute erleben, noch erbringen?'[27] Contemporary writing in German-speaking

Switzerland, with its range of talent and theme, provides a variety of responses to this urgent question.

Notes

1. Carl Spitteler, 'Unser Schweizer Standpunkt', in *Gesammelte Werke*, ed. Gottfried Bohnenblust, Wilhelm Altwegg and Robert Faesi, 10 vols, Zurich, 1945–1958, vol. 8, pp. 577–94; Karl Schmid, 'Die kulturelle Lage der Schweiz 1944', in *Zeitspuren. Aufsätze und Reden II*, Zurich and Stuttgart, 1967, pp. 14–31, especially p. 20f.

2. 'Vorwort', in Bruno Mariacher and Friedrich Witz (eds), *Bestand und Versuch. Schweizer Schrifttum der Gegenwart*, Zurich, 1964, pp. 7–10 (p. 9); and 'Vorwort', in Hugo Leber (ed.), *Texte. Prosa junger Schweizer Autoren*, Zurich, 1964, pp. 7–16 (p. 8).

3. A full documentation of the 'Zürcher Literaturstreit' is provided in *Sprache im technischen Zeitalter*, vol. 22, 1967, pp. 83–206 and vol. 26, 1968, pp. 87–179.

4. Reto Hänny, *Zürich. Anfang September*, Frankfurt am Main, 1981, p. 131.

5. Dante Andrea Franzetti, 'Letzter Tango auf die schweizerische Eigenart', *Texte*, no. 4, Summer 1987, pp. 14–15 (p. 14), reprinted in Wilhelm Solms (ed.), *Geschichten aus einem ereignislosen Land*, Marburg, 1989, pp. 91–7.

6. For Marchi, see Otto Marchi, *Schweizer Geschichte für Ketzer*, 5th edn, Zurich, 1985, pp. 200–5; for a selection of readers' letters; for Frisch, see 'Der Friede widerspricht unserer Gesellschaft', *Die Weltwoche*, 23 November 1989.

7. Niklaus Meienberg in *Vorschlag zur Unversöhnlichkeit. Realismusdebatte Winter 1983/84*, ed. Fredi Lerch, Zurich, 1984, p. 12; Adolf Muschg, 'Hunger nach Format', in *Begegnungen. Eine Festschrift für Max Frisch zum siebzigsten Geburtstag*, ed. Siegfried Unseld, Frankfurt am Main, 1981, pp. 154–76 (p. 174).

8. Walter Matthias Diggelmann, 'Die Schweiz – provinziell solange nicht entdeckt', *Die Weltwoche*, 25 September 1964.

9. Max Frisch, *Gesammelte Werke in zeitlicher Folge*, ed. Hans Mayer, 7 vols, Frankfurt am Main, 1976–86, vol. 2, p. 474.

10. Ibid., vol. 2, p. 349.

11. See Marianne Burkhard, 'Diskurs in der Enge. Ein Beitrag zur Phänomenologie der Schweizer Literatur', in Albrecht Schöne (ed.), *Akten des VII. Internationalen Germanisten-Kongresses Göttingen 1985*, Tübingen, 1986, vol. 10, pp. 52–62.

12. Klaus Pezold, 'Die deutschsprachige Literatur der Schweiz in den sechziger und siebziger Jahren. Probleme, Thesen und offene Fragen', in Klaus Pezold (ed.), *Entwicklungstendenzen der deutschsprachigen Literatur der Schweiz in den sechziger und siebziger Jahren*, Leipzig, 1984, pp. 7–40 (pp. 30ff.); Pezold's thesis has since been relativised by János Szabó, *Erzieher und Verweigerer. Zur deutschsprachigen Gegenwartsprosa der Schweiz*, Würzburg, 1989, p. 141, who refers, more convincingly on the basis of the evidence, to the 'fruchtbaren Frisch- und der kaum präsenten Dürrenmatt-Linie'.

13. Hermann Burger, 'Schreiben in der Ich-Form. Zur Literatur in der Schweiz', *Schweizer Monatshefte*, vol. 53, 1973, pp. 45–54 (p. 46); and Egon Ammann, 'Die Schweiz – kein Thema mehr. Rezeption aus der Sicht eines Schweizer Verlegers', in *Geschichten aus einem ereignislosen Land*, pp. 135–46 (p. 138).

14. O. F. Walter, 'Unbewältigte schweizerische Vergangenheit', *Die Weltwoche*, 11 March 1966.

15. See, for example, Carl Ludwig, *Die Flüchtlingspolitik der Schweiz seit 1933 bis zur Gegenwart*, Bern, 1957; Alice Meyer, *Anpassung und Widerstand. Die Schweiz zur Zeit des deutschen Nationalsozialismus*, Frauenfeld, 1965; Alfred Häsler, *Das Boot ist voll. Die Schweiz und die Flüchtlinge 1933–1945*, Zurich, 1967; Edgar Bonjour, *Geschichte der schweizerischen Neutralität*, 9 vols, Basle, 1965–74 (vols 4, 5 and 6 relating to the period 1939 to 1945 were published in 1970).

16. See Klaus Dieter Schulz, 'Untersuchungen zum literarischen Leben in der Schweiz der sechziger Jahre. Die deutschsprachige Literatur im Spiegel von Literaturkritik und öffentlicher Diskussion', unpublished PhD thesis, University of Leipzig, 1980, pp. 59ff.

17. See Gerda Zeltner, *Das Ich ohne Gewähr. Gegenwartsautoren aus der Schweiz*, Zurich and Frankfurt am Main, 1980.

18. Hugo Loetscher, 'Der Auftritt des Engagements', in Dieter Bachmann (ed.), *Fortschreiben. 98 Autoren der deutschen Schweiz*, Zurich, 1977, pp. 194–8 (p. 198).

19. See Anton Krättli, 'Labyrinthen und Höhlen. Beobachtungen an der deutschschweizerischen Gegenwartsliteratur', *Neue Rundschau*, vol. 95, 1984, pp. 71–87.

20. 'Poetik-Vorlesungen' at the University of Frankfurt: Adolf Muschg, *Literatur als Therapie?*, Frankfurt am Main, 1981, Peter Bichsel, *Der Leser. Das Erzählen*, Darmstadt and Neuwied, 1982, Paul Nizon, *Am Schreiben gehen*, Frankfurt am Main, 1985; at the University of Munich, Hugo Loetscher, *Vom Erzählen erzählen*, Zurich, 1988; and, at the University of Graz, a member of the third generation, Jürg Laederach, *Der zweite Sinn*, Frankfurt am Main, 1988.

21. See 'Unbewältigte schweizerische Vergangenheit?', *Die Weltwoche*, 11 and 25 March, 1 and 22 April 1966; and *Vorschlag zur Unversöhnlichkeit*.

22. See Peter Grotzer (ed.), *Aspekte der Verweigerung in der neueren Literatur aus der Schweiz*, Zurich, 1988.

23. Gertrud Leutenegger, quoted by Elsbeth Pulver in Elsbeth Pulver (ed.) *Zwischenzeilen. Schriftstellerinnen der deutschen Schweiz*, Zurich and Bern, 1985, p. 23.

24. Peter André Bloch, 'Aspekte und Tendenzen der deutschschweizerischen Gegenwartsliteratur. Von Frisch und Dürrenmatt zu O. F. Walter und Peter Bichsel', in Albrecht Schöne (ed.), *Akten des VI. Internationalen Germanisten-Kongresses Basel 1980*, Bern, 1980, vol. 4, pp. 202–11 (p. 208).

25. Ralf Schnell, '"Fremd und fern wie in Grönland". Schweizer Gegenwartsliteratur aus deutscher Sicht: Eine dissidente Poesie', in Gürsel Aytaç, Viktoria Rehberg and Sara Sayin (eds), *Dokumentation der Beiträge des II. Izmirer Colloquiums*, Izmir, 1987, pp. 91–100 (p. 95).

26. See also Michael Böhler, 'Swiss Literary Culture since 1945: Productive Antagonisms and Conflicting Identities', *German Quarterly*, vol. 62, 1989, pp. 293–307.

27. Otto F. Walter, 'Zehn Noten zum Schreiben', in *Gegenwort. Aufsätze, Reden, Begegnungen*, ed. Giaco Schiesser, Zurich, 1988, pp. 95–9 (p. 95).

II

Challenge and Example

3

Max Frisch and Friedrich Dürrenmatt

Michael Butler

From the vantage point of the last decade of the twentieth century it is difficult to capture accurately the situation of Switzerland over fifty years ago. The images of stable financial power in the international arena and solid prosperity at home have long since blunted memories of the weakness and fragility of a small democratic country surrounded on all sides by hostile, fascist powers. And yet it was the unique experience of being both incarcerated within their own borders and cut off from the momentous events beyond them that shaped the intellectual and cultural horizons of the new generation of writers which emerged after 1945. There was a sense of liberation and relief that a frightening nightmare had after all passed them by. The proud tradition of Swiss neutrality, underpinned militarily by a determined Citizen Army and ideologically by the concept of 'geistige Landesverteidigung', was seen to have come through the severest test of its long history. The reality, of course, was somewhat different.

For despite the official policy of neutrality and the widespread opposition towards the excesses of fascist Germany and Italy, the exigencies of *Realpolitik* led to a series of compromises with Hitler and Mussolini. For example, strategic supplies between the Axis powers were allowed to flow unhindered across the Alps throughout the war, and the refusal to admit many Jewish refugees seeking asylum in the country at the height of the Nazi pogroms – following the slogan 'das kleine Rettungsboot ist voll' – sharply relativised the country's vaunted humanitarianism. Whilst official propaganda continued to stress Switzerland's courageous 'Igelstellung', the more complex, and thus less flattering, truth was laconically expressed by Dürrenmatt over twenty years later in his fragment, 'Zur Dramaturgie der Schweiz' (1968/70):

> Neutralität ist eine politische Taktik, keine Moral. Neutralität ist die Kunst, sich möglichst nützlich und möglichst ungefährlich zu verhalten.

–41–

Wir waren auch Hitler gegenüber möglichst nützlich und möglichst
ungefährlich . . . Wir lavierten uns zwischen den Beinen des Dino-
sauriers hindurch ins Freie . . . wir hielten an unseren Idealen fest, ohne
sie unbedingt anzuwenden, wir schlossen die Augen, ohne gerade blind
zu werden. Tell spannte zwar die Armbrust, doch grüßte er den Hut ein
wenig – beinahe fast nicht –, und das Heldentum blieb uns erspart.
(WA/28 63f.)[1]

Dürrenmatt's essay, of course, was written at the end of a decade
which in Switzerland was – as in West Germany, if not quite so
violently – a time of reckoning, when critical sons and daughters
began to question their parents' interpretation of the world. In
1945, for the vast majority of the population, matters were more
comfortingly black and white. The ideological undertow of 'geistige Landesverteidigung', sharply boosted by the repression of the
East German workers' rebellion of 1953 and the 1956 Hungarian
Uprising, ensured that anti-fascism evaporated and anti-com-
munism, always a feature of Swiss public policy, came more to
the fore.

However, during the 1930s and 1940s one institution above all
was untainted by compromise: the Schauspielhaus in Zurich. From
1933 to the end of the war the Schauspielhaus was the centre of
German-language theatre. Under Ferdinand Rieser and later Oskar
Wälterlin, it attracted the cream of theatrical refugees from Nazi
Germany – not to the unalloyed pleasure, it must be admitted, of
every local actor and director – and these new arrivals helped to
turn a provincial enterprise into a theatre of world stature. The
success of Frisch and Dürrenmatt in so quickly establishing themselves on the European stage after 1945 is incomprehensible outside
the context of this theatre which despite its isolation maintained a
vibrant international repertoire, which included the world
premières of Brecht's *Mutter Courage* (1941), *Der gute Mensch von
Sezuan* (1943) and *Leben des Galilei* (1943).

The lack of competition from an exhausted Germany naturally
gave the Swiss dramatists a flying start, but talent of a high order
was also required. And, although both writers originally began
with narrative fiction – Frisch's first major publication was the
novel *Jürg Reinhart* (1934); Dürrenmatt's first stories date from 1943
– it was their plays of the late 1940s and 1950s, culminating in
Biedermann und die Brandstifter (1958) and *Andorra* (1961), and *Der
Besuch der alten Dame* (1956) and *Die Physiker* (1963), which established their reputation both as Swiss iconoclasts and as creators of
critical models of wider European significance. Inevitably, the two

men were yoked together, and indeed in the early days, when they were in close contact with each other, a friendly rivalry spurred both to greater dramatic efforts. To the more reflective reader or spectator, however, it was clear that Frisch and Dürrenmatt were very different writers. Understandably irritated by the constant juxtaposition, Frisch himself once remarked that the difference between them lay in the fact that Dürrenmatt's creativity had its roots in theology (his father was a parish priest), whereas his own could be traced to the rational humanism of the Enlightenment.[2] This has proved an oversimplification, for although Dürrenmatt had indeed once planned to write a doctoral thesis on Kierkegaard, there is a great deal of Enlightenment thought in his later philosophical essays, just as the challenging ironies of Kierkegaard's theology inspired a major theme of Frisch's greatest achievement, *Stiller* (1954). Heinz Ludwig Arnold characterised the essential difference when he pointed, on the one hand, to Frisch's antipathy towards all abstract theorising and, on the other, to Dürrenmatt's fascination with epistemology: 'Frisch literarisiert seine Erlebnisse; Dürrenmatt literarisiert seine Erkenntnisse.'[3] This crucial insight helps to explain the different Swiss reactions to Frisch and Dürrenmatt. Despite occasional scandals, for example over Dürrenmatt's first play, *Es steht geschrieben* (1947), or in 1969 when he decided to pass on his 'Großer Literaturpreis des Kantons Bern' to three well-known nonconformists, including Arthur Villard, the controversial initiator of a highly unpopular campaign for the institution of 'Zivildienst' as an alternative to military service, Dürrenmatt rarely aroused the fierce animosity which all too often was Frisch's lot. For right up to his sudden death on 14 December 1990 Dürrenmatt's relationship with Switzerland was characterised more by ironic distance, his criticism – often just as hard-hitting as Frisch's[4] – usually rendered more palatable by his idiosyncratic humour. Frisch, on the other hand, always demonstrated a high degree of personal involvement with his environment, exhibiting at times a hypersensitivity to criticism which occasionally alienated friend and foe alike.[5]

Indeed, Frisch's intensely subjective response to his environment was the key to his significance for many younger German-Swiss writers. No work of Dürrenmatt's, for example, has had the persistent resonance of *Stiller*. The story of a man who cannot accept society's image of himself, who flees its suffocating smugness in order to locate a more creative identity, but returns to Switzerland only to discover that such radical transformations are not possible – this novel seemed to speak for a whole generation of younger writers and intellectuals, who felt similarly paralysed by the exemplary 'Konkordanzdemokratie' of post-war Switzerland. Thus the themes of thwarted 'Aufbruch', the symbolic antimony of 'Enge' and 'Weite', became dominant in the work of such writers as Adolf Muschg, Peter Bichsel and Paul Nizon and reached perhaps their most damning, if neurotic, expression in Fritz Zorn's *Mars* (1977), the astonishing dissection of the Zurich 'Goldküste', the right bank of Lake Zurich where the very rich live.[6]

By contrast, Dürrenmatt's imagination was predominantly inspired by the classical myths and legends he had absorbed in his childhood. The structure of *Die Physiker*, for example, is Oedipal. The physicist Möbius, in his attempt to escape the frightening consequences of his own discoveries, flees into the assumed safety of the madhouse, only to discover that he has delivered his terrible secret straight into the hands of the power-crazed Mathilde von Zahnd. Dürrenmatt, in other words, was fascinated by intellectual and moral problems which he could think through dramaturgically, while Frisch's work concentrates on more subjective, existential concerns.

Another reason for Frisch's greater importance for Swiss writers of the younger generation lay in his willingness to become directly involved in political issues or cultural controversies. Whereas Dürrenmatt always refused to see Switzerland as a specific problem beyond the framework of a general cultural malaise, Frisch remorselessly attacked his fellow countrymen for their narrowness of vision and cultural myopia. Throughout the 1960s, for example, it was Frisch who took the leading role in such varied polemics as the problem of 'Heimat', the public amnesia over the Swiss record in the war, the unpleasant racist debate on 'Überfremdung' or the violent suppression of the youth revolt in Zurich in 1968. Thus, much more than Dürrenmatt, Frisch was seen as central to the often bitter arguments about Swiss identity which were linked to the catchwords of the 1960s, 'helvetisches Malaise', 'Unbehagen im Kleinstaat', 'Diskurs in der Enge'.

The different roles played by the two senior Swiss writers were well exemplified in the so-called 'Zürcher Literaturstreit' of 1966. The intemperate attack on contemporary German literature unleashed by Switzerland's most prominent Germanist, Emil Staiger, on the receipt of the Zurich Literaturpreis, led to a controversy which swiftly escalated beyond Switzerland's borders. The counterattack was launched by Frisch in his famous essay, 'Endlich darf man es wieder sagen', but the acrimonious debate which followed drew in many of the best known literary figures in Switzerland and the Federal Republic.[7] Dürrenmatt was conspicuous by his silence. Only a year later, on the occasion of the same award to the painter Varlin, did he add his support in a witty, but by that stage superfluous, speech, 'Varlin schweigt'.

Although Frisch's public battles in the 1960s won him esteem from his younger colleagues,[8] they achieved very little outside sympathetic intellectual circles. Similarly, the reception of his creative work was patchy. Whereas the novel *Mein Name sei Gantenbein* (1964) underlined his skill at articulating the problem of lost or precarious identity through a fascinating exploration of language as an unreliable compass in the charting of memories and experience, *Biografie* (1967), his first play since *Andorra*, achieved merely a *succès d'estime* for all its assured theatricality and brilliant dialogue. Dürrenmatt, on the other hand, after his great successes of the 1950s, including a number of idiosyncratic detective stories which characteristically overturn the genre's comforting conventions, had to cope with a series of theatrical disappointments: *Der Meteor* (1965), *Die Wiedertäufer* (1966, a radical reworking of *Es steht geschrieben*) and *Porträt eines Planeten* (1970) all flopped. Indeed, the end of the decade marked a turning point in the careers of both writers. Frisch, for example, demonstrated his impressively resilient imagination in his *Tagebuch 1966–1971* (1972) which with its mixture of short stories, political commentary, witty 'Fragebögen' on marriage, violence and the problem of ageing, recalls but does not repeat the techniques of the earlier *Tagebuch 1946–1949* (1950). As for Dürrenmatt, the failure of *Der Mitmacher* (1972), together with his negative experiences as a director in the mid 1970s in the Zurich Schauspielhaus, led him to withdraw from the theatre and concentrate on narrative fiction and philosophical speculation, which the unexpected success of *Play Strindberg* (1969) did little to alter.

By the end of the 1960s the major role played by Frisch and Dürrenmatt in contributing to and promoting the conditions for a vital literature in German-speaking Switzerland was clear. The matter of assessing their influence on individual writers is altogether more problematic. There may be some justification in grouping Adolf Muschg, Peter Bichsel and Otto F. Walter temperamentally around the 'Frisch' pole, and more loosely perhaps, E. Y. Meyer, Hugo Loetscher and Hermann Burger around the 'Dürrenmatt' one; but the overlaps and cross-references are too complex to render such categorisations more than fleetingly plausible. What ultimately counts is the example the older writers set for their younger colleagues in the way they challenged the social, political and spiritual reality of their environment.

As later generations of writers came to the fore in the 1970s and 1980s, neither Frisch nor Dürrenmatt retired from the scene. The last two decades have seen, in fact, major work from both, in each case marked by an astonishing consistency. Where the 'Bildnis' theme, first articulated in his *Tagebuch 1946–1949*, continued to underlie Frisch's later work, Dürrenmatt's dominant obsession with the twin concepts of labyrinth and rebellion became even clearer. Frisch, for all his moral scepticism, continued to write from an Enlightenment point of view with its battered utopian belief in the possibility of change; Dürrenmatt continued to dissect the illusory nature of all utopias, setting only the rebellious mockery of the creative spirit against a pervasive determinism.

Frisch's *Wilhelm Tell für die Schule* (1971), originally meant as part of the *Tagebuch 1966–1971*, fits into his long struggle to confront his fellow countrymen with the rigidity of their self-imposed image. Despite the well-known historical facts – for example, the Nordic origins of the Tell myth – the Swiss, in Frisch's view, cling complacently to a worn-out tradition and thus impede any possibility of spiritual or moral growth. With great virtuosity he retells the old story from the point of view of a tired, well-meaning Gessler, the supposed representative of Habsburg tyranny. Proceeding via a series of hypotheses and adding to his text lengthy, mock-academic footnotes, Frisch subtly deconstructs the heroic pretensions that still help to underpin the ideology of the state. Indeed, it was these footnotes, with their caustic references to contemporary scandals and political expediency, rather than the witty story itself, that provoked the little book's hostile reception in Switzerland.

With *Montauk* (1974) Frisch made his own idiosyncratic contribution to a general trend in the writing of the 1970s, which came to be known in West Germany as 'Neue Subjektivität'. Frisch's extraordinary meditation on his 'Leben als Mann' certainly appeared to fit into the current vogue for autobiography. However, *Montauk* bears the significant description 'Erzählung' and acknowledges its debt to the sceptical tradition of Montaigne. What is presented ostensibly as the account of a brief love affair, a weekend 'out of time' with a young American girl in Montauk, a small fishing village on the tip of Long Island, becomes a much more complex exploration of the nature of memory and experience. The older man reflects on the impossibility of repeating the spontaneity of youth, for each new experience is lived via the structures of earlier ones. This pattern of programmed responses insidiously undermines all vitality. The fact that the book's protagonist is called 'Max Frisch' and quotes constantly from the writer's works adds a piquant immediacy (certainly not prurience) to themes most fully explored in *Mein Name sei Gantenbein*. Like the anonymous 'Buch-Ich' of the earlier novel, Frisch – despite himself – turns into an equally insubstantial character in an imagined story. The attempt at total honesty founders on the very nature of narration to thrust distorting patterns onto the shapelessness of lived experience.

The fear of 'Wiederholung', which underpins such false coherence, was of course a principal theme of *Stiller*. It is taken to its logical conclusion in Frisch's last play, *Triptychon. Drei szenische Bilder* (1978). The work is a stylish presentation of the cruel finality of the images we make of ourselves and others. In the grey permanence of an imagined Hades, the characters are transfixed in the negative attitudes of their previous lives. The necessarily static quality of the play makes it difficult to stage successfully, but the 'triptych' is structured as an elegiac 'Warntafel', in whose three bleak panels the audience can see reflected with uncomfortable precision its own trivial preoccupations.

In *Der Mensch erscheint im Holozän* (1979) the equally 'private' story of an old man, retired to a remote Ticinese valley from a busy life in the city, becomes a resonant metaphor for a very 'public' crisis. Momentarily cut off by bad weather and difficult terrain from civilisation, Herr Geiser is forced to confront both his own mortality and the meaning of the vast intellectual and cultural edifice mankind has constructed as his 'permanent' habitat. Like a confused Noah, Geiser attempts to reconstruct in his head, and with the help of a 'Zettelwand' on which he pins notes and cuttings from reference books of all kinds, the world as he has known it. With his memory defective and his physical strength diminishing, his efforts are doomed to failure as the laws of nature assert their dominance over man and his creations. The text, for all its linguistic sparseness, is one of Frisch's most richly suggestive. For example, the passage describing Geiser's exhausting attempt to break out of the oppressive gloom of his valley and climb to freedom over the mountain pass echoes both Plato's cave simile and Sisyphean heroism, thus bringing the short tale close to Dürrenmatt's mythical concerns. *Der Mensch erscheint im Holozän* clearly has reference beyond the immediate case to a world threatened by nuclear or ecological apocalypse. Its impact, however, is all the stronger for posing at a basically 'private' level the philosophical question of how an intelligible world can survive the demise of the individual mind which fashioned it.

Blaubart (1982), at first sight, appears to return the reader to a more conventional fictional mode, since the story suggests the dimensions of a detective novel. However, Frisch begins his tale with the acquittal of his paradoxically named protagonist, Felix Schaad, of the brutal murder of a call-girl, his sixth wife, for lack of evidence. Though pronounced innocent, Schaad in fact cannot disentangle himself from the web of deceit and guilt produced by a lifetime of defective personal relationships, not least with his various wives. Like Walter Faber, Schaad appears suspended in a capsule of timelessness from which no distractions can free him. He lives on only in the words and gestures of his ex-wives, friends and acquaintances – all of whom cling to their particular graven images of his personality. Stylistically similar to *Der Mensch erscheint im Holozän*, *Blaubart* explores the contradictory nature of memory both as the key to individual perception and as the most important single source of its distortion. Unhappily, *Blaubart* turned out to be Frisch's farewell to a distinguished career as a novelist; it is thus fitting that the story should recapitulate his central theme of the fatal propensity of human beings to fix crippling definitions on each other. What the text conjures up with stringent economy is the increasing isolation of an individual forced to recognise with a mixture of horror and detachment the labyrinthine nature of guilt.

The unexpected appearance of *Schweiz ohne Armee? Ein Palaver* (1989) underlined the point that though Frisch had fallen silent as a creative artist, his involvement with the political culture of Switzerland was undiminished. Although in a moving speech to the eighth 'Solothurner Literaturtag' on 10 May 1986 he had appeared to pass on to his younger colleagues the baton of half a century's committed opposition to the status quo,[9] this contribution to the debate over the proposal to abolish the Swiss army surprised many with its self-deprecatory humour. The short text, with its voluminous footnotes recalling the ironic method of *Wilhelm Tell für die Schule*, raised the debate to a markedly higher level: it sold well over 80,000 copies and was reprinted five times before the referendum was held in November 1989. Conceived as a dialogue with his grandson, who seeks advice on whether to go for promotion in the army or stay a lowly corporal and thus risk his middle-class career in civilian life, the text wittily reverses the Socratic method by having the grandson draw out his taciturn grandfather with a series of pointed questions about the past and, in particular, Frisch's own experience of military service recorded in his critical memoir, *Dienstbüchlein* (1974), itself a caustic revision of his earlier, benignly patriotic *Blätter aus dem Brotsack* (1940).[10] Frisch acknowledges the vastly different world confronting his grandson, but is unable to resolve a dilemma which encapsulates the whole notion of Swiss identity. Nevertheless, the fact that he dedicates the book to two eighteenth-century eccentrics, the irrepressible *philosophe*, Denis Diderot, and the obscure autodidact and former army deserter, Ulrich Bräker, gives a neat indication of Frisch's utopian position. For in their very different spheres, these two forerunners each combined a rich imagination with a thirst for knowledge in the best tradition of the Enlightenment.[11] Thus Frisch's 'Palaver' suggests that only a restoration of this creative dialectic can point the way forward for a Switzerland faced with a myriad unsettling challenges to its customarily comfortable modes of thinking. The astonishing result of the referendum gives a hint that this process is already underway.[12]

In common with most nonconformist writers who have emerged since the 1960s, Frisch took an unequivocal stance on the political left. Dürrenmatt, on the other hand, never showed much interest in such overt allegiance. In accepting the 'Literaturpreis der Stadt Bern' in 1979, Dürrenmatt himself indicated his preferred position: 'Die Stadt Bern hat ein Anrecht zu wissen, wem sie den Preis erteilt. Nicht einem Rechten oder Linken, sondern einem Queren' (WA/28 170). And a decade earlier, in a speech occasioned by the crushing of the Prague Spring, he spelt out his role as a writer: 'Ich bin kein politischer, ich bin ein dramaturgischer Denker, ich denke über die Welt nach, indem ich ihre Möglichkeiten auf der Bühne und mit der Bühne durchspiele, und mich ziehen demgemäß die Paradoxien und Konflikte unserer Welt mehr an als die noch möglichen Wege, sie zu retten. Ich bin Diagnostiker, nicht Therapeut . . .' (WA/28 35f.).

Such quasi-scientific detachment, with the dominant motif of the labyrinth suggesting a fatalistic determinism governing human affairs, has led to frequent misunderstandings, indeed charges of cynicism or even nihilism. What makes such criticism absurd, however, is the fact that Dürrenmatt sets against or within the labyrinth the grand counter-myth of the rebel. Against the confusions, dead ends, endless complexities of ideological systems, against the human psyche, the implacable and threatening obscurities of modern technology and the unknowable vastness of cosmic space, Dürrenmatt creates courageous analogues to Atlas, Sisyphus, Theseus, Prometheus – but frequently in such grotesquely distorted versions that the underlying mythical structure is not readily apparent. The plays of the 1950s and 1960s, for example, are full of what Dürrenmatt termed 'mutige Menschen', individuals

whose revolt, however ineffectual or doomed to failure, nevertheless undermines the power of the relevant 'Minotaur' by simple
defiance of its dominion. Defeat worked out in terms of the
theatrical model paradoxically points to the possibility of human
dignity which imposes its own image on the otherwise overwhelming chaos of reality.

As German theatre grew increasingly political in the Brechtian
mould, and directors became more important than the text, it was
perhaps not surprising that Dürrenmatt's depictions of human
existence as characterised by ludicrous blunders and the blind
workings of Chance should fall out of fashion.

The fascinating *Der Mitmacher. Ein Komplex* (1976) was the
immediate result of Dürrenmatt's withdrawal from the theatre. Far
more than a mere justification of his own idiosyncratic concept of
theatre, the text is an extraordinary fusion of philosophy, drama-
turgical treatise and imaginative fiction. The target is the reductive
nature of ideology and its anaesthetising effect on both art and
politics. Dürrenmatt argues for a personal vision as the only
method of unmasking communal lies. As always in his work, he
shows how the human mind, by refusing to think through the
frightening implications of relativity, falls continually into the trap
of tyrannical absolutes. The *Mitmacher-Komplex* thus links up to the
Monstervortrag über Gerechtigkeit und Recht (1969) and provides the
stimulus for the controversial *Zusammenhänge. Essay über Israel*
(1976). For Dürrenmatt, the Israeli struggle for existence, brought
about by the 'arch-blunderer' Hitler, had become a crucial test case
for Western civilisation. And here, too, the argument is illuminated
by passages devoted to language criticism, theology, philosophy
and parabolic narratives. Taken together with the 'Nachgedanken',
specially written for the 1980 *Werkausgabe*, the book asserts with a
passionate clarity, not seen in German literature since Lessing's
Nathan der Weise, the moral, spiritual and intellectual interdependence of the great religious constructs of Judaism, Christianity and
Mohammedanism, to which Dürrenmatt adds the secular 'religion'
of Marxist humanism. Dürrenmatt saw himself as a latterday
Sisyphus pushing his thoughts up a mountain of prejudice, drawing his energy from one dominant insight: that freedom is indivis-
ible, that the Arab Abu Chanifa and the Jew Anan ben David share
a common prison from which they will emerge as a pair or not at
all.

Dürrenmatt described the *Mitmacher-Komplex* and *Zusammenhänge* as the first two parts of a grand trilogy to be concluded with
an ambitious 'history of his writing', called simply *Stoffe*. Before

his untimely death 'nine' books had appeared in two volumes, *Stoffe I-III* (1981, reissued in a revised edition under the title *Labyrinth*, 1990) and *Turmbau. Stoffe IV-IX* (1990). Begun in June 1969 in response to a serious illness, *Stoffe I-III* charts not only the structures of Dürrenmatt's thinking, but also its roots in his childhood. The Emmental village into which he was born gave him his first experience of existential paradox: it represented both an idyllic refuge and a place where violence, sexuality and death were undisguised and inescapable. His move to the more abstract structures of Bern and his later experiences in Zurich merely refined the concept of the labyrinth. In the stories which round off the three 'books' – 'Der Winterkrieg in Tibet' (the final reworking of the early texts, *Die Stadt* and *Aus den Papieren eines Wärters* of 1952), 'Mondfinsternis' (an early version of *Der Besuch der alten Dame*) and 'Der Rebell' – the individual is presented as the archetypal rebel, lurching confusedly in the subterranean passages of his own mind. But human freedom, Dürrenmatt makes clear, lies precisely in the rebel's ability to fashion images of his predicament and thus establish the necessary preconditions for transcending its stifling constrictions.

Turmbau continues the method of *Stoffe I-III*, but in this second instalment it is clear that Dürrenmatt himself had become aware of the paradoxical nature of his mammoth undertaking. The more he attempted to reconstruct the history of his writing, the more the reconstruction assumed a life of its own: 'Ein Einfall rief einen anderen, eine Erinnerung eine andere und eine Assoziation eine weitere hervor' (T 7). In trying to plot the inexhaustible twists of the labyrinth, Dürrenmatt merely succeeded in creating a formidable 'Manuskriptdschungel', a literary Tower of Babel. *Turmbau* is perhaps for this reason a slimmer volume than its predecessor; more space is given to Dürrenmatt's fruitful struggle with philosophy, especially Kant and Kierkegaard (on whom he had once planned to write a doctoral dissertation), and to reflections on the nature of reality and perception. Apart from the light thrown on the origins of such plays as *Ein Engel kommt nach Babylon* (1953), *Die Physiker* (1962) and *Der Meteor* (1966), the book is particularly memorable for a brief sketch of a bleakly inconclusive meeting with Paul Celan and a devastatingly witty parody, 'Das gemästete Kreuz' (T 74–82), which offers a potted history of Switzerland and Swiss identity in terms of international football. Dürrenmatt traces the fortunes of 'FC Helvetia 1291' from the club's glory days to its decline into the lower divisions of provincial soccer, culminating in the dubious refusal to take part in the last World Championships

(= '1939–45'). The club's cessation as a coherent playing unit is matched only by its absurd addiction to constant training and nostalgic adherence to an ideology which totally ignores the fact that 'FC Helvetia 1291' has long since abandoned such heroic simplicities for the vast and anonymous world of international business which plays by quite a different set of rules.

The most unambiguous statement of Dürrenmatt's obsession with the labyrinth metaphor is to be found in a wide-ranging conversation with Franz Kreuzer, *Die Welt als Labyrinth* (broadcast on Austrian radio, 10 June 1982, published 1986). 'Der Winterkrieg in Tibet', for example, the absurd depiction of a third world war in a far-off land (which nevertheless bears an unmistakable resemblance to Switzerland), fought endlessly for ends long since forgotten, is linked both to a sense of approaching apocalypse and the experience of Switzerland's position in the Second World War: 'Es ist einfach aus diesem Erlebnis des Eingeschlossenseins entstanden und des im Eingeschlossenen noch einmal einschließenden Prinzips, das das Eingeschlossensein verstärkt.'[13]

Achterloo (1983) represented a surprising return to the scene of earlier disappointments, the Zurich Schauspielhaus. But despite the initially respectful reception, the play, like its predecessors of the 1970s, has not established itself in the repertoire. Inspired by the declaration of martial law in Poland by General Jaruselski on 12/13 December 1981, *Achterloo* (the stage setting is given as 'Achterloo in Acherloo irgendwo bei Waterloo') depicts a theatre within a theatre, a chaotic collage of political jokes and literary allusions which brings together Napoleon as the Polish General and Jan Hus as the contemporary rebel, Lech Walesa. With the unique freedom from time and space which the theatre offers, moral absolutists such as Richelieu and Robespierre are confronted with Benjamin Franklin, five characters claiming to be Karl Marx, and Büchner's oppressed anti-hero, Woyzeck. In Dürrenmatt's parabolic madhouse, 'Waterloo' is the culmination of all Grand Designs and the long-suffering Woyzeck their perennial victim. The combination of 'Waterloo' and 'Achterbahn', plus the random echo of C. F. Meyer's poem, 'Fingerhütchen' ('Tief im Tal von Acherloo'), points to the notion of history and human endeavour as an absurd switchback of unpredictable disasters.

Dürrenmatt's constant delight in refashioning and reinterpreting his own inventions was demonstrated also with *Achterloo*. Under the influence of his second wife, the film maker Charlotte Kerr, he radically rewrote the play as *Achterloo III* (with typical mischievousness Dürrenmatt refused Germanists sight of the putative 'second' version!). The new play acquires Büchner himself as the central figure who claims to be writing *Achterloo* as a continuation of *Woyzeck*. This version (premièred on 17 June 1988 in the small West German Festival Theatre in Schwetzingen) was published together with a 'Protokoll einer fiktiven Inszenierung', drawn up by Charlotte Kerr, under the title *Rollenspiele* (1986). Kerr's record of their discussions gives an illuminating insight into Dürrenmatt's method, and it is clear that her intervention has led to a dramaturgically tauter play in which the 'Irrenhaus' is delineated as a wry reversal of Kantian optimism – 'die banalste, aber einzig mögliche Metapher für unsere Welt der selbstverschuldeten Mündigkeit des unmündigen Menschen' (R 200). Thus the action is made more intelligible as a series of ludicrous episodes in role-therapy that continually escape Büchner's authorial control. Mental patients, already locked in their own fantasies, are encouraged to play historical rebels, heretics and tyrants in dizzying succession until roles dissolve into roles in an infinite regression.

On a different level, the same principle of shifting perspectives is exploited to more convincing effect in the short 'ballad' *Minotaurus* (1985), which is lavishly illustrated with Dürrenmatt's own idiosyncratic drawings. For the first time the focus is squarely on the wretched Minotaur who lives in a world of reflections, insubstantial selves, with which it slowly learns to live peaceably enough in the subterranean gloom. Disaster strikes with the appearance of humanity in the shape of a young girl. Typically, Dürrenmatt shows how the 'mythical' horror of the beast stems from a simple misunderstanding: the girl is accidentally killed in a would-be joyous embrace. The subsequent human revenge prompts both the Minotaur's rebellious self-assertion and the construction of the labyrinth as the only way of controlling its primitive power. Paradoxically, Dürrenmatt's monster dreams of being a man, the recipient and giver of love and friendship. His treacherous murder by Theseus is simply the result of another error of perception.

Faulty perception is also the theme of the novel *Justiz* (1985). The story was in fact first drafted in the 1950s, then put aside until 1985 when the fragment was reshaped and equipped with a final chapter as a personal epilogue. This lengthy genesis has left its mark on the text, which is both confused and confusing. Isaak Kohler, a leading Zurich politician and financier, murders a local Professor of German in front of numerous witnesses in the city's leading restaurant. The crime is clear, the punishment exemplary: twenty years in gaol. Startlingly serene in his cell, Kohler invites a struggling young lawyer, Felix Spät, to re-examine the case on the absurd assumption that Kohler is innocent. The novel consists mainly of Spät's embittered report on how he gradually became aware that Kohler had been manipulating him in a power game beyond his comprehension. The plot loses itself in its twists and turns, but reveals the main contours of Dürrenmatt's theme: the inevitable discrepancy between the notion of absolute justice ('Gerechtigkeit') and the grubby machinery ('Justiz') that men have invented to pursue it. The author's belated Epilogue fits awkwardly on to this earlier material with its black jokes, farcical interludes and side-swipes at the Swiss Establishment. Yet these final pages show Dürrenmatt's speculative energy at its best. He claims no narratorial superiority nor does he make excuses for the provocative puzzle he puts before the reader: 'Doch ist die Geschichte, die nur in meiner Phantasie wirklich wurde und die nun, geschrieben, von mir weicht, sinnloser als die Weltgeschichte, weniger erdbebensicher als der Boden, auf dem wir unsere Städte bauen?' (J 369).

The short 'Novelle' *Der Auftrag* (1986), with its programmatic subtitle 'Vom Beobachten des Beobachters der Beobachter', takes up the theme of the fragility of perception in a more tightly organised form. The twenty-four chapters, each of a single, extended sentence, are modelled on Bach's variations for 'das wohltemperierte Klavier'. But where Bach's genius explored musical ideas to a satisfying resolution, Dürrenmatt shows language to be yet another labyrinthine structure, entrapping the unwary. The outward paraphernalia of the detective novel – murder, rape, exotic locations: echoes of Dürrenmatt's early potboilers – litter the surface narrative, only to mock and eventually defeat both the protagonist's and the reader's efforts to assemble them into conventional narratorial patterns. The heroine F., a film reporter, accepts a commission to seek the facts behind a vicious murder in North Africa. Her researches bring her into contact with the world of espionage and secret rocket stations, but at a metaphorical level lead her deep into the problems of her own identity. Increasingly sophisticated systems of observation are turned on themselves in a vicious circle of fatuity. As a clue to his meaning, Dürrenmatt places a quotation from Kierkegaard's *Either/Or* at the head of his tale, the image of a spider hurtling towards its own centre: 'So geht es mir; vor mir stets ein leerer Raum; was mich vorwärtstreibt, ist eine Konsequenz, die hinter mir liegt. Dieses Leben ist verkehrt und grauenhaft, nicht auszuhalten.' This strange little tale is clearly rooted in the same crisis of personal inadequacy that drove Anatol Stiller into his own private wilderness of mirrors and, despite its brevity, raises the existential theme to a cosmic level.

The very title of Dürrenmatt's last novel, *Durcheinandertal* (1989), suggests a continuation of the theme of *Der Auftrag*. The focal point of the eponymous valley, situated in an isolated part of Switzerland, is a huge Kurhaus which a local preacher, Moses Melker, turns for the summer season into a 'Haus der Armut' where millionaires can recover from their stressful lives. The same graceful villa serves in the winter as a refuge for international gangsters where plastic surgery gives them new identities. The interplay between these two grotesque worlds and the village that unwittingly harbours them gives Dürrenmatt ample scope to display once again his baroque imagination. But what intrigues within the discipline of the 'Novelle' form, here frequently becomes merely tiresome. At its best, the novel is like a Bosch painting in words, interweaving the machinations of finance capital with the ruthless violence of the underworld in a comic mafia of the absurd.

Dürrenmatt's awareness of modern science, particularly cosmology, and his predilection for reworking myths and legends set him apart from most of his fellow Swiss writers. And yet his critique of universal human folly is securely rooted in his observations of contemporary Switzerland. Frisch, too, for all the more intensely 'private' quality of his later work, clearly responded to Swiss stimuli. Both authors tended to see their country, most clearly perhaps in their speeches and essays, not as a 'Sonderfall' but as a paradigm for universal problems. Frisch's later work was more sparse, more concentrated than Dürrenmatt's – not just because of waning powers, although the ten-year age difference played an unavoidable role. Dürrenmatt's exuberance remained undiminished to the end, but he often paid the price of formlessness. What linked both authors, the embattled moral sceptic Frisch and the more philosophical, speculative Dürrenmatt, was their deep antagonism towards social structures that imposed a rigid conformity on the individual. In both cases the apparent pessimism of their frequently bleak diagnoses was counterbalanced by the unmistakable principle of hope inherent in the creative act itself.

The development of a vigorous, contentious German-Swiss literature since the war would have been unthinkable without the challenge and example of Frisch and Dürrenmatt. Switzerland faces many problems in the 1990s. As she tries to locate a new role in the context of the dominant economic power of a European Community growing closer together and of the opening up of Central and Eastern Europe to democracy and trade, their humane and critical voices, together with those of the younger writers they have inspired, will be needed more than ever.

Michael Butler

Notes

1. References are to the *Werkausgabe in dreißig Bänden*, Zurich, 1980 = WA, followed by volume and page number; J = *Justiz. Roman*, Zurich, 1985; R = *Rollenspiele. Protokoll einer fiktiven Inszenierung und Achterloo III*, Zurich, 1986; T = *Turmbau. Stoffe IV-IX*, Zurich, 1990.

2. Heinz Ludwig Arnold, *Gespräche mit Schriftstellern*, Munich, 1975, p. 25.

3. 'Max Frisch und Friedrich Dürrenmatt: Zwei Möglichkeiten literarischer Artikulation', *Germanica Wratislaviensa*, vol. XXXVI, 1980, p. 8.

4. See, for example, the cold bitterness of his 'Schweizerpsalm III' (1971), reprinted in WA/28 180–2.

5. Just days before his own death on 4 April 1991 Frisch characteristically sent back a personal invitation to a Jubilee Dinner from Marco Solari, the man in charge of the country's 700th anniversary celebrations, on the grounds that he had no wish to sit at the same table as representatives of a regime that had kept him under secret surveillance for the last 43 years. In the wake of the so-called 'Fichen–Affäre' (see above, p. 20), many Swiss writers and intellectuals called for a boycott of the 700th anniversary celebrations. For a full documentation of the scandal, see *Schnüffelstaat Schweiz. Hundert Jahre sind genug*, ed. Komitee Schluß mit dem Schnüffelstaat, Zurich, 1990.

6. To gauge the impact of Zorn's novel against the background of the 1980 'Jugendunruhen' in Switzerland, see Adolf Muschg's 'Frankfurter Vorlesungen', *Literatur als Therapie? Ein Exkurs über das Heilsame und das Unheilbare*, Frankfurt am Main, 1981, especially pp. 67–81: 'Aus einem einsamen Lebens- und Todesbericht ist eine Projektionsfigur, ja ein Mythos für eine ganze Generation geworden. Sie nimmt *Mars* nicht mehr nur als eine gesellschaftliche Krankheitseinsicht ab. Sie findet darin die tröstlich-summarische Schuldigsprechung der Eltern' (p. 71).

7. The controversy is well documented in *Sprache im technischen Zeitalter*, vol. 22, 1967, pp. 83–206 and vol. 26, 1968, pp. 87–179. (The latter volume contains Dürrenmatt's speech, 'Varlin schweigt'.)

8. See the contributions of Peter Bichsel, Silvio Blatter, Jürg Laederach, E. Y. Meyer, Adolf Muschg, Paul Nizon, Erica Pedretti, Jörg Steiner and Otto F. Walter to *Begegnungen. Eine Festschrift für Max Frisch zum siebzigsten Geburtstag*, ed. Siegfried Unseld, Frankfurt am Main, 1981.

9. 'Am Ende der Aufklärung steht das Goldene Kalb', *Die Weltwoche*, 15 May 1986, pp. 57–9. (The speech is reprinted in: Max Frisch, *Schweiz als Heimat? Versuche über 50 Jahre*, ed. Walter Obschlager, Frankfurt am Main, 1990, pp. 461–9.) Cf. Martin Roda Becher's report of a Swiss friend's view: 'Mit diesem Datum, Mai 86, [ist] eine Epoche zu Ende gegangen . . . "Was bleibt ist Frisch, wir müssen weiter."' 'CH-Literatur im Swatch-Zeitalter. Anmerkungen zur Schweizer Literatur', *Litfaß*, no. 43, October 1987, p. 152.

10. Benno Besson directed a stage version of *Schweiz ohne Armee* under the title 'Jonas und sein Veteran', as a co-production of the Zurich Schauspielhaus (première: 19 October 1989) and the Théâtre de Vidy, Lausanne (French text, première: 20 October 1989).

11. See Frisch's comment on Diderot in the Solothurn speech: 'Bei aller Brisanz seines Intellekts ein empfindsamer Entdecker der Subjektivität und ein Befreier eben dadurch; Vernunft als Inspiration.' *Schweiz als Heimat?*, p. 464.

12. In a country where the army plays such a central role, it was astonishing enough that the 100,000 signatures required to launch a referendum could be collected at all. In the event the turnout was exceptionally high (68.6 per cent), and the motion was only defeated by a margin of 64.4 per cent. The cantons of Geneva and Jura actually voted for abolition.

13. *Die Welt als Labyrinth. Ein Gespräch mit Franz Kreuzer*, Zurich, 1986, p. 25.

III

New Directions

4

Otto F. Walter: Literature and the Strategies of Revolt
Ian Hilton

Born in 1928, and therefore, in the wider German context, of the same generation as Grass, Enzensberger, Walser and Kunert, Otto F. Walter spearheaded the second literary surge in Switzerland after the Second World War. He has been an influential publisher, is a formidable 'Publizist' and longtime supporter of the 'Sozialdemokratische Partei der Schweiz' (SPS), and not least a successful and thought-provoking novelist. He celebrated his sixtieth birthday with the publication of his most ambitious novel to date, *Zeit des Fasans* (1988). Characteristically, that same year saw the appearance of *Gegenwort*, a selection of essays and speeches from the previous quarter of a century, which eloquently illustrates his dual role as 'Publizist' and goad of the public conscience. The very title of the volume is symptomatic of Walter's penchant for challenging conventional views and values, for adopting a counter-stance ('eine singuläre, revoltäre Haltung') that surfaces so readily in his creative writings. Terms such as 'Gegenfrage', 'Gegen-Wort', 'Gegen-these', 'Gegen-Satz', 'Gegensignal', 'Gegenbild', 'Gegenargument', 'Gegenentwurf', 'Gegenmacht' dominate these essays and speeches on subjects ranging from nuclear weapons and ecological problems to press freedom, corporate business and patriarchy. And what Walter himself says of these essays and speeches could in turn be applied to his creative writings:

> In ihrer Summe sind sie Plädoyers gegen das Prinzip Hierarchie, im Namen der Befreiung hin zu Selbstverantwortung, zu Autonomie in Solidarität. (G 246)[1]

Walter had turned thirty when his first novel, *Der Stumme*, was published in 1959,[2] marking his breakthrough as a writer. Critics regarded it as following in the mould of Frisch's influential novel *Stiller* (1954). The story is set in remote wooded, hilly and rocky terrain some nineteen kilometres northwest of the fictional town of

Jammers in the Jura (a recurrent location throughout Walter's work), where a gang of workers is engaged in a road construction project. In narrative terms, the time span covers twelve days in autumn, though the narrated time embraces earlier years in the life of the novel's protagonist, the dumb teenager Lothar Ferro, who now seeks a confrontation with his father because of former family strife.

The apartness of father and son is paradoxically accentuated in that they are both accepted as integral members of the road work gang by the other labourers, who themselves prove to be an odd assortment of individuals drawn together by work that requires team effort, and by equally enforced communal living in site huts, cut off from the town of Jammers.

At a mock-trial conducted by the gang, Lothar 'confesses' to protect his father, who he thinks has stolen a petrol can for his motorbike. His punishment is to set the explosive charges necessary to clear the remaining obstacles to the road and he thereby becomes innocently responsible for the accidental death of his father who fails to hear – or to heed? – the warning signal. Only in the final moment of human tragedy does Lothar's voice return, the voice he had lost when witnessing an earlier deed of violence, the sight of his father hitting his mother in one of his drunken rages. As in Walter's other writings, violence is never far removed from the veneer of ordered, patterned society. But in *Der Stumme* the specifically Swiss sociopolitical issues, characteristic of his later fiction, are virtually absent in favour of a symbolic clash of generations in the bourgeois literary tradition, coupled with generalised ideas of guilt and identity crisis.

The novel beautifully illustrates Walter's striving to establish his own literary form. There are sustained passages of realistic description associated with the traditional novel. But Walter modifies conventional narrative technique by adopting a 'modern' approach in apportioning the different chapters to the individual viewpoint of each of the members of the work gang (with the exception of the Ferros, father and son), accompanied by narratorial commentary on the thought processes of the characters. The shifting perspectives are matched by Walter's predilection for the use of the subjunctive to pose questions, to suggest possibilities, to qualify sentences often with 'vielleicht', 'oder', 'wahrscheinlich'. The technique suggests the inadequacies of language to cope with expressing reality fully. The traumatic restoration of speech to the youth is encapsulated in the single word that he succeeds in uttering as a warning that comes too late: 'Vattr' (DS 282). The intention is clear. The cry represents 'Eigenartikulation', yet at the same time an act of reconciliation. For the word itself betokens the language – and moral values – of tradition; it anticipates Lothar's eventual return to society at the end of the novel when he emerges from his hide-out in the forest to accept the due processes of law and order imposed by society.

Walter's second novel, *Herr Tourel* (1962), also concentrates on the problematic existence of an individual trapped in the inadequacies of language. At the same time it employs an even more complicated narrative structure and chronological layering, again involving the flashback technique and the analytical interior monologue.

The novel tells of a wildcat strike at a cement factory and a show of solidarity with the labour force to whom Tourel is drawn out of sympathy with their plight. This is the first time Walter has placed the social issue of industrial pollution in the foreground in his major creative writing. But the social antagonisms are ultimately – and deliberately – subsumed in the private fears of the problematic hero in his crisis of identity.[3]

The narrative time covers a few days in the middle of June following Tourel's *second* return to Jammers almost a year to the day since his first. The narrated time is primarily the period of this earlier stay, though reference is made to other episodes in his life. After his involvement with Beth Ferro (familiar names – and setting – establish a thread of continuity in Walter's writings), Tourel had spent the next half year wandering 'zigeunerisch', as if fleeing responsibility, through French Switzerland. His mode of living there casts Tourel as an 'outsider' who is very aware of crossing linguistic boundaries and hence of the disparateness of life. The selling of his camera equipment to survive infers a further step towards isolation in that this action cuts off the means of his livelihood. Indeed the relinquishing of the equipment in one sense contributes to his loss of identity, for with the camera Tourel had been able to impose form and permanence on the fleeting moment:

Das war eine Welt, die ich bestimmen konnte, hier war mir wohl, nichts blieb mehr, was mich daran hätte stören können, und was wichtig war: sie blieb unveränderlich, blieb so, wie ich sie aufgenommen hatte. (HT 70)

The maxim he had been taught in his photographic apprenticeship was: take pictures that are 'genau und klar'. What he achieves is undoubtedly artistry, but not necessarily the penetration of surface reality in the search for truth, a point which is emphasised when he attempts to superimpose twelve pictures of a face to influence the 'Mienenspiel'. 'Ein interessantes Bild, aber es fehlt ihm etwas, die Zeit vielleicht' (HT 71), he concludes. It is the interface of reality and imagination that is lacking. Can language improve on that?

In no way does Tourel suffer from Lothar's disadvantage; quite the opposite. It is the sound and the sight of martens around the boathouse in June that evokes early childhood memories of fear which he had sought to allay then – as now – by talking aloud. As fear had driven him in the first instance, now a sense of guilt too spurs Tourel to continual talk, to absolve his conscience. He speaks of matters not necessarily as they had been in actuality, but more as the narrator himself would prefer them to be viewed. Various episodes therefore offer different, alternative interpretations to fit in with the narrator's wilful reconstruction of reality. Even language itself is seen to disintegrate. Mohn, the well-meaning outsider who befriends Beth during the birth of her child at the car dump (itself a symbol of the materialism of affluent society), proves to be Tourel's major informer, though, for his part, Tourel believes Mohn's tale to be far-fetched. But it is the feeble-minded Mohn who brings the novel to its close with a résumé of the preceding events, the final pages constituting confused, incomprehensible, stream-of-consciousness outpourings. In the end the reader is aware of the overshadowing sense of waste – not only waste caused by pollution, but the waste of potentially beneficial human re-lationships, for the real tragic outcome of the story is the death of Beth within that patterned context of disorder.

The success of *Herr Tourel* brought Walter the Charles Veillon Prize. Incidentally, it is pertinent to observe how in the course of that one year 1962 Walter's crisis in his personal and business life, mirrored in his creative writings in such figures as Tourel and Elio,[4] is balanced by his public voice that finds expression, for example, in his forthright 'truisms and theses', 'Das Positive und die zeitgenössische Literatur' (G 16–18), and the joint 'Aufruf' with Kurt Marti and others, 'Keine Atomwaffen!' (G 130–4). At the same time, however, Walter's 'Notiz zu Hugo von Hofmannsthals "Brief des Philipp Lord Chandos an Francis Bacon"' (1963, G 13–15) showed how Hofmannsthal's famous words on the despair of the writer being able to express himself adequately struck a responsive chord:

> Hier, so sah ich . . . hat einer die Erfahrung unseres Jahrhunderts – den Zerfall der bürgerlichen Ordnungen, die Unmöglichkeit jeglicher Ideo-

logie, den Massentod, die Unzulänglichkeit unserer Sprache, die Einsamkeit –, hat sie ahnend kurz nach der Jahrhundertwende formuliert,
gewiß als erster in dieser gespenstigen Überdeutlichkeit. (G 14)

His subsequent role as publisher in West Germany[5] was so
demanding both in political and personal terms that a long hiatus
occurred before the appearance of his next book, *Die ersten Unruhen*. The work, begun in 1967 but only completed and published in
1972, was a response to the political atmosphere of West Germany.
Walter actually describes the book as 'ein Konzept' – rather than use
the more conventional term 'novel' – proceeding from his desire
'ein Kollektiv auch formal adäquat darzustellen. Ich versuchte das,
indem ich in der ersten Person Plural erzählte. Das wies zweifellos
in die Richtung der Darstellung gesellschaftlicher Prozesse'
(G 234). Jammers is once again the focal point and the reader is
immediately made aware of its modernity and materialism – a
Swiss Manhattan or Chicago (DU 11). We witness the city come to
life at the start of another day with the appearance of both workers
and middle-class professionals, all swept along in self-contained
groups: 'Wir. Wir. Vereint mit uns selbst. Ja, so ist's gut!' (DU 14).
   The city then is the collective subject of the book. The time span
is five weeks leading up to the city elections held on 5 June. But the
materialism that has brought prosperity and change to the town of
Jammers has also shown an adverse side, expressed in the fears and
frustrations of its inhabitants. Almost invariably the object of their
dissatisfaction turns out to be the minorities in the social system –
Gastarbeiter and the *Rätoromanen* (and, let it be noted, fellow Swiss
citizens), who are dubbed 'die Flicker'. Disturbances in the shopping areas, on the streets, necessitating the involvement of the
police to restore law and order, intensify in the run-up to the
elections into ugly violence in the concrete jungle. The community
is encapsulated and threatened not only by the feuding factions but
also ultimately by the army, which has been summoned to intervene. What Walter therefore seeks to mirror in this political
work is the notion of an incipient fascism and terrorism in the
industrialised society of a traditionally stable and conservative
Switzerland. The six-lane highway has become the road to self-
delusion and self-destruction in a city of dehumanising high-rise
blocks of flats, increased road traffic, pollution. A visionary scene
of the future is provided in the episode of the townsfolk lining the
banks of the river Aare and watching 'in stummen Grausen' as the
cadavers of animals float downstream, panicked into the waters like
lemmings.

Only one individual is permitted by Walter to stand out in this collective 'Wir'. A distant echo of a character from a novel in the nineteenth-century bourgeois tradition (see G 235), Barbara Frankenstein is depicted as an obvious outsider; her old kiosk-shop is an anachronism in the thrusting world of an affluent society. As in his other stories, Walter ensures that in *Die ersten Unruhen*, too, death through violence leaves its mark. The tragic outcome is Barbara's death when she tries to intervene neutrally in the street fighting. Walter has imbued her with an almost legendary aura; she is, as it were, a collective invention, 'eine Art von Fabelwesen' (G 236). The ironic use of the surname Frankenstein points to this modern mythical context.

The narrative thread is deliberately fragmented by Walter in accord with his belief, outlined in his critical essay 'Literatur als Revolte' (1967, G 30–4), that literature should challenge accepted conventions. *Die ersten Unruhen* comprises collages of fact and fiction. Prehistory is juxtaposed with the present day; reports on rapidly rising crime with statistical surveys; regulations governing elections with TV programmes and folk songs; party political propaganda with day-dreams; theories with judgements. In short, the montage technique threatens to overwhelm the reader; it is as tantalising in its way as the linguistic discontinuity of *Herr Tourel*.

His first work of fiction after his return to Switzerland in 1973 is *Die Verwilderung* (1977). Against the backcloth of the economic recession in Switzerland around 1973, Walter proffers the radical choice of a 1968-inspired utopian, alternative society – 'eine schweizerische Gesellschaft in Selbstverwaltung' (a theme taken up in 'Brief an eine junge Frau' (1979, G 73–81), 'Eine geschichtliche Wende ist fällig' (1981, G 107–13) and 'A im O, Alpha und Omega, Anfang und Ende' (1983, G 120–7)). Walter argues for 'Selbstverwaltung als gesellschaftsbestimmendes Prinzip', seeing it as a step towards emancipation; at the same time he acknowledges the limitations in the prevailing sociopolitical climate of such a decentralised system of self-governing communities. This novel traces the rise and fall of one such grouping in which the search for a utopian renewal of Swiss society is checked and neutralised by the provocation of its dystopian 'faschistoides Potential' (G 240).

Not for the first time a story by Walter opens with a hint of violence to come. A young car mechanic, Robert Allemann, is beaten up in a seemingly motiveless attack by some thugs. At his 'home' in the now disused 'Huppergrube' on the edge of the town of Jammers he is joined by the young student Leni (Helen Bloch). They in turn befriend the journalist Blumer and invite him to share their home and lifestyle. Blumer is thirty-seven, has travelled extensively and been present at the student riots in Germany, France and elsewhere in the late 1960s. But those movements and what they stood for have long passed, and Blumer's frustrations with his job and disappointments over his personal life have led him to massive resignation, even the contemplation of suicide. Indeed it is Leni who fortuitously appears in time to save him. In their company he sees a glimmer of hope – the 'Keimzelle einer neuen Gesellschaft' (DV 192).

Rob and Leni seek to establish a cooperative, a freer lifestyle at the 'Huppergrube'. In time the group of three becomes six, nine, grows into a democratic and moderately successful cooperative, rejecting notions of exploitation, the *Leistungsprinzip* and jealousy over property and possessions, all of which are shown as characteristics of a bourgeois, affluent society. The 'Huppergrube' community suggests a utopian concept of *Heimat* where sanctuary, self-determination and self-sufficiency are offered to those feeling threatened in a hostile, materialistic society. But the urgent question of whether Blumer's problems of individuation can be overcome, or whether they are merely suspended, through his involvement with the group and the dissolution of traditional social ties remains unanswered. For the commune at the 'Huppergrube' is viewed with suspicion and then hostility by the inhabitants of Jammers, and the novel ends characteristically with an act of violence in the breaking up of the commune and the killing of Rob and Leni by self-appointed representatives of law and order and upholders of bourgeois respectability and values. Thus the glimmer of spiritual renewal is brutally overshadowed by fear and the novel closes on an ambiguous note: 'Aber wir machen doch weiter, du he! – wir machen doch weiter?' (DV 279).

Though Walter creates and sustains realistically individualised characters in *Die Verwilderung* (as against *Die ersten Unruhen*), the author nevertheless does continue to strive for formalistic innovation as an emancipatory 'Protest gegen Traditionen und Konventionen' (G 239). Thus narrative discontinuity is still predominant. Succeeding chapters present a mixture of narrative flow; extracts from theoretical works on patriarchy and the mass-psychology of fascism (see the 'Quellennachweis' at the end of the novel and Walter's accompanying comment); extracts from reports in *Zeitdienst, Zürich*; and, not least, extracts from Keller's *Romeo und Julia auf dem Dorfe*, which provides the motto and title for Walter's novel and which he deliberately employs to parallel his own love story of Rob and Leni in a hostile social environment. Walter envisages

Keller's story as serving a double function – as a kind of 'historische Folie' and as an example of a bourgeois concept of love, 'gegen die dieses Buch eigentlich revoltiert' (G 237). Walter's familiar ironic and barbed comment is manifested throughout this political realist novel. Characteristic too is the mixed stylistic approach adopted: a hypothetical, non-affirmative technique is interwoven with passages of more directly controlled material. Furthermore the narrator offers the reader two endings – the possible and the probable. *Die Verwilderung*, like *Die ersten Unruhen* and *Herr Tourel*, thus makes no popular concessions to the reader.

Walter's next narrative, *Wie wird Beton zu Gras* (1979), is, in contrast, more straightforward. Again Walter's polemical writing can be linked with his prose fiction. In 'Literatur in der Zeit des Blindflugs' (1978, G 61–6), for example, he argued for a 'Literatur, die – bei aller Selbstkritik – den Mut hat, informiertes Warn-System zu sein, die aber ebenso fähig ist zum Entwurf der Gegen-welten' (G 66). The immediate stimulus for *Wie wird Beton zu Gras* was the Whitsun March to the nuclear power station at Gösgen, where on 30 May 1977 Walter delivered in dialect his first Gösgen address, 'Das Veto des Volkes' (G 58–60).[6]

The bulk of the story concentrates on the consequences of that occasion, the reaction of ordered society (family, school board, local council, police, big business), which bands together against the protesters. The vital nuclear issue as such with its attendant threat to mankind and the environment is therefore not the sole target of Walter's concern, but also the financial, commercial and industrial world (to say nothing of the predicament of women in a patriarchal society). Throughout the story the writer is at pains to contrast the natural with the unnatural (as embodied, for instance, in the nuclear power station, seen as an unwelcome blight on the landscape, on life itself). Yet the natural world of Africa's forests, lakes and rivers, the Niagara Falls, the Garden of Eden no less, of which the seventeen-year-old Esther Moll dreams, must for her remain just that, dreams that vanish with the ringing of the alarm clock in the early morning or symbols of longing on travel posters. Closer to hand is the river Aare with its own rocks and miniature waterfall to which Esther and her younger brother Koni retreat: for them, this represents the microcosmic ideal, the innocence of the natural world that is within their childhood grasp and experience. For the sceptic, it represents youthful, romantic escapism.

The final chapter of the book records the 'happening', as Esther and Koni drive an old tank, long abandoned by the army but secretly restored to working order by the boy, towards the nearby town with the desperate determination of idealistic youth in its crusade for justice against the familiar objects of Walter's critical wrath – the manipulative power of the press, of big business. The spectacle of the tank being driven through the police cordon and smashing into the newspaper offices, with the crowd cheering in the background, is pure fantasy. Yet Walter intends the episode to serve symbolically. Significantly, he employs for his cautionary tale a motto from the nineteenth-century story by Kleist, *Michael Kohlhaas*, in which the protagonist seeks to correct injustice single-handedly. Here in *Wie wird Beton zu Gras* the teenagers' naive idealism becomes ensnared in the harsh, unpalatable realities of life. But in fact Walter wishes the book to be anything but a story of resignation. As he makes clear in his speech attacking the *Berufsverbot*, 'Zürich 80, Hammer und Traum' (1980 G 82–5), the act of solidarity must be undertaken and it is good that youth display initiative in the fight:

Ich habe einen Traum. Die Jungen auf der Straße haben bewiesen, wie Spontaneität, lustvolle Aktion, Phantasie diese Gesellschaft wieder in Bewegung bringen. Ich träume davon, daß wir diese Kreativität in uns allen freisetzen. Daß wir ihr und ihren großartig subversiven Qualitäten endlich vertrauen. Daß wir – solidarisch – sie befreien in uns. Nur so wird aus Beton wieder Gras. (G 85)

The thematic importance for the novelist of the effect of political power and big business operating together in the media in Switzerland carries over into *Das Staunen der Schlafwandler am Ende der Nacht* (1983). Indeed this novel could well be taken in tandem with his 1980 speech 'Erst wenn das letzte Wort dagegen verstummt ist' (G 86–94), reflections on intellectuals in the media, and the 1981 speech 'Binsenwahrheit' (G 100–6), delivered in the Volkshaus, Zurich, on 10 October on the occasion of the Day of Action for a Free Press against the background of the 'Zürcher Unruhen'.

Thomas Wander, a middle-aged writer and newspaper columnist, has just published his book *Ein Wort von Flaubert*, which is more than just a love story, the affair between the journalist Winter and a younger woman Ann, for it centres essentially on the responsibility of the writer to society in troubled political times, on the search for a synthesis between art and commitment. Walter's novel constitutes his most comprehensive examination of the question since it was first raised in *Herr Tourel*. Two young people, Ruth and Schorsch, come to see Wander because they find his book potentially useful in their own quest to shake the blind, sleeping majority of people from their lethargy (hence the implications of the title of Walter's novel) and even to combat their own resignation ('unser winziges Dennoch auch gegen unsere eigene verdammte Resignation', SS 148). The key polemical section is chapter twenty-two, where Wander, the 'Wortarbeiter', the 'Sprachprofi', is confronted with his public and private conflicts:

> Schreiben, wie ich's betreibe, sei, bestenfalls, subversiv, ich meine: es könne vielleicht indirekt die kulturellen Voraussetzungen, die Vorurteile, unser Verhältnis zur Sprache, zu unseren Codes, auch zu den meinen unterhöhlen und damit, immer bestenfalls, unser Verhältnis zu unseren Wertvorstellungen und unseren Gefühlen ein bißchen verändern – ach, was weiß ich! (SS 156)

Nevertheless he is won over to the cause, albeit with reservations (rather like Blumer, the older journalist, is won over by Rob and Leni to a sympathetic understanding in *Die Verwilderung*).

The trip Wander makes with Ruth, with whom he has embarked upon an affair, forms the extended central sequence in the novel. Circumstances decree that they make a detour that takes them into the very heartland of Switzerland in Canton Uri, passing through Altdorf with its memorial to Wilhelm Tell. In the hope of finding accommodation they drive up a remote valley where they are eventually forced to leave their car and finish the journey on foot to the *Kurhaus*. The *Kurhaus* in its splendid isolation turns out to be a piece of the past – a crumbling nineteenth-century building redolent of tradition. It is due to close for the winter, perhaps for good because of the prohibitive costs needed to repair the collapsing structure. It serves as a metaphor for Switzerland, just as the crumbling villa fulfils a similar function in Walter's next novel, *Zeit des Fasans*. Significantly, the topic of conversation between Wander and Ruth in their bedroom before dinner centres on press freedom and the dubious political practices of international corporate concerns. The following morning they take another walk into the woods and come across a cataract; they are in 'Urschweiz', the heartland of democracy. It could almost be paradise, 'Naturromantik':

> Wieder jedenfalls war's so, als wären Ruth und ich hinausgeraten aus den Mustern unserer gemachten, verbauten, verwüsteten Landstriche ins Vorzivilisatorische: in diese Zone, worin Zeit sich bemaß nach dem Tempo, mit dem das Wasser sich in die Granitplatten fraß, zwei Zentimeter in siebzig Jahren. (SS 213)

But the blue sky they have enjoyed briefly is illusory. There in the heartland of Switzerland the owner of the *Kurhaus*, Adalbert Gamma (who himself had been one of the participants at the ritual slaughter of the bullock the night before, involuntarily witnessed by Wander and Ruth) talks of the ecological disaster befalling them all around (SS 212).

Wander's decision to head back to the centre of Swiss politics, corporate finance and business represents his facing up to the reality of a commitment, as conscience dictates that solidarity be displayed with the journalists threatened not only with the loss of press freedom but also with the takeover of the newspaper by a corporate concern which will inevitably introduce streamlining and redundancies. Thus the return to Zurich – instead of heading south for Italy – is for Wander a form of reintegration into society as a politically involved individual.

At the personal level, however, Wander's life remains ultimately unsatisfactory, as Ruth is reluctant to enter into any commitment with him in her desire to retain her autonomy. Wander, then, is made to realise that he is paying the consequences of playing with people's feelings in real life, be it with his wife Lisbeth, Helga, or now with Ruth, who had more than once pictured herself, ironically, as a character in Wander's next novel. Wander is forced now to face the consequences of living the lie of his own fiction (in the shape of the relationship of Winter with his wife Susann and his friend Ann in the *Flaubert* book) that now pursues him relentlessly. On more than one occasion Walter has Wander excise passages from his projected novel. Similarly, at the newspaper offices Peter criticises Wander for cutting the trenchant (in other words, politically engaged) passages from the proofs for his column. Are the passages rejected because they are too near the truth, *are* the truth? Should the truth be excised and an obfuscation substituted? Wander becomes guilty of telling 'Lügengeschichten', fantasies of deception; ironically, he is caught out when Ruth herself indulges in an elaborate ploy of storytelling that makes him jealous.

In the end, then, Wander steps out from his fictions (as Ruth had encouraged him to do) onto the path of commitment. The plan of action is decided upon and Walter reiterates the metaphor of the snowflake to conclude his novel on a cautionary note. We observe how he has employed the fairytale style 'und es war einmal' and emphasised the transient nature of things: 'Märchenglück und Schnee sind flüchtige Erscheinungen' (SS 251). But again we may sense the importance for Walter of the word 'dennoch': 'Dennoch und für diese eine Nacht: etwas wie Glück' (SS 251).

Where *Wie wird Beton zu Gras* was essentially a straightforward, simply told tale, this novel is multi-layered and complex, to the point of confusion for the reader. The extended parallelling of scenes and situations with minor yet significant variations, the matching of actions and reactions of characters (Winter and Wander; Ann, Helga and Ruth; Lisbeth and Susann) reveal the contrived artistry of the novelist, achieving a symmetry that is deliberately and ironically overstretched to make his point as to the difficulty of synthesising art and commitment.

Arguably Walter's most readable and satisfying novel is *Zeit des Fasans*. It certainly is his most ambitious project thus far, amounting to some six hundred pages. Here he turns to a much wider historical sweep, to face four-square the question posed by Max Frisch back in 1966, 'Ist unser Land für seine Schriftsteller kein Gegenstand mehr?'[7] In *Zeit des Fasans* Walter addresses himself to the broad issue of Switzerland in the period of Nazism and reaction to those times and events as viewed in the current sociopolitical climate. Walter actually started work on his novel the year after the death of Walter Matthias Diggelmann, who had aroused considerable discussion with the publication of his own book on the theme, *Die Hinterlassenschaft* (1965).

Walter's novel imaginatively tackles the question of 'unbewältigte schweizerische Vergangenheit' through the researches of Thomas Winter. The 44-year-old historian had been gathering depositions for a historical study on the 'Politik des Generals', relating to the wartime policy of the Swiss General Guisan and the secret arrangement he made with the French War Office, and to the dangers for Switzerland after documents were seized by the Germans at La Charité-sur-Loire. To work on the notes, Winter comes back to the parental home in Jammers in June 1982 with his German girlfriend Lisbeth Bronnen. Having belonged to his industrialist father who is long dead (as indeed is Thom's mother, who had suffered from cancer), the villa is now occupied by the sherry-drinking, cigarillo-smoking Aunt Esther, Thom's sister Gret and her family. Thom's promise to follow Lisbeth to Provence on holiday soon rings hollow when he comes across a host of old family papers in the house, including a diary containing a note in Esther's handwriting to the effect that Thom's mother had not died from natural causes. Twenty years have since elapsed but the seed of suspicion and curiosity impels Thom to delve into the family past, to search for the truth.

The quest turns into an examination of his own past as well as of that of the whole family, but the family history that gradually becomes unravelled is inextricably interwoven with that of the town of Jammers, and indeed Switzerland itself, with particular reference to the period from 1936 to 1945. Bit by bit the pieces of the family jigsaw are fitted together as Thom investigates the roles of his father and mother and his two sisters Gret and Charlott, which in turn encompass the history of the family clan going back to the nineteenth century. The success of the industrial firm of Winter is seen against the build-up of a family tragedy. But this of course is also treated by Walter within the context of the wider national tragedy of Switzerland itself over the relevant span of time in the twentieth century (though historical references go back through the ages – inevitably to 1291). We learn therefore of the strident and bloody clashes of right- and left-wing organisations at various demonstrations; the political relationship of Switzerland and Germany (the international football match in 1938 between the two countries proving an enormous emotional outlet); the economic and social position of people at the time; the emphasis on the *Leistungsprinzip*; the role of the Swiss army. But beyond that, Walter keeps inserting through statement or question, as in a general-knowledge quiz, snippets of information that keep the reader abreast of what was occurring on the world front in those same years. Moreover, the events of the earlier decades are set alongside current world affairs (i.e. of the 1970s and 1980s), so that Walter presents to us in the span of the novel a panoramic portrayal of epic proportions.

Gradually the crumbling house yields up its secrets. But as Winter comes nearer the truth, the dawning awful reality poses intolerable burdens upon him. He is finally forced to face the relevance of Esther's earlier warning that the day would come when he would have to distinguish between those who live a lie and those who live by the truth (ZF 113). Of course the personal and family responsibility for the tragedy (crime?) that has occurred within the clan assumes symbolic dimensions. The family history is a fragment of Swiss history, a fragment of one great confession. The facing and overcoming of one's own past with its toll on human awareness and acceptance of personal guilt sets the perspective of national guilt – in short, of Switzerland's role on the national and international political scene from the 1930s to the end of the war. Importantly, it is his *German* friend Lisbeth, a modern Ariadne, who returns from Provence to comfort Thom and lead him towards recovery from the dark recesses of the suppressed family history.

Unsurprisingly, Walter finds the opportunities to ride some

familiar hobby-horses too: the oppressive nature of patriarchy; the corresponding role of woman; the declining value of the individual in a computerised world; the threat to democracy itself. Familiar imagery is also present. The 'Marderjagd' in *Herr Tourel* reappears and is also matched by the pheasant-shoot. The eponymous pheasant had been tended by Charlott after it had been injured. She nurses it back to health only to see the hapless bird eventually killed by her father out with a hunting party. Animal, bird, human life is seen at risk, all potential victims of 'Mordlust'. The construction of the novel too follows a familiar pattern. There is no strict chronological sequence of narrated time. And the reader encounters a mixture of fact and fiction assembled in the form of diary fragments, reports, letters, conversation, reminiscences, Greek and Celtic mythology – all of which are used to weave together the strands of the long novel.

Walter's oppositional stance manifests itself throughout his writings from *Der Stumme* to *Zeit des Fasans*, whether it is expressed thematically, formalistically or linguistically. The clash of his progressive, socialist ideas with the conventional views of a deeply conservative Swiss society produces the dialectical element in his work. The posing of questions – and not least of one's self – remains ever essential. Self-analysis, reflecting a crisis of identity, is the responsibility of both intellectual (Winter, Wander, Blumer, Tourel) and non-intellectual (Esther, the Mute). For the uncritical acceptance of one's self and one's situation in society leads to the danger of being 'nicht offen, nicht auf Veränderung zum Menschlicheren hin offen', of having '"dicht" gemacht' (G 41). Etymologically, 'dicht' is connected with 'dichten' ('"dicht" machen'), and also 'Dickicht'. Walter's works creatively examine the very legitimacy of writing, and, as he reminded us in his essay on the *Chandos-Brief*, 'jede *bedeutende* [my italics] Dichtung schafft Unruhe in uns' (G 15). Only thus can literature, in Walter's eyes, fulfil its proper function as an 'informiertes Warn-System' (G 66). Within his framework of social commitment, Walter treats issues which vitally affect Switzerland but are by no means unique to the Swiss. The wealth of cultural references at his fingertips betrays his immersion in the European tradition. His political beliefs transcend purely national bounds. And the themes and the characters in his works register this wider dimension.

Notes

1. References to Walter's works are to the following editions: G = *Gegenwort*. *Aufsätze, Reden, Begegnungen*, Zurich, 1988; DS = *Der Stumme*, Munich, 1959; HT = *Herr Tourel*, Munich, 1962; DU = *Die ersten Unruhen*, Reinbek bei Hamburg, 1972; DV = *Die Verwilderung*, Reinbek bei Hamburg, 1977; BG = *Wie wird Beton zu Gras. Fast eine Liebesgeschichte*, Reinbek bei Hamburg, 1979; SS = *Das Staunen der Schlafwandler am Ende der Nacht*, Reinbek bei Hamburg, 1983; ZF = *Zeit des Fasans*, Reinbek bei Hamburg, 1988.

That Walter is an exponent of 'littérature engagée' is not in question. His regular utterances over the years in respect of the legitimacy and function of literature (e.g. 'Notiz zu Hugo von Hofmannsthals "Brief des Philipp Lord Chandos an Francis Bacon"' (1963); 'Literatur als Revolte' (1967); 'Literatur in der Zeit des Blindflugs' (1978); 'Es hat sich verändert' (1979); 'Zehn Noten zum Schreiben' (1981)) reflect Walter's conception of the central role of the writer in society.

2. Werner Weber, the literary editor of the *Neue Zürcher Zeitung*, first encouraged Walter's writings, publishing his short story 'Einfahrt' in that newspaper on 5 February 1956. Several others appeared in the *NZZ* over the next eighteen months. Arguably the best known is 'Ein Unglücksfall' (originally 'Das Floss', first published in *NZZ* in October 1957, and subsequently anthologised on several occasions).

3. 'Der Roman kreiste um das Grundproblem Lebenslüge' (G 230).

4. Walter turned briefly and unsatisfactorily to the theatre in his search for an adequate form of expression. Two pieces were conceived in 1962: *Elio oder eine fröhliche Gesellschaft* (first performed in 1965) and *Die Katze* (first performed in 1967). Both pieces were received politely but not enthusiastically by the critics.

5. Walter's contract with the Walter Verlag was terminated at the end of 1966, following his publishing of the Austrian Ernst Jandl's *Laut und Luise*. Two months later he formed the Luchterhand Verlag, where he stayed until 1973 on a full-time basis. Walter started the year 1967 in challenging mood in another direction by entering the 'Zürcher Literaturstreit' with his own response to Emil Staiger, namely 'Vorschlag zur Unversöhnlichkeit' (G 27–29).

6. A second address, 'S'wär langsam Zyt!' (G 148–52), followed on 21 June 1986 on the occasion of the demonstration at the Gösgen site some weeks after the Chernobyl accident.

7. See his essay 'Unbewältigte schweizerische Vergangenheit?' (1966), reprinted in Max Frisch, *Schweiz als Heimat? Versuche über 50 Jahre*, ed. Walter Obschlager, Frankfurt am Main, 1990, pp. 215–18 (p. 217f). In fact Walter had already responded to Frisch in the same year with his own essay 'Das "Soll" der Literatur' (G 19–26), effectively arguing that, for him, Switzerland did not represent a special case. The essay was the occasion of Walter's celebrated dictum: 'Schweizer bin ich in etwa dritter Linie' (G 23). Is it a question of the 'Linse zu eng eingestellt?' 'Warum Literatur nicht auch einmal mit dem "Weitwinkel-Objektiv" betrachten?' (G 24).

5

Peter Bichsel: 'In Geschichten leben'

Ronald Speirs

By the standards of many of his contemporaries, Peter Bichsel's literary output is not extensive. Since 1964 his fictional writing has amounted to just four slim volumes of short prose. On the other hand he has also put his talents to other uses, writing a lively and popular newspaper column,[1] provocative political essays,[2] essays on educational and related matters[3] (having originally trained and practised as a primary school teacher), and contributing, through discussion and writing, to the political work of the Bundesrat Willy Ritschard. As a journalist and essayist Bichsel has criticised repeatedly the inertia of Swiss public life engendered both by the country's political–institutional arrangements and by the pride – or smugness – felt by a deeply conservative citizenry for Swiss democracy, Swiss neutrality, the Swiss army, Swiss industry, indeed most things Swiss.[4] The aim of such writing is to promote change. Bichsel's fiction, too, is much concerned with the experience of stagnation and with various longings for some kind of fresh start. Here, however, one finds not the vehement tone of the polemicist but an anxious circling around the question of whether any fundamental change is possible. Bichsel's various theoretical pronouncements on literature are similarly stamped by the same central contradiction that lies at the heart of his practice as a creative writer. While on the one hand insisting that the function of literature is to provide access to a 'Gegenwelt' by the adoption of a conjectural mode of thinking (the principle of 'Was wäre, wenn . . .'),[5] Bichsel concedes that invention is not strictly possible because 'die menschliche Fantasie ist begrenzt durch all das, was es gibt'.[6] The conflict between the desire to conceive of a new and better way of living and the realisation that the capacity even to *imagine* life differently is profoundly constrained by the experiences of the past is to be found, in one form or another, in each of his collections of prose.

The world of *Eigentlich möchte Frau Blum den Milchmann kennen-*

lernen (1964) does not display its Swissness as obviously as did, say, the 'Seldwyla' stories or the *Zürcher Novellen* of Gottfried Keller, but numerous incidental details make the point plainly enough. Unmistakably in 'Vom Meer', where a woman receives an envelope addressed to 'Svizzera' (FB 38),[7] or in references to Locarno, Davos or Aarau, and clearly enough for anyone at all familiar with the country in the 'zehn Rappen zu wenig' left out by Frau Blum for the milkman, or the pocket knife registered by a prison officer ('ein rotes Taschenmesser mit zwei Klingen, einem Zapfenzieher und einem Schraubenzieher', FB 40), or the 'Bundesrat' opening a newly electrified stretch of railway, or the hat worn by the official Bühlmann ('einen Haarfilzhut mit grüner Kordel', FB 27). Less obviously, but more importantly, Switzerland is *implicitly* present at virtually every point in these stories in the form of the idyllic image of Swiss life held, in Bichsel's view, by too many of his compatriots, an image challenged in detail after detail by these miniatures of daily life. Precisely aimed as these stories are, however, they are neither intended nor suited for home consumption alone. Indeed the fact that the generally unhappy lives shown here represent, at most, local variants on the unsatisfactory quality of life as it is widely lived throughout contemporary European society is a major part of Bichsel's challenge to the notion of the 'Sonderfall Schweiz',[8] and more particularly to the idea that it could serve as a *positive* paradigm for the rest of Europe.

In part the problems experienced by Bichsel's characters have material causes. Despite Switzerland's enviable gross domestic product, the touchstone of many political decisions (too many in Bichsel's view), and in spite of the anachronistic but still cherished ideal of the family house in its own garden,[9] the people in these stories mostly live in apartment blocks, some of them in the least desirable flats at the top of several flights of stairs. The opening piece, adopting the perspective of a 'Hausierer', takes the reader up and down the stairs of one such cramped building ('ein Haus . . . auf teurem Boden, hineingezwängt zwischen andere', FB 7), the kind of building occupied by the old woman Adele for whom an acquaintance leaves a bunch of peonies in the letter box rather than climb up five flights to call on her, or in which Frau Blum lives, carefully counting every copper in the change from the very modest order of milk and butter left by the milkman in her 'verbeulten Topf'. These are lives which show no benefit from the steady growth of the economy in which so much national pride is invested.

Nor does the work ethic on which the wealth, efficient management and self-image of the country depend bring happiness to the individuals whose lives are governed by it. Although dutiful, the official who registers a new prisoner's belongings (in 'Das Messer') is too aware of the length of his own working day to be bothered to exchange a friendly word with the clearly nervous new inmate. The sound of a passing brass band, in which the warder's son plays, reinforces the contrast between leisure time and 'Dienstzeit', adding to it the contrast of inside with outside, so that the prison becomes a metaphorical as well as a literal setting and the lifelong constraint of duty becomes, if anything, more oppressive than the prison term which the young man has to serve for what looks like an act of civil disobedience. Neither of these lives, the one spent enforcing the country's laws and the other punished for breaking them, indicate that there is much scope within daily life for the individual freedom so prized in official ideology. For the prison warder, as for the officials (in 'Die Beamten') who detest their work ('sie lieben ihre Arbeit nicht', FB 35) or the embittered old man approaching retirement (in 'Sein Abend'), work is accompanied by alienation just as surely in work-proud Switzerland as it is elsewhere.

The isolation experienced by most characters in *Frau Blum* illustrates concretely Bichsel's general fear that the 'Bürgersinn' of which his countrymen boast does not mean they are endowed with any true sense of community. In the first piece in the collection the occupants of a block of flats are all referred to as 'jemand' and many of the figures in subsequent stories are simply 'er' or 'sie'. Frau Blum's milkman is 'einer von denen, die ihre Pflicht tun' (FB 30). If asked, he would say that he 'knows' Frau Blum, but this means simply that he associates her name with the 'verbeulten Topf' in which he leaves her small order for butter and milk. Apart from such transactions he has no interest in her life: 'Den Milchmann interessiert es nicht, in welchem Stock Frau Blum wohnt, der Topf steht unten an der Treppe. Er macht sich keine Gedanken, wenn er nicht dort steht' (FB 30); in other words it would not occur to him that she might be ill or even dead. She would like to speak to him some day. He in turn thinks, but does not actually write, '"Nicht der Rede wert" oder "keine Ursache"' in reply to her apology for leaving out too little money. In her case the inhibition is prompted by fear of what he or the neighbours might think of such unusual behaviour.

Bichsel's keen awareness of isolation in his society is reflected in the topography of the stories, in which familiar features of Swiss life acquire a symbolic dimension. The collection closes with a reflection on the effects of snow: 'Aber er dringt in die Schuhe, blockiert die Autos, bringt Eisenbahnen zum Entgleisen und macht entlegene Dörfer einsam' (FB 61). But separation was already present as a theme in the opening sentence of the very first piece, a reflection on the stairway in a block of flats: 'Behelfsmäßig kann man sich ein Haus vorstellen, ein Haus mit vier Stockwerken, mit einer Treppe, die sie verbindet und trennt' (FB 7); the odd-sounding 'behelfsmäßig' and the explicit definition of the stairway as something which both links and separates are devices – Brecht would have called them 'Verfremdungseffekte' – designed to bring out the general, metaphorical significance of what otherwise might be passed over as a mere recording of visual detail.

Once the theme has been established in this way the reader is alert to further details which take it up and vary it, as in this passage: 'Der Dachboden ist mit Latten unterteilt, jedes Stockwerk hat ein Abteil, jedes Abteil ist mit einem Vorhängeschloß gesichert, sicher werden hier auch alte Matratzen aufbewahrt, Fotoalben und Tagebücher, Spiegel' (FB 8). The tenants close themselves off not just from the outside world, but from one another in the shared space of the loft, each preserving his or her privacy with a padlock. In 'Die Beamten' the scurrying of officials between office and work, where their roles are reassuringly defined, becomes a symbol of the neurotic sense of threat in the society they represent: 'Und jetzt gehen sie schnell, denn die Straße scheint ihnen verdächtig. Sie bewegen sich heimwärts und fürchten, das Pult nicht geschlossen zu haben . . . Beim Mittagessen fürchten sie sich vor dem Rückweg, denn er scheint ihnen verdächtig und sie lieben ihre Arbeit nicht' (FB 35). Although he satirises it in this story, Bichsel's response to the fear that perpetuates isolation is generally one of sadness. In 'November' the chill of winter provokes despair about another, more penetrating chill that cannot be kept out by a good overcoat. This prompts a need for the comfort of communication but the need remains undetected behind the conventional formulae that pass for conversation in this inhibited society:

Er fürchtete sich und wenn er zu jemandem sagte: 'Es ist kälter geworden', erwartete er Trost.
'Ja, November', sagte der andere. (FB 17)

The mutual isolation which people cultivate in this society as a protection against intrusion leaves the individual trapped with his existential fears within a prison house of conventional politeness.

Bichsel does not imagine that all the problems experienced by his characters can be attributed to socialisation. One of the stories, 'Holzwolle', carries the suggestion that the archetype of the Fall is re-enacted in each individual's life when the child, by seeking to grasp the elusive 'Etwas' at the heart of a beloved teddy bear or snowman, destroys the very thing he is fond of: 'Man wird es nie finden. Sobald man es sucht, ist der Schneemann keiner mehr' (FB 24).[10] On the other hand the stories often prompt anger at the unnecessary *additional* disappointments people inflict on one another, as often as not within the family. In 'Die Löwen' a grandfather, now dead because he drank too much, once dreamed of becoming a lion tamer, but was cowed by the disparagement of others into accepting the unsatisfying compromise of keeping a few ducks on a pond; sadly the same suppression of the imagination is perpetuated in the life of his grandchildren: 'Die Enkel haben die Löwen mitgenommen und sie sorgfältig unter ihren Betten versteckt' (FB 20). A husband with a passion for music boxes has to hide his collection – and their bigger brother, the fantasy fairground organ which he keeps in the cellar – from the disapproving gaze of a wife whose education has taught her that such things are kitsch. She, possessed of a greater will to power than her husband, buys the piano she wants (but which he does not), while he loses the courage to play his music-boxes:

> Und er wagte immer seltener, seine Musikdosen zu spielen, er saß im Zimmer, hörte ihr zu, sah das Klavier und ihre ungeschickten Finger und abends umarmte sie ihn und sagte: 'Ich weiß, daß du Musik gern hast.' (FB 22)

Bichsel knows that we live by making 'Geschichten' out of our lives,[11] and that the death of the heart will come about all too soon if society, by putting too high a premium on the values of common sense and conformity – and here Switzerland is simply a marked example of a widespread tendency – suffocates all attempts to 'tell' – i.e. to live out – the kind of stories which deeply felt wishes prompt the imagination to conceive. Happiness may ultimately be unattainable, but without at least some illusions life ceases to seem worth living.

The tension between the wishes that feed the imagination, stimulating it to tell the stories needed in order to go on living, and the daily, monthly, yearly routine that constricts and deadens the imagination is the central theme of *Die Jahreszeiten* (1967), Bichsel's second, longest and most demanding work. Like *Frau Blum*, *Die Jahreszeiten* begins with the description of a block of flats, seen in this case with the critical eyes of a reluctant prospective tenant:

> Jemand sagte: 'In diesem Haus könnte ich nicht wohnen, es ist so
> tomatenfarbig angestrichen.' Dagegen gibt es nichts zu sagen. Das Haus
> ist auch viel zu hoch, zu schmal oder zu hoch, der Garten zu klein. (J 5)

The narrator now lives in the building, his dramatic pose of
rejection ('In diesem Haus könnte ich nicht wohnen') having been
cut down to size by the need to find somewhere affordable to live.
As if to rub in his own defeat at the hands of reality, the narrator
next opens a detailed catalogue of the deficiencies in his flat – damp
walls, lack of heating, peeling paint, a defective boiler – which will
grow steadily as the work unfolds. His room lies 'auf der Nord-
seite, der Schattenseite des Hauses' (J 6), his bed facing the window. In a half-asleep state he sometimes has the feeling that the bed
has turned through 180 degrees, but he only has to open his eyes to
see the hope or illusion of change dashed:

> Ich mache die Augen auf, sehe die wirkliche Situation und erlebe eine
> zeitlos schnelle Drehbewegung um 180 Grad. Die Augen schließen, die
> Situation umstellen und das Bett wieder mühsam drehen.
> Nach einigen Versuchen gelingt es nicht mehr, die Wirklichkeit zu
> verleugnen. (J 6)

The defeat of wish and fantasy by known reality is, however,
only temporary. No sooner has the narrator declared his intention
simply to describe the room ('Aber ich will das Zimmer beschreiben, auch wenn es mich nicht interessiert, also irgendwo
beginnen', J 6), than he suddenly changes tack, shifting from the
description of a water pitcher to the abrupt assertion that 'Kieninger hat in Tarragona einen Wasserkrug gekauft' (J 7). Who is this
Kieninger and what has he to do with the narrator's Spanish water
jug? Kieninger is a figure of fantasy constructed in part from
fragments of the narrator's biography, such as the visit he once paid
to Tarragona over a decade ago,[12] and the function of this character
in *Die Jahreszeiten* is to be the central figure in an attempted story of
romance and adventure. Kieninger was supposedly travelling back
to Vienna after a holiday in Tarragona, where he had fallen in love
with an English girl called Carole, when, reluctant to return to his
wife Elfriede, he arbitrarily decided to leave the train in a strange
town. In this way he has come to live in the narrator's flat, so that
the narrator is now able to assign his water pitcher to Kieninger and
romanticise its supposed origin:

> Oder man könnte wie Kieninger den Krug einer Zigeunerin in Tarra-
> gona abhandeln, eine Zigeunerin beschreiben, alte, windgegerbte Haut,
> unter der viel Schönheit liegen muß und ganz nebenbei der Frau einen
> Krug in die Hand geben. So ist der Krug weder glockenförmig noch
> unlasiert. Er ist jetzt Erinnerung, Olivenhaine, die rote Erde der
> Pyrenäen, Gitarren und Flamenco. (J 7)

By the end of this passage, at the latest, the reader has sensed the
cliché quality of the romance that is being attributed to Kieninger.
Yet still the hunger for a 'story' persists, and to satisfy it the
narrator reaches further down into the store of memory and
emerges with a fairy tale, told in the words one might use when
speaking to a child, in which the jug has a part to play in a young
girl's quest for happiness:

> Es gibt aber eine bessere Geschichte, die von dem kleinen Mädchen, das
> seine sieben verschollenen Brüder suchen geht und das neben einem
> Ringlein als Andenken an seine Eltern nichts anderes mitnimmt als einen
> Krug für wenn es Durst hat, einen Laib Brot für wenn es Hunger hat
> und ein Stühlchen für wenn es müde ist. (J 7f.)

But the naive pleasure of the child who once heard this story is no
longer available to an adult mind irritated by its own
knowingness.[13] For such a mind the 'Märchen' is simply part of
literary history, hence its repetition in its 'correct', literary – but no
longer magical – formulation. The path back to childhood being
blocked, the narrator's desire to write about a quester-hero has to
make do with the unsatisfactory story of Kieninger, unsatisfactory
because his stereotype romance can command no credence even
before it has been told.

The two main topics of *Die Jahreszeiten*, the house occupied by
the narrator and the story of Kieninger, are intimately related to
one another: 'Außerhalb dieses Hauses gibt es keinen Kieninger. Es
gibt ihn, wenn er hier ist, wenn er weggeht und zurückkommt'
(J 58). Just as Kieninger is an experimental literary figure, the
house is the 'house of fiction', a metaphorical setting built from
words and designed to reveal the processes of literary construction.
Common to both topics is further the narrator's desire to avoid
writing about himself: 'Alles dem Kieninger unterschieben' (J 8);
'Ich versuche, nicht von mir zu schreiben, sondern vom Tisch,
Zimmer, Haus und Straße' (J 9). In neither case is the diversionary
tactic successful, however, as the narrator's mind keeps returning
to his own situation:

Er sitzt an einem Pult, schreibt einen Brief nach Wien. Ich sitze an einem kleinen Pult, genaue Maße 98 auf 53 Zentimeter, Höhe 73 Zentimeter, hell lackiert. Ich bin der, der das schreibt. (J 8–9)

The evident and increasing hostility felt by the narrator towards Kieninger has to do with the fact that the fictional character keeps turning his creator's thoughts back on himself. There are two mirrors in the narrator's room, one of them being Kieninger. Thus Kieninger's writing to Elfriede about his decision not to return home is an extension of the narrator's attempt to construct a story of romance around Kieninger. Ego and alter ego share the same writing desk. Kieninger's role in the novel, as intruder and *Doppelgänger*, confirms Elsbeth Pulver's observation that hostility towards the 'Fremden' who appear so frequently in contemporary Swiss fiction arises from the fact that such figures reflect, in an unwelcome manner, repressed features of their hosts' *own* lives.[14]

Kieninger exists in a half-way house between Tarragona and Vienna, between Carole and Elfriede.[15] He lives alone, like a bachelor, but remains married. The narrator, too, is a married man with a family, but he is irritated by the problems and duties involved in maintaining a household and would like to be able to isolate himself: 'Ich hasse das Geräusch des Windes in der Wohnung. Ich will, daß die Fenster geschlossen werden. Ich will, daß die Zimmertüren geschlossen werden, ich will die Wohnung in einzelne Räume unterteilt haben' (J 10). His awareness of the regressive character of such wishes is expressed in numerous features of Kieninger's imagined behaviour. When Kieninger is given a room of his own it promptly resembles nothing so much as the territory of a rebellious adolescent, and an anachronistic one at that, since several of the stage props through which he asserts his 'individuality' are leftovers from an earlier phase in teenage culture, redolent of the mid-1950s rather than the late 1960s:

Seit Kieninger mit einem Filzstift an die Tür seines Zimmers MR. KILROY WAS HERE geschrieben hat, ist vieles besser. Auch trägt er jetzt Gegenstände in sein Zimmer. In einem Acker fand er eine rostige Hacke ohne Stiel, im Garten ein riesiges Horn, das wie ein Mammutzahn aussieht, im Keller ein Bild Marilyn Monroes aus einer alten Illustrierten – sie hat Selbstmord begangen – und in einem Kehrichteimer die Mütze eines Bahnarbeiters mit einem Silbergalon auf gauloisesblauem Grund und einem Flügelrad als Kokarde. (J 28)

A couple of these objects also have associations with childhood.

The bone was first brought into the narrator's home by his son Matthias, whose childish imagination first declared it to be a mammoth's tooth (J 9). The railwayman's cap, too, is a reminder both of Matthias playing at trains and of the impulsive interruption of his train journey that has supposedly given Kieninger his freedom from the constraints of marriage ('Er hat sich daran gewöhnt, keine Post zu bekommen. Elfriede antwortet nicht', J 28).

Here again Kieninger can be seen to be an extension of the narrator. Not only is Kieninger a creation of fantasy, he is also a character given to indulging his fantasies, and the things which appeal to his imagination are often the same as those which appeal to the narrator. In chapter four the narrator introduces a figure of whimsy (later revealed to be a quotation from Fellini's film *Otto e mezzo*), a small girl dressed as a melancholy white clown who executes a mysterious dance up the stairs of the apartment block each week. She is given the name Annemarie. Kieninger takes a liking to the figure, so that when she goes missing the narrator knows that Kieninger will take on the task of searching for her ('Er nimmt mir das ab', J 116). Annemarie seems to be another of the mirror images in the work, embodying a vision of childhood as graceful-purposeless play, although tinged also with the melancholy of such a dream. Kieninger's eye was attracted to a similar figure in the museum in Tarragona, a 'Gliederpuppe aus Elfenbein' (J 91). The attraction of both narrator and Kieninger to figures or objects of play reflects in turn their own regressive inclination to play.[16] Thus the name Annemarie is later transferred to a pretty young girl to whom Kieninger is attracted, and then transformed into Marianne. Kieninger's tendency to use women as objects of fantasy-play, which underlies his decision to leave the train before Vienna in order to preserve in memory the story of Carole, leads the narrator to think of him as a window dresser: 'Kieninger könnte auch Schaufensterpuppen auf die Schulter laden und ins Schaufenster tragen, er könnte sie anziehen mit neuen, makellosen Kleidern und ihnen Falten stecken . . .' (J 57).

Implicit in this is self-criticism on the part of the narrator, since Marianne or Annemarie, in whatever guise, are in origin playthings of *his* fantasy, as indeed is Kieninger: 'Kieninger kann die Arme bewegen, den Unterarm und den Oberarm, aufwärts und abwärts . . . Er kann ein Bein vor das andere setzen . . . Aus Kieninger kann man einen Soldaten machen. Aus Kieninger kann man einen Schreiner machen, einen Bauzeichner, einen Schaufensterdekorateur' (J 57). In a later passage the narrator describes himself in similar terms: 'Ich kann die Arme bewegen. Ich kann ein

Bein vor das andere setzen. Ich habe Mühe mit Fremdsprachen' (J 115). The narrator, too, is a character/marionette in the story that he is writing of his life. His anger with Kieninger is anger at his own inability to write a less stereotyped, more credible romance for Kieninger, and this in turn reflects his inability to write a more satisfying plot for his own life. Unable to be anything other than the character which the plot of his life so far has made him, the narrator in the end remains in the family home, redecorates it, rearranges the furniture and sends Kieninger back to Elfriede in Vienna.

'Immer wieder der Versuch, Papier zu füllen, Erkundigungen bei der Bauverwaltung, ein Baugesuch vom 17. Februar 1927, in Peter Dürrenmatts Schweizergeschichte steht, daß es 1926 14,000 Arbeitslose gab. Günstige Zeit, billige Häuser zu bauen' (J 55): this is a typical example of the narrator's many excursions into various features of house building, but one which indicates more clearly than most why this diversionary tactic must fail. The definition of writing as an endlessly repeated but otherwise unexplained 'Versuch, Papier zu füllen' hints at its symbolic–existential function: filling the empty sheet in front of the writer is an attempt to fill out those empty spaces in his life, comparable to Studer's slow way of checking his golden pocket watch: 'Er erfüllte mit seinen Bewegungen einige Sekunden und brachte sie hinter sich' (J 35). These underlying existential concerns keep finding expression in the features of the house 'described' by the narrator. The narrator defines a house as a place of protection, but one that is necessarily inadequate: 'Häuser bieten Schutz vor Regen, vor der Witterung im allgemeinen, bieten einen gewissen Schutz vor Dieben, vor Mördern, sind abschließbar, aber sie sind vor nichts gefeit' (J 48). Above all the house is experienced as a place of decay: first one boiler bursts, then another, paint peels from the walls, doors jam, carpets fray, the light switch in the stairway is broken, the walls are out of true, there is woodworm in the roof joists, tiles are ripped from the roof during storms, are replaced and fall out again so that, 'durch das Dach dringt Schnee' (J 52). But the cold that penetrates this house is not just that of winter, for it is also a place of death. The narrator attends the funeral of the second-floor tenant who has committed suicide. He later attends the funeral of an old neighbour who has evidently died after a long period of suffering ('Der Pfarrer sprach von Hiob', J 94). The early deaths of Marilyn Monroe and Billy Holiday haunt the narrator's memory. The garden of the house is buried under concrete in order to provide car parking.

The house, then, and its occupants constantly remind the

narrator of the transience of things. They also bear in on him another feature of the passing of the seasons, namely the sense of stasis produced by the recurrence of the same things year after year. The routine of the neighbours seems as inevitable as the rising of the sun: 'So geschah jeden Tag das Unvermeidliche, daß es Tag wurde, daß Studer das Haus verließ, um halb acht, daß er zurückkehrte, daß die Frau im Parterre das Haus verließ, daß sie es um zehn Uhr schloß, daß man irgend einmal am Morgen erwachte' (J 38). A passing description of a house within the house, namely the cage occupied by Matthias's pet hamster, sums up the narrator's feeling of imprisonment within the family home and of pointless stasis within the cycle of time: 'Goldhamster hält man in einem Metallkäfig. Darin ist eine Tretmühle, in der sie nachts rumrennen' (J 27). Such are the experiences that prompt the fantasies of escape enacted by the character Kieninger, through which the narrator in turn attempts to flee back down the corridor of time to the irresponsible, self-absorbed condition of an adolescent.

Although Bichsel has insisted that *Die Jahreszeiten* is not a novel but rather a loose collection of short pieces of prose[17], there is a development in the work, and the end of Kieninger's story is long foreshadowed. It is not simply that the narrator eventually decides to get rid of Kieninger, for his irritation at the character has been evident from the beginning ('Keine Lust zu beschreiben, Kieninger abgeschrieben. Kieninger taugt zu nichts', J 12). Kieninger's disappearance is dictated rather by the logic of the narrator's imagination. If he imagines Kieninger taking on 'real' existence, he has to think of the character as acquiring progressively the attributes of a bourgeois, with a passport, a residence permit, a job as a draughtsman, regular habits. The figure of fantasy is thus eventually 'zu Tode gequält', for it is proved to him 'daß es ihn nicht gibt' (J 192). He might as well go back to Vienna, rejoin his wife and two children, promise to take them to Spain with him next time, in fact so insubstantial has the romance surrounding him become that his life is in the end indistinguishable from the narrator's: 'Aber auch Wien kann man fallenlassen und damit auch seinen Namen und den Namen seiner Frau; dann ist er von hier aus weggefahren und nach hier zurückgekehrt' (J 115).

The 'embourgeoisement' of Kieninger stems from and anticipates a growing tendency to resignation in the narrator. First it is Kieninger who drinks a beer after work with the archetypal 'Pfahlbürger', Studer, then it is the narrator who does so: 'Auch trinke ich nachmittags um fünf in der Wirtschaft mein Bier mit Studer. Ich sehe keinen Anlaß, seine Meinung zu korrigieren, und ich höre ihn über die Russen sprechen. Er wiederholt, was in der Zeitung steht, und bildet sich nichts darauf ein' (J 106). Here again the mirror principle is at work, for Studer's repetition of the opinions he has read in the newspaper reflects the ultimate conformity of the narrator's imagination to the life story which he absorbed in childhood from his craftsman father and which he is now, albeit reluctantly, repeating. In a sense his excursions into the past of the house have been an excursion into the world of his father, and the reconstruction of the story of the house simultaneously a reconstruction of his life along lines his father would have approved of. The initial gesture of refusal ('In diesem Haus könnte ich nicht wohnen', J 5), repeated and varied in Kieninger's escape attempt ('Ich halte das nicht aus', J 31), and issuing for a long time in depressive apathy on the part of the narrator, is eventually channelled into active improvement of the house:

> Das Zimmer ist gestrichen. Es war eine mühsame Sache. Ich bin stolz darauf. Ich ließ auch einen Spannteppich legen, einen grauen; ich stellte die Möbel um und hängte die Bilder neu.
>
> Der Hausmeister weiß nichts davon, die Farbe war billig. Ich mußte endlich etwas unternehmen; ich hielt es nicht mehr aus, in einem zerbröckelnden Haus zu leben. (J 98)

Not only does the narrator repeat his father's work (like Bichsel's own father, he was a house painter by trade), but his motives for doing so reinstate the values of his class. It appears that his upbringing compels the narrator either to dismiss Kieninger's attempt at a fresh start as adolescent fantasy or, when he attempts to imagine a 'new' life for Kieninger, to turn him into just another respectable citizen. Nevertheless the narrator's pressing sense of life's transience does not allow his resignation to become total. *Die Jahreszeiten* ends where Kieninger's story began, on a train, a deserted commuter train in the early, still dark hours of New Year's morning. The last sentence ('In Olten umsteigen', J 120) shows the narrator still clinging at least to the possibility of branching out in a new direction.

Although the intricate, private world of *Die Jahreszeiten* may seem far removed from the issues of Swiss public life to which Bichsel addresses himself in his essays and newspaper articles, it raises questions central to Bichsel's political work, namely what are the possibilities for change, to what extent is fundamental change precluded by the conditioning force of the past? Bichsel's play with the possibilities of narration in *Die Jahreszeiten* is no mere formal self-indulgence but an uncovering – well before the advent of the 'Neue Subjektivität' of the disillusioned 1970s in the FRG – of the problems of imagining an alternative future, for the constraining effect of conditioning even on the individual's imagination has worrying implications for social and political renewal. However, for his next work of fiction, *Kindergeschichten* (1969), Bichsel chose a genre in which he could give more scope to hope or defiance, the emotions that make change at least still thinkable even when the odds are against it.[18] Not that these are merely jolly or harmless children's stories. In fact they are mostly populated by old men who engage in undertakings which are either pointless or doomed to failure. As such, however, they are the slightly comic literary descendants of Camus's heroic Sisyphus, asserting the dignity of spirit and will in the face of absurdity.

The relation between these defiant old men and the emotional and imaginative world of the child is expressed most clearly, and most movingly, in 'Jodok läßt grüßen', a story which, in a sense, rewrites 'Die Löwen' from the *Frau Blum* collection. 'Die Löwen' was elegaic in tone, mourning not only the death of a grandfather but also the suppression of his dream of becoming a lion tamer which led to his death ('Nun ist er tot, er trank zu viel', FB 19). At first 'Jodok läßt grüßen' seems to tell the story of a quite different old age. The story is narrated by the grandchild of an old man who claimed to have had an uncle with the unusual name of Jodok. All the narrator ever learned about Jodok was told to him by his grandfather, and all the grandfather's stories were not descriptions of Jodok but tales about the times when Jodok was alive, about the time when he visited his uncle Jodok, or the time when Uncle Jodok presented him with a Jew's harp. It seems that the grandfather talked of nothing but Jodok, applying the name Jodok to everything and every action, substituting the long vowel 'o' for all other vowels, and he persisted in doing so in the face of opposition from those around him: 'Aber er hörte nicht auf. Er hörte sein ganzes Leben nicht auf, und mein Großvater ist sehr alt geworden, und ich habe ihn sehr geliebt' (K 53–4). The child's love for his grandfather that is evident in the way he recounts his life was elicited by the love conveyed by the way the grandfather had once told his tales of Jodok: 'Und wenn er zum Schluß auch nichts anderes als Jodok sagte, haben wir zwei uns doch immer sehr gut verstanden. Ich war sehr jung und der Großvater sehr alt, er nahm mich auf die Knie und jodokte Jodok die Jodok von Jodok Jodok' (K 54). But there is a twist to this seemingly idyllic tale. The narrator finally reveals it to be a sheer invention, as the grandfather did not live to an old age and his attempt to tell a tale about Jodok was stamped on by his wife:

> Und meine Großmutter, die ich nicht gern gehabt habe, schrie ihn schroff an: 'Hör auf mit deinem Jodok', und der Großvater wurde ganz still und traurig und entschuldigte sich dann. (K 55)

Thus the story as a whole is an attempt to rewrite history, to restore to the grandfather the happy old age he was deprived of, and to give back to the narrator the love of the grandfather which he lost so early. The story, issuing as it does from a mixture of love and defiance, offers itself as a model of how an acceptable future might be imagined and realised: 'Da bekam ich eine große Wut . . . Und wenn das mein Großvater getan hätte, wäre er vielleicht älter geworden, und ich hätte heute noch einen Großvater, und wir würden uns gut verstehen' (K 55).

In his latest collection of stories, *Der Busant* (1985), Peter Bichsel has developed his interest in the emotional and imaginative deformations produced by society in new directions. The title story of the collection alludes to an old Provençal tale in which two noble lovers, Peter of Provence and 'die schöne Magelone', daughter of the King of Naples, are separated during their elopement when a legendary bird – 'der Busant' – steals from Magelone one of the love rings given to her by Peter, who then sets off in pursuit of the bird. The two lovers spend their lives wandering in search of one another and are at last reunited in old age in Provence. In Bichsel's version Peter has become 'Ueli', a drunken down-and-out, slow of speech and apparently of understanding, one of the eternally exploited and despised. Magelone has become Mage Lehmann, a secretary given to bouts of drinking until she vomits. In sudden shifts of time-setting the pair of them are shown as having been the 'lowest of the low' throughout the centuries.[19] Nevertheless these two still preserve within them a flicker of genuine, intense human longing which leaves them untouched by the patronising attitudes of the solid, respectable citizens of Solothurn who have accommodated themselves profitably to an exploitative social system, but for whom the cost has been the loss of all genuineness from their lives. In Bichsel's rewriting of the legend the two lovers, although living in close proximity, never recognise one another as Peter and Magelone; but Mage, while in her cups, suddenly has a vision of the approaching Peter, while Ueli is characterised as being for ever on the move, with no secure employment, seemingly searching vacantly for something he has forgotten. By describing him as 'nie angekommen' (B 12), a man whose characteristic place is 'im Niemandsland' (B 21), Bichsel defines Ueli as the negation of the static, 'arriviert' lives of the citizens of Solothurn, which is represented as the epitome of picture-book, small-town Swiss life, affluent, smug and utterly false: 'So verlogen wie der Wirt ist die Stadt, aufgeputzt und mittelalterlich wie ein Tiroler Ferienort' (B 13). In Ueli the romantic figure of the 'Taugenichts' is brought back to life, but now transformed into an embodiment of melancholy in a world where the narrator sees no hope of bringing about the changes that might give the errant souls of Peter and Magelone the sense of having found their lost home.[20]

In several stories of the collection ('Laufbahn', 'Eisenbahnfahren', 'Diese Sätze', 'Warten in Baden-Baden') Bichsel uses the technique he first used in *Die Jahreszeiten* of confronting the focal character with a 'Fremden' or 'Doppelgänger' who embodies some repressed feature of his psyche. In 'Eisenbahnfahren', for example, a travelling insurance agent finds himself seated opposite a long, insubstantial figure who can roll himself up like Peter Schlemihl's shadow and who is a comic symbol of the '*Lange*weile' not just of such regular train journeys but of the whole way of life of the insurance agent.

The longest and most innovatory story in the collection is 'Warten in Baden-Baden'. Here Bichsel uses his mirroring technique to put into question his own satirical questioning of contemporary (Swiss) society. It is a framework story (a form beloved of German novella writers, particularly in the nineteenth century), whereby the brief 'Rahmenerzählung' is told by the 'Stadtschreiber' of Bergen-Enkheim (a post held by Bichsel in 1981–2). This narrator has supposedly had the 'Binnenerzählung' sent to him by a successful businessman, Karl Bönzli (the name has negative associations both with 'Bünzli', epitomising narrow-mindedness, and with 'Bonze', a person in power) whom he knows and heartily dislikes. The narrator of the 'Rahmenerzählung' is disturbed by this experience in two main ways. Firstly, the fact that Karl Bönzli has sent him the story suggests to him that this man is so sure of himself that he has failed completely to recognise that the story about a hated Charles Bönzchen refers to himself: 'Sein Brief . . . ist der Brief von einem Mann, der immer im Recht ist und dem nichts geschehen kann' (B 94). Even more disturbing is the narrator's compulsive feeling of identification with the narrator of the 'Binnenerzählung' and the consequent worry that this story is a trap for him personally.

The 'Binnenerzählung' in turn shows that the 'Stadtschreiber' has every reason to be disturbed by his identification with its narrator. The latter is a waiter from Lucerne (Bichsel's birthplace) now working in Bergen-Enkheim, having fled Switzerland: 'Ich hatte dieses Land endlich hinter mir' (B 70). This waiter feels threatened by the arrival of another Swiss in his hotel, the successful businessman Charles Bönzchen, also a native of Lucerne. Not only does Bönzchen's arrival rob the waiter of his stereotyped and thus protective identity as 'der Schweizer' (since there are now two of them), it also destroys progressively his illusion that the job of waiter gives him a peculiar form of power: 'Der Beruf des Kellners hat den Vorteil, daß man fremd bleibt und distanziert, daß einen die berufliche Servilität überlegen macht. In keinem anderen Beruf gibt es soviel Macht mit so wenig Verantwortung, so wenig Freizeit und so wenig Person' (B 70). Not only does he discover that no inner strategies can compensate for the deep-seated inferiority felt by the 'Knecht' towards the 'Herr', he also has to listen to this man of achievement (whose power he so clearly envies) as he reveals the melancholy beneath the mask of success. Like the waiter, Bönzchen too just wants to 'have everything behind him', a discovery which prompts the waiter to repeat (or think of repeating) the suicide bid which had once made him leap from his window in St. Moritz. The 'Knecht', it seems, needs the resentment he feels towards the imagined success of the 'Herr' in order to fill his own otherwise empty life with at least that emotion and the compensating strategy of inner superiority. The waiter's story is disturbing for the 'Stadtschreiber' because of the all-too-clear analogy with the relation of writers and intellectuals to the holders of power in society. Part of Bichsel's own answer to the question as to why he became a writer is the fact that he was a 'schlechter Fußballer' at school, and that, like the greatly admired James Joyce, he sought to compensate for his physical inferiority by developing his intellectual and imaginative gifts: 'Wer ein "widerwilliger Indianer" ist wie Joyce, dem bleibt noch der Kopf. Wer das Leben nicht lebt, der muß es sich erzählen.'[21]

As the reference to Joyce indicates, Bichsel's literary and intellectual horizons are clearly open across time and space, however much his subject matter may be drawn from life in contemporary Switzerland. In particular, whether one considers the unsparing exposure of the interdependence of power and *ressentiment* in 'Warten in Baden-Baden', or the thinly disguised will to power evident in his cameos of unhappy marriages ('Jodok', 'Die Löwen', 'Musikdosen'), or Bichsel's dissection of his own motives for writing as an intellectual compensation for physical inadequacy, one repeatedly finds parallels with the psychological insights of a much earlier critic of provincial philistinism, Friedrich Nietzsche. There is an echo – fortuitous or deliberate? – of Nietzsche's *Unzeitgemäße Betrachtungen* in the witty title Bichsel gave to one volume of his critical essays, *Geschichten zur falschen Zeit* (1979). More significantly, Bischsel's concern to encourage his contemporaries to adopt a freer, more creative relationship to history is remarkably similar to the arguments advanced by Nietzsche, as a newly appointed Professor of Classical Philology at Basel, a hundred years previously. In the second of his *Unzeitgemäße Betrachtungen* Nietzsche argued that his contemporaries had largely lost the ability to see themselves as the agents of history, masters of the present moment, confident of their right and power to shape the future as their own needs dictated because of an 'Übermaß von Historie'.[22] Bichsel, readily sympathetic to the revolutionary stirrings of 1968, recognises in the present exactly the same threat of personal and social stagnation that is posed by a paralysing awareness of the impersonal, determining force of history: 'Wer nur in der Geschichte lebt – im Sinne von Historik – und nicht in Geschichten, dessen Leben wird sinnlos . . . Die Geschichte ist den Geschichten feindlich, und nur in Geschichten sind Menschen zu erkennen.'[23] Yet, though Bichsel would like to challenge the enclosure of history with defiantly open 'Geschichten', and attempts to do just this in a number of his stories (particularly the *Kindergeschichten*), his longer pieces, *Die Jahreszeiten* and 'Warten in Baden-Baden', demonstrate rather the inescapability of the past and the consequent failure of the narrators to rewrite their lives along more desirable lines. Nevertheless, like the 'Selbstdenker–Selbsthenker' Nietzsche, Bichsel is not deterred by the results of social and self-analysis from pursuing truth even when this becomes a very uncomfortable activity. What clearly sustains him is the act of communication – in 'Geschichten' – itself.

Notes

1. A good deal of Bichsel's journalism has been collected in two volumes: *Geschichten zur falschen Zeit*, Darmstadt and Neuwied, 1981, and *Irgendwo anderswo. Kolumnen 1980–85*, Darmstadt and Neuwied, 1986.
2. See *Des Schweizers Schweiz*, Zurich, 1969; 'Ich beschimpfe gern, was ich liebe', Ex Libris Gespräch mit Peter Bichsel, *Ex Libris*, no. 12, 1981, pp. 17–23; 'Das

Ende der Schweizer Unschuld', *Der Spiegel*, 5 Jan. 1981, pp. 108–9.

3. Collected in *Schulmeistereien*, Darmstadt and Neuwied, 1987.

4. See *Des Schweizers Schweiz, passim.*

5. *Der Leser. Das Erzählen. Frankfurter Poetik-Vorlesungen*, Darmstadt and Neuwied, 1982, p. 20.

6. *Der Leser. Das Erzählen*, p. 12.

7. All references in this form are to *Eigentlich möchte Frau Blum den Milchmann kennenlernen*, Olten and Freiburg, 1964. Short references to Bichsel's other fictional works are given as follows: J = *Die Jahreszeiten*, Darmstadt and Neuwied, 1967; K = *Kindergeschichten*, Darmstadt and Neuwied, 1969; page references to 1974 edition; B = *Der Busant*, Darmstadt and Neuwied, 1985.

8. 'Europäer haben im ganzen bestimmt so viel Gemeinsames wie die Schweizer im ganzen', *Des Schweizers Schweiz*, p. 26.

9. See the essays by Malcolm Pender and Mary Stewart in this volume.

10. Bichsel believes 'daß Glück nie erreichbar ist' and that the task of literature is to help us live with sadness: 'Traurigkeit ist nicht überwindbar. Sie kann abgelehnt werden oder angenommen werden, und Geschichtenerzählen hat etwas damit zu tun, Trauer anzunehmen.' *Der Leser. Das Erzählen*, p. 11.

11. 'Der Jüngling, der unbedingt eine Honda kaufen will, kauft sich dieses Motorrad ja nicht als Transportmittel, sondern als Mittel zur Herstellung von Geschichten.' *Der Leser. Das Erzählen*, p. 82.

12. Bichsel himself went on a school trip to Spain in 1955. Just as the narrator is using Kieninger to cope with his problems, Bichsel is presumably using the narrator for similar private purposes. In an interview with Werner Bucher, Bichsel called *Die Jahreszeiten* 'mein privatestes Buch' ('Peter Bichsel: "Mich interessiert, was auf dem Papier geschieht"' in *Schweizer Schriftsteller im Gespräch*, ed. Bucher and Ammann, vol. 1 Basle, 1970, p. 44). Elsewhere in the same interview (p. 35) he denounced writing as 'ganz einfach ein unanständiges Geschäft, weil es doch eine dauernde Selbstbespiegelung ist'.

13. 'Behauptung: Der Mensch, der – auch auf der untersten intellektuellen Stufe – ein reflektierendes Wesen ist, es auch sein kann und will, leidet doch darunter, daß ihn die Reflexion daran hindert, original, erstmalig und einmalig leben zu können. Er sucht das Originalerlebnis.' *Der Leser. Das Erzählen*, p. 17. One of the reasons why Kieninger so irritates the narrator is the 'fact' that he is a year older and has thus always anticipated any experience, particularly with women, which the narrator might have (J 98).

14. Elsbeth Pulver, 'Von einem nächtlichen Fassadenkletterer, von Ambrosio, dem Spanier, und der neuen Lindauerin', *text + kritik*, Sonderband *Bestandsaufnahme Gegenwartsliteratur*, Munich, 1988, pp. 267–81.

15. Suzanne Steiner writes aptly of the 'Qualität des Dazwischen-Seins' in the lives of the characters of Robert Walser and Bichsel. Suzanne Steiner, *Schreiben im Dazwischen-Sein*, Bern, 1982, p. 15.

16. 'Letztlich ist Literatur eine Spielform, die einigen, den Schreibern und den Lesern, gefällt.' *Der Leser. Das Erzählen*, p. 21.

17. 'Die *Jahreszeiten* waren nie als Roman gedacht', 'Mich interessiert, was auf dem Papier geschieht', *Schweizer Schriftsteller im Gespräch*, p. 37.

18. See Bichsel's comments to Carl Paschek: 'Anfänglich versuchte ich nichts anderes als kindliche Denkmodelle an Geschichten zu erklären . . . "Trotz", "Widerstand", "Selbstbehauptung", das sind kindliche Themen und das ist der Inhalt kindlicher Denksysteme.' In '"Wenn einer Pfeife raucht, dann ist das eine Geschichte". Gespräch mit Carl Paschek', in *Peter Bichsel: 'Mich interessiert der Vorgang des Veränderns durch Beschreibung'*, Begleitheft zur Ausstellung der Stadt- und Universitätsbibliothek, Frankfurt am Main, 1982, p. 13.

19. Bichsel's early religious beliefs are still evident in his preference for social

outcasts over today's pharisees. See his essays 'Abschied von einer geliebten Religion' and 'Wie christlich sind die Christen?', in *Schulmeistereien*, Darmstadt and Neuwied, 1987, pp. 120–34 and pp. 134–44.

20. Bichsel's affinity with Romanticism is evident in his sympathy for the need of people in everyday life to model their lives on an imaginary 'Geschichte' that appeals to them: 'Hier in der Kneipe geschieht Selbstdarstellung in Imitation. Hier leben die Cowboys und die Seefahrer, die Kraftprotzen und die Einsiedler . . . Romantisch jedenfalls sind alle Imitationen. Romantisch als Stilform, als Kunstform meinte ja auch die Imitation – die Imitation des einfachen Lebens in der Natur zum Beispiel.' *Der Leser. Das Erzählen*, p. 42.

21. *Der Leser. Das Erzählen*, p. 57.

22. 'Vom Nutzen und Nachteil der Historie für das Leben', *Unzeitgemäße Betrachtungen*, Munich, 1964, p. 139.

23. *Der Leser. Das Erzählen*, pp. 78–9.

6

Adolf Muschg: Glimpses
of Freedom

H. Morgan Waidson

In the early 1960s Adolf Muschg spent two years as Lektor in German at Tokyo University. On his return to Switzerland he wrote up some of his impressions of Japan in prose. When he was encouraged to use these essays as a basis for a work of larger dimensions, his first novel took shape – *Im Sommer des Hasen* (1965). The book achieved an immediate success and showed that its author had a distinctive prose style, complex in its nuances and virtuosity, and that he could present convincingly to Swiss readers an exotic environmental setting. He had earlier had aspirations to become a poet, but now gave up writing verse and devoted his major literary energies to fiction and, less successfully, to drama, including plays for radio and television. Parallel with the novels run the five volumes of short stories, which some readers may find more immediately accessible than the longer fiction. He further underpinned his work with critical writing that has made clear his affinities with Keller, Goethe and psychoanalytical thought. In addition, he has written numerous reviews of other German-Swiss authors' work, beginning in 1961, and as Professor of German at the Eidgenössische Technische Hochschule in Zurich he has proved a knowledgeable and sympathetic champion of contemporary German-Swiss literature.

With the appearance in 1981, twenty years after he first began publishing, of *Literatur als Therapie?*, a treatise based on lectures given a year previously at Frankfurt University, Muschg expounds his approach to literature for the first time in detail and explains his association of imaginative writing with therapy, in part drawing on the stages of his own personal development. Perhaps it will be helpful to direct our attention in the first place to this 'Traktat', as he calls it (LT 153)[1], before considering some of the author's prose fiction. The printed treatise of 1981 corresponds, the author tells us, only to a minor degree to the lectures he gave in January and February 1980 as visiting lecturer for poetic theory at Frankfurt

University. The course of lectures and seminars was duly held, but when the time came for preparing the material for publication, the author had mislaid and lost his script. The outbreak of youth disturbances in Zurich and elsewhere had recently rocked Swiss society, and against this backcloth he felt obliged to produce a largely new version. The essay opens with the author contrasting the obsessions and mistakes of the 1968 generation with the different preoccupations of the young in 1980. Whereas the former had entertained grandiose visions of the overthrow of the bourgeois system, announcing among other things the 'Tod der Literatur', today's young people had eschewed utopian thinking in favour of apolitical escapism from the pressures of their parents' society, based, as they saw it, on exploitation and the ruthless pursuit of materialism. The 'Jugendunruhen' in Switzerland, unleashed by the violent reaction to the demand for an 'Autonomes Jugend-Zentrum' in Zurich, merely underlined the gulf which existed between the prevailing bourgeois ideology and the demand for private happiness.[2]

Since the early 1970s, marked in West Germany by the so-called 'Neue Subjektivität' as a reaction to the failed hopes of 1968, writers of Muschg's generation had somewhat sheepishly returned to more traditional notions of the value of literature. And the central thrust of *Literatur als Therapie?* is a critical discussion of the 'Therapie-Erwartungen . . . die heute bei Schreibern und Lesern in der Luft liegen' (LT 11). Muschg's main theme is the contention that literature and psychotherapy, to which many had turned after 1968, are in no sense substitutes for each other, but nevertheless share a common aspiration: 'Befähigung zum eigenen Leben.' For whilst neither can offer cures for individual neurosis, both essentially aim to liberate the imagination and thus restore vitality to the individual:

> Kunst – oder Literatur – ist keine Therapie, aber sie macht Mut dazu, den Weg der Therapie im Ganzen weiterzugehen. Die Therapie ist nicht Kunst, aber sie dient der Kunst als Bürgschaft für die Verbindlichkeit, für die Gangbarkeit der lebensändernden Phantasie . . . Aus beiden ist die Einsicht zu schöpfen, daß Überleben erst dann keine Sorge mehr wird, wenn wir leben gelernt haben. (LT 203)

Thus the function of art and literature is to give form to those glimpses of freedom which are accessible through the imagination; to demonstrate not the attainment of, but the *need* for utopia: 'Die Künstler sorgen dafür, daß wir die Defizite an Freiheit *und* Ordnung mit Händen greifen können' (LT 202). The subtext, for Muschg, is always the pointer to 'die *andere* Ordnung'. This view implies a mistrust of civilisation which depends for its well-being on the deferment of individual gratification. Muschg's approach here, of course, echoes Freud's scepticism in *Das Unbehagen in der Kultur*, and the disaffection of the young in Zurich appeared to underline the point. For the 'Unruhen' reflected not only youthful frustration, but also the marginalisation of art itself – unless it took the non-controversial 'bourgeois' form of acceptable opera.[3]

It is in this context that Muschg discusses the extraordinary impact of Fritz Zorn's *Mars* (1977), the autobiography of an upper-middle-class scion of the wealthy Zurich 'Goldküste' who savagely equates the cancer which is killing him with the ethos and lifestyle of his parents and their society. No form of therapy can save this young rebel, either spiritually or physically, but the book serves its purpose of using physical and mental collapse to indicate the *possibility* of emancipation and creativity. For Muschg, who wrote a foreword to the book, the parallel between the ill-fated Zorn, whose immense social and educational advantages became a crippling burden, and the autonomous artist in bourgeois society was clear.

Not surprisingly Muschg accepts that childhood impressions are all-important for the modelling of the adult writer, and the themes of *Literatur als Therapie?* are often disguised forms of his own personal biography. He gives an account of some earliest experiences in the essay. For example, he relates that his father was embarrassed and ashamed when his wife, twenty-six years younger than he, gave birth to their son Adolf. His father knew black from white, sin from virtue, and was himself a writer of stories which feature conflicts between the weak and the strong. Having been put to bed as a small boy, Adolf could regularly hear the tapping of the paternal typewriter in an adjoining room. When his father, a teacher, retired, the small family experienced some hardship. After his father's death from cancer, his mother became a patient in a psychiatric hospital (before her marriage she had been a nurse), and the boy was sent to a boarding school where he did not feel at home. She was excessively punctilious about treating her child's ailments, but she dismissed them as insignificant; at the same time, her confidence that her son would be a success in life exerted a subtle pressure: she would have liked him to become a doctor or a pastor. For many years Muschg concealed, even from himself, his psychological dependence on his parents. He underwent psychoanalysis, but looking back, he concluded that the treatment had not benefited him greatly. Against such an oppressive background the roots of his fascination and empathy with Zorn's *Mars* are painfully clear.

A work of art, however, that Muschg accepts without reservation as fulfilling his requirement of emancipation is *Die Zauberflöte*. The opera takes place in a world where Providence intervenes and where games are played with an ironic awareness; the beauty and splendour of the music have a unique power. But although this may well be a healing power, we must also be prepared to acknowledge that which is incapable of being healed:

> Das Kunstwerk ist auch für seine Empfänger nicht gemacht zur Heilung von Not und Angst. Es behebt die Mißstände nicht, die Not und Angst auslösen. Schon ihrem Urheber hat *Die Zauberflöte* keine Sorge abgenommen. Die Kunst erleichtert keinem den Umgang mit den andern oder mit sich selbst. (LT 145)

For art is not a therapeutic 'Lebenshilfe', but 'Form gewordene Sehnsucht . . . Kunst ist, wie jede Geburt des Eros, ein Kind des Mangels *und* des Reichtums. Der Mangel ist die Wahrheit, der Reichtum ist die Kraft, mit der der Mangel offenbart wird' (LT 147). In other words, art (literature) cannot provide 'answers', but serves as a unique method of awakening and clarifying the desire to search for answers; intimations of wholeness provoke a productive awareness of the fragmentation of modern existence.

Im Sommer des Hasen traces the reactions of a group of Swiss men to the impact of Japan. Muschg explains in *Literatur als Therapie?* that his own stay in that country was a 'Flucht nach vorn' disguised as the fulfilment of a longing for travel that had been with him since his childhood; as with his other wishes, this was double-edged – he *had* to travel to disguise his fear of leaving home, like a child whistling in the dark. And so there is ironic humour, but also a wish to identify sympathetically with the protagonists in their often serious and tragic experiences. The narrator, Bischof, a man of not quite fifty, is a public relations officer who is writing a report for his employer, Manuel Inauen, who has had the idea of celebrating the centenary of the involvement and representation of the firm 'Inauen Suisse' in Japan. It is Bischof who has carried out the plan and who has chosen the six young Swiss writers who are to spend six months in Japan as guests of the firm, in the hope that they will each be able to write an account that will bring credit to their employer. Bischof looks back on the six days he has spent in Japan, during which he has come to know the scholarship-holders and their immediate concerns more intimately.

The six authors are treated in varying detail; sometimes their ways of spending the six months in Japan appear to be trivial, and almost always they can be seen as of dubious value to the firm that has sponsored them. One of their number has spent much of his time watching Japanese television and films, whilst another arouses sharp criticism with his story about three old people. A radio technician presents a fictitious account of a military strategy on tape, and is gently chided for never writing but making recordings instead. A man with stomach troubles is not able to see through his concern to explore Zen Buddhism. In spite of having good opportunities for fruitful cultural contacts, another man sees his own life as sad and flawed – to such an extent that he commits suicide. A married man becomes passionately involved with a young student of theology; the narrative of this failed love affair forms the most graphic and fully rounded episode in the novel. The Japanese environment has posed a threat to this group of Swiss visitors, an alien force which they have hardly understood and whose effect on their lives is at times destructive.

Muschg's second novel, *Gegenzauber* (1967), is located on predominantly familiar Swiss terrain. A group of largely young people determine to resist local government plans to demolish 'Soldanella', the family house of one of their members, in order to make way for road improvements. Übersee was a countrified village by Lake Zurich when the house was built in 1910, but as Soldanella was never listed as a building of architectural interest, there appeared to be no reason why it should be preserved. Nevertheless, the planning officials are persuaded to leave the house undisturbed on the grounds that one of its former residents has made a unique contribution to the arts as a sculptor. The Soldanella community can only expect to have a temporary reprieve in opting out of official society; the false claims on behalf of the posthumous sculptor are eventually exposed by one of the group, and Klaus Marbach, the first-person narrator, sets down his account to vindicate the Soldanella group. In his last days at school Klaus Marbach finds an alternative home in the Soldanella community, an escape from his parents' constant quarrels which culminate in their divorce. Klaus's role as youthful rebel against society has been compared to that of Oskar Matzerath in Grass's *Die Blechtrommel*, Hans Schnier in Böll's *Ansichten eines Clowns* and Siggi Jepsen in Lenz's *Deutschstunde*.[4] Although the main motivating plot of *Gegenzauber* is rather slight, this novel is nonetheless a subtle and complex work with a rich variety of scenes, a range of colourful characters, and skilfully wrought descriptive sections.

Mitgespielt (1969) is a novel centring upon two Zurich teenagers, with the disturbing but never really threatening figure of Hämmerli, a teacher with homosexual tendencies, in the background. Andres is in a difficult domestic situation; after his mother's death, his father has unstable relationships with women and is alienated from his son. After Andres' disappearance in the course of a school expedition, his friend Ulrich does not accept that he is dead, and in due course he is proved right when the boy returns to normal society. The earlier part of the novel has Andres as a narrator, while Ulrich, whose family is considerably better-off and more stable, becomes the protagonist for the later section of the work, where there is a feeling of greater confidence in the outcome. It is evident that Andres is too easily assumed to be dead, while his subsequent reappearance likewise evokes less surprise than one would have imagined. Hämmerli is not, as is suspected for a time, responsible for any murderous threats to Andres or Ulrich, but he is fearful of being blackmailed because of his association with a homosexual prostitute. His death from natural causes while sunbathing at a public swimming pool effectively removes him from the scene, but leaves his personality and motives in some obscurity. The novel is not altogether clear in its story line and is uneasy in its portrayal of death; it is, however, felicitous in its description of the group of school students, and one senses how much at home the author was with this age group (Muschg notes in a short preface that he and his pupils at the Zurich Oberrealschule in 1959 had planned a group narrative project that would include the murder of a teacher).

Albissers Grund (1974) has thematic links with *Gegenzauber* and *Mitgespielt*, but has greater reason to be considered as a more completely satisfying work. Albisser fires three shots at Zerutt whom he has chosen to consult as a personal counsellor; he then gives himself up without delay, acknowledging his personal responsibility for the act. Zerutt is severely injured, but disappoints hospital staff by refusing to assume the role of trusting and appreciative patient. He is fundamentally at odds with the hospital authorities; Dr Kündig, the head surgeon, refuses Zerutt's request that a bullet should be removed from his lung, but the patient, when supposedly dying, at the end of the novel attacks Dr Kündig with bizarre violence, and succeeds in getting the bullet out of his own body himself, and is thus at last in a position to let life return with confidence. Zerutt, the victim, is regarded with suspicion and hostility, partly because he is habitually uncommunicative, but also because his wish to be accepted as a Swiss citizen is viewed with misgiving by the examining magistrate. For the society in which Zerutt has been living for many years and also in which he might well expect to be tolerated in the future is often hostile to aliens who wish to immigrate, especially if their records are at all obscure. Albisser is certainly willing to talk about his personal problems, while Zerutt gives no indication of being interested in or sympathetic to the man, from whom he takes an unusually high fee. As a man of sensitivity and feeling, with aspirations and ideals, Albisser, who is more than a little absorbed in himself, has features in common with Faust, while Zerutt appears like Mephistopheles, indifferent to the man he serves and quietly and severely estranged from the conventions of polite amiability; he is an outsider, and the examining magistrate tells him that he understands how as a refugee Zerutt distrusts representatives of state authority. Did Zerutt return to Switzerland in May 1945 with the papers of a dead Rumanian soldier, and was he born in Graubünden, Switzerland, in 1918? The authorities harass Zerutt, a helpless patient, and because of the lack of proof of his Swiss origin, the victim has to suffer much more than the aggressor.

Not quite forty, Albisser was an only child on whom his mother lavished her full attention, and after her death his aunt Anna provided the finance for his higher education. He becomes more pronouncedly hypochondriacal, and this is the main reason for the breakdown of his marriage. Zerutt speculates that Albisser only felt truly loved when he was ill, for his mother loved him then with a possessiveness that aimed to direct the boy from human ordinariness to identification with an awareness of saintly status. Albisser has told Zerutt that he has come to him because he needs an alternative model to that of the socially acceptable, ambitious achiever which has been held up to him for so long. In the autumn of 1970, after Albisser has been having counselling sessions with Zerutt for about a year and a half, he begins an experimental type of group teaching, and a little later he refuses to give students marks for their work. In March 1971 he defends an objector to military service, and in August refuses to take part in the normal military exercise to which he has been summoned. The inevitable result is imprisonment. A radical apprentices' group makes contact with Albisser, inviting him to express solidarity with them. He makes considerable efforts to feel at ease with this group of young people, but mistrust remains. After Albisser loses his post as a teacher, he sees himself as victim and sacrifice, an attitude that had formerly been his mother's. However, having lost his teaching post in one

canton, Albisser finds that this by no means excludes his finding
another in a neighbouring one. The student revolt of 1968 is having
an effect on Albisser's teaching; but authority can absorb Albisser's
eccentricities. On the other hand such pliancy is not offered to
Zerutt as an assumed alien. Dr Meret Leumann, who has replaced
the first examining magistrate, reproaches Zerutt for his lack of
sympathy with Albisser's troubles; Zerutt is accused of lacking
human feeling as well as being of dubious origins. *Albissers Grund*
contains many vivid episodes which provide a variety of incident
and background. Narrative devices include tape recordings and
memoranda, as well as conversations; the reporting can be ironically distanced. The considerate way in which Albisser is treated by
the representatives of Swiss legal and medical authorities is in
marked contrast to the treatment received by Zerutt. Albisser is an
accredited local Swiss figure, a member of the teaching profession,
and enjoys talking about his personal background and motivation.
Zerutt's origins cannot be established beyond all doubt, and consequently although he is a patient who has suffered grave injury and
whose life is threatened, he is considered even more as an alien who
has no right to be in Switzerland and whose death is anticipated by
hospital staff with indifference. Zerutt, however, asserts in a su-
preme effort his will to live, resisting the pressures around him in a
form of retaliation born of the belief that the people responsible for
his hospital treatment are his enemies. The theme of discrimination
in hospital treatment had been previously presented in the radio
play *Das Kerbelgericht* (1969). Here Muschg shows hospital staff as
perfunctory in their treatment of a student demonstrator of 1968
who consequently dies, whereas a retired law-court reporter who is
not at all seriously injured receives particularly favourable treatment. Thus the medical profession is seen to pass judgement on
their patients in ways which have more to do with ideology than
the Hippocratic Oath.

Das Licht und der Schlüssel. Erziehungsroman eines Vampirs (1984) is
a generously proportioned novel, formally the author's most ambitious to date. After the ending of the main narrative, where
events are seen from the point of view of Samstag, an expert on fine
art, there follows an appendix where the narrator lays down his
views on art and society in more general terms. The work as a
whole focuses attention on art, sickness and death, circling about
these themes with fine poise and an often elusive combination of
serenity and resignation. It opens with a doctor's abrupt statement
to Samstag that he must die and the latter's indignant comments to
Mona, a fellow invalid, about the manner in which he has been

told. The subtitle already prepares us for the incursion of the fantastic. Samstag feels that he is not a human being but a living corpse, a vampire, who looks for surrogate satisfaction in the narration of stories. During the daytime he becomes rigid and sleeps, unseen and alone, in a cellar store-room beneath Mona's elegant apartment in the patrician quarter of Amsterdam. He sustains himself in part by biting the necks of women and drawing their blood, while they enjoy his 'therapy'; he is the shadow in which Mona walks and thus he draws from her the vitality he needs to sustain his own wan identity. He claims to be a Count who, as in the legend, lives alone in a God-forsaken castle in Transylvania and who needs thirty boxes of unhallowed earth for his transportation to London, so that he may suck the blood of innocent British women there. Mona at this point interprets Samstag's story and lifestyle as a self-delusion that will shelter him from the awareness that he badly needs psychiatric help. He refuses, however, to admit this and pretends to be already dead because he believes that he can no longer be helped; he is solitary, desperate, vain and fearful. Jan Willem van Helsing, a curator at an art gallery who also works for the police, is reading Bram Stoker when they first meet, and he addresses Samstag as 'Dracula'. Jan Willem becomes Mona's lover, but they are both killed on a Dutch motorway in the early morning of 28 August (Goethe's birthday) and their bodies disappear mysteriously. The three doctors' wives (Myrna, Jeannette and Maaika) give notice to Samstag that they no longer wish to continue with his blood-sucking treatment; Samstag's references to 'Mijnheer', a blind tobacco-king, as his employer, on whose behalf he is looking out for a unique work of art from the seventeenth-century Dutch School, are seen by van Helsing as a fabrication; he throws doubt on the existence of this eccentric employer who is said to collect still-life pictures. Samstag later asks in one of his letters to 'Mijnheer' what meaning there would be for the two of them to become one person; he then points to their earlier identities as Bischof, the public relations officer of *Im Sommer des Hasen*, and then as Zerutt, 'the dubious graphologist and victim of an angered boy' in *Albissers Grund*, and now finally as a 'bachelor vampire'. It is clear that the two characters are two halves of the same consciousness, and with this split identity, the novel turns into a parody of the classical German *Erziehungsroman*, where identity is basically secure and merely needs nurturing to maturity through experience. *Das Licht und der Schlüssel* raises the central problem, discussed in *Literatur als Therapie?*: is art an efficacious cure for cultural malaise or paradoxically an obvious symptom of it? The 'key' and the 'light' are set against each other in a complex, and often confusing, dialectic.

While Muschg's novels and plays are often concerned with political and social ideas and unfold their themes in a frequently leisurely and expansive flow of language, his five collections of short stories tend to focus on conflicts and contacts on the individual level and to present problems and people that are neatly and sharply drawn. Many of the short stories make an appeal to the reader's enlightened scepticism and his or her sympathy with the dispelling of intolerance and superstition. Their protagonists are often at home in prosperous middle-class circles. *Fremdkörper* (1968) contains stories which bring out features of alienation and incompatibility in personal relationships, and also emphasises environmental factors which can override individual initiatives. 'Der Ring' centres upon the situation at a party where all present are aware of the suicide of one of their friends some days previously. The advent of Robert, the author of a play that has recently been produced with success in Berlin, brings to the group someone who has not yet heard of the death of Jan; his attempts to fit in with what would be the atmosphere at a normal party of this kind fail to evoke the response he would normally expect and he is puzzled. However, his apparently tactless and thoughtless remarks to Roswitha are welcomed by her as helpful rather than hurtful; she finds Robert's approach therapeutic. The story's theme of misunderstanding is employed in such a way that an optimistic outcome can be envisaged, however reluctantly.

The volume *Liebesgeschichten* (1972) consists of stories where love is associated with fear and misfortune rather than with happiness and freedom. The narrator of 'Der Zusenn oder das Heimat' frames his story in the form of a letter to the authorities; he wishes to reveal the events in his life which will explain why he is open to the charge of incest. The farmer is concerned to defend his relationship with his two daughters against the condemnation of society. What is regarded as a punishable offence by society as a whole represents a valid expression of self-fulfilment and consolation in face of the disasters and difficulties that have confronted him – his original farm was destroyed by fire, his wife died a year later, and the farm which he took over was isolated and difficult to work. The father and his two daughters have sexual relationships which bring stability and fulfilment to the three of them. A young man who works as 'Zusenn' (assistant cheese-farmer) finds out about this situation and informs the authorities, which leads to their arrest. The narrative is the farmer's written statement, drawn up in his unique style: 'Der Frieden war die Hauptsache, und haben wir ja keinen

Menschen gestört, sondern sind nie auf Rosen gebettet gewesen' (LG 40). Their life has been hard, and it is understandable that they should have no regrets for a relationship which for all its shocking breaking of ancient taboos has brought them happiness.

'Hindukusch', in the volume *Entfernte Bekannte* (1976), throws light upon the relationship between mother and son, and reveals the self-indulgent selfishness of both of them. The mother, accompanied by her son, is taken to the hospital where she has arranged to stay for an operation; she is concerned to withdraw from the outside world and has chosen private facilities. After the matron has left the two together, the son is angry with his mother for opting for expensive private accommodation when alternative cheaper facilities are available. His mother reacts by referring to his long absence on an expedition to investigate developmental problems in a remote part of the world. She has no interest in his experiences away from home and resents their interference with her own expectations of him. After leaving, the son drives around in his car and thinks of the phrasing of a letter that he might send to his mother, in resigned and conciliatory language. The problem of their relationship with one another is not solved; it will presumably continue to preoccupy him into an indefinite future.

In 'Christel', in *Der Turmhahn und andere Liebesgeschichten* (1987), the narrative dwells on a number of motifs and scenes in a way that does not reveal immediately what the focal points of the story are. The narrator is a Swiss literary figure who is on tour in various Pacific locations and who is curious about Christel, her past in Austria and her present life in New Zealand (at sixty she has been assaulted by three Maori boys). The claim of her mother to have been used as a character in Musil's *Der Mann ohne Eigenschaften* Christel dismisses as fantasy. In Vienna in the summer of 1938 Christel, aged thirteen, is undergoing treatment for tuberculosis, and in this context becomes acquainted with Dr Salomon Pollack, a fellow sufferer. The central crisis of the story takes place when he and Christel's mother, meeting again for the first time after a long period, discuss the urgency of arranging for Christel and her elder sister Isolde to leave Austria to escape the Nazi régime. It is Salomon Pollack who has to convince her mother that Hitler is a threat to be taken seriously and that flight from Austria is an urgent matter. Christel and Isolde are sent to England, while Salomon, who, it is revealed, is Christel's father, becomes a refugee in Switzerland; they correspond for a time after the end of the war, and this is seen by Christel as a major formative influence on her development. Her subsequent emigration from England to New

Zealand, her marriage to a Frenchman there and her decision to stay on in New Zealand after he returns to Europe are phases of her life that are without the deeper level of experience that characterises the episodic contacts with her father. The visiting author presents his picture of the background to the story in a ruminative, leisurely manner; it is an apt framework to Christel's narrative, which is both measured and dramatic.

The world of Adolf Muschg's fiction is predominantly that of the prosperous Swiss middle class, caught most vigorously perhaps in *Albissers Grund*. And it is the sharp, ironical light that he throws on its subterfuges, dishonesties and suppressed fantasies that places his work firmly in the category of 'Kunst als Widerstand'. In this sense, Muschg belongs to the Enlightenment tradition of seeing art as a principal method of drawing men and women out of the treacherous comfort of self-imposed immaturity. The negative evaluation of society which runs through the relative simplicities of his first novel, *Im Sommer des Hasen*, to the less accessible complexities of *Das Licht und der Schlüssel*, is always relativised by the implication of more positive structures. As he put it in *Literatur als Therapie?*: 'Das Poetische ist widerstandsfähig. Die Verwalter der Macht haben die Kunst zu fürchten – am meisten die autonome, die unbeirrbar selbstgefällige Kunst' (LT 177). Thus against the constrictions of contemporary Swiss society, blindly intent on releasing and utilising the full power of the *Leistungsprinzip*, Muschg sets the anarchic, free play of the imagination. In a slight, but crucial variation of a famous line from Brecht's *Leben des Galilei*, he remarks: 'Wehe dem Staat, der Dichter nötig macht; er hat Grund, ihre Subtilitäten übelzunehmen' (LT 178). For Muschg, literature – no less than psychotherapy – remains an essential and complementary component in the continuing struggle for human emancipation.

Notes

1. References to Muschg's work are to the following editions: LT = *Literatur als Therapie? Ein Exkurs über das Heilsame und das Unheilbare*, Frankfurt am Main, 1981; DLS = *Das Licht und der Schlüssel. Erziehungsroman eines Vampirs*, Frankfurt am Main, 1984; LG = *Liebesgeschichten*, Frankfurt am Main, 1972.

2. For an account of the 'Jugendunruhen' in Zurich, see *Der Spiegel*, 22 December 1980, pp. 33–52; and Peter Bichsel's article 'Das Ende der Schweizer Unschuld', *Der Spiegel*, 5 January 1981, pp. 108–9. A useful documentary pamphlet has been published by Pro Helvetia: *Youth Disturbances in Switzerland*, Zurich, 1981.

3. It was youthful protest at the massive expenditure on the restoration of the Zurich Opera House, combined with the forcible closure by the police of the 'Autonome Jugend-Zentrum' in the Limmat-Straße, on the grounds of suspected drug peddling, that intensified the disturbances.

4. See Renate Voris, *Adolf Muschg*, Munich, 1984, pp. 38–9.

7
Hugo Loetscher: The Committed Intellect

Hans Seelig

Am liebsten wäre er in alle Richtungen gegangen und aus allen Richtungen zurückgekehrt, bis jeder fremde Ort ein vertrauter wurde, jeder vertraute sich einem fremden anglich und es keinen Unterschied mehr gab zwischen vertraut und unvertraut. (I 63)[1]

Gern hätte er jedes Wort, das es gab, mindestens einmal benutzt. (I 418)

These two quotations reveal not merely Hugo Loetscher's awareness of the diversity of human experiences, but also a passion to be all-embracing, to intertwine and interlink experiences, indeed to project himself into the consciousness of 'Andersheiten',[2] as he once called them, a task which requires an immense diversity of linguistic means, styles and vocabularies. Although, apart from one unsuccessful play, his creative writing is confined to prose fiction, Loetscher is also prominent as a journalist, broadcaster and critic. He is an ardent traveller, obsessed with widening his experience of other continents and cultures. His particular concern has been Portugal and Latin America, and he has written extensively on their history, politics and culture. More recently he has been preoccupied with the Far East. Such myriad interests make Hugo Loetscher one of the most critically minded, liveliest and most versatile writers of the generation following Frisch and Dürrenmatt.

This international dimension, however, has not brought Loetscher a widespread reputation in the other German-language countries, despite the fact that he spent 1979/80 as writer-in-residence at the University of Southern California in Los Angeles, was the first incumbent of the 'Swiss Chair' at the City University of New York in 1981/2, and professor of poetics at Munich in 1987/8 – a post which produced the illuminating series of lectures *Vom Erzählen erzählen* (1988). The explanation for this relative neglect may be partly that he does not fulfil the expectations foreigners have of a Swiss writer, partly that his publishers have been mainly Swiss. Whatever the case, he does not conform to any Swiss stereotype, certainly not to the conservative *Heimatdichter*, nor to the nonconformist rebel suffering from an identity crisis and yearning to break out from the narrow confines of a small state and its bourgeois constrictions. He is perhaps like Heinrich Böll, a resister rather than a rebel.

In some of his public statements and autobiographical sections of his writings Loetscher presents himself clearly as an intellectual of working-class origins, but one who has become, as far as possible, liberated, socially and culturally as well as politically. However, autobiographical material interests him 'nur inwiefern sich da auch schon Gesellschaftliches drin spiegelt; also nie im Sinn "Ich habe erlebt, mir ging es so, mein Gott wie ging es mir!", sondern ich kann mich als Beispiel nehmen, wie in einer Gesellschaft wie der unseren einer lebt'.[3] Thus, although his proletarian origins are reflected in *Der Immune* (1975) in an early section where Loetscher gives an objective account, tinged with affection and pity, of a character obviously resembling his own father, he declares: 'Der Immune konnte diesem Manne nur ein Leben geben, indem er aus diesem Fall eine Figur machte' (I 53). Whether the details of this paternal portrait are accurate or not is immaterial; important is the technique of transforming autobiographical material into generalisations which can sustain a complex and convincing fiction.

Much can be deduced about Loetscher's views – a politically undogmatic sympathy with exploited workers, the poor and the oppressed – from the personalities he chooses for his articles or radio talks. Independent-minded nonconformists with high humanitarian principles are favoured subjects, even when he does not necessarily agree with the directions in which these principles drive them. Thus, for example, in 1973 he wrote an article on the Swiss art historian and communist Konrad Farner, with the significant subtitle 'Ungewöhnliche Stichwörter zu einem ungewöhnlichen Marxisten'.[4] The picture given is of a liberated Marxist who, without changing his political attitudes, both protested against the Russian invasion of Czechoslovakia and kept open a dialogue with progressive Christians. Equally revealing is the article on the Swiss painter Varlin: 'Varlin ist Realist, indem er das Problem, wie erfährt man Wirklichkeit, mit allem Mut und mit jedem Zweifel angeht . . . das Modell übernimmt dabei die Stellvertretung dieser Wirklichkeit . . . Als der besessenste Realist, den die moderne Schweizer Malerei mit ihm kennt, erlebt er immer wieder, wie er dem Gegenüber ausgeliefert war . . . Denn dieses Gegenüber änderte sich von Moment zu Moment, von Lichtbedingung zu Lichtbedingung. Er aber wollte es als Ganzes; alles andere wäre ihm wie Verrat vorgekommen.'[5] The representative nature of the 'Modell', the elusive nature of reality, are essential aspects of Loetscher's own work.

Just as his proletarian childhood in Zurich made its mark on Loetscher's personality, so did his growing up in the Switzerland of the war years, the inward-looking period of 'geistige Landesverteidigung' during which Switzerland was spared the worst and survived, but neither unscathed nor uninvolved. Here we have the probable roots of his most important novel, *Der Immune*, with its central preoccupation with an individual's survival in the world whilst not escaping involvement. The theme becomes universalised and Switzerland, Zurich and his family background merely provide convenient motifs and examples. But if his novels rarely directly reflect his attitudes to his country, Loetscher's articles and interviews certainly do. In the delightful series of satirical and ironic newspaper essays revised and published in book form, *Der Waschküchenschlüssel und andere Helvetica* (1983, enlarged 1988), for example, his main aim is the explosion of myths, clichés and misconceptions, both on the part of foreigners and on the part of the Swiss about themselves. His particular target is the 'Sonderfall Schweiz' mentality. This concept was inhibitingly prevalent during the war years. For in Loetscher's view, no country can thrive on the assumption that the world around it does not change, and his own travels, acts of release rather than escape, revealed to him, 'daß der Mythos des Sonderfalls wie der Melkschemel nur auf einem Bein steht' (W 141). Although Loetscher recognises the impossibility of entirely shedding one's origins, it is important that one is not imprisoned by them. Certainly he believes his novels would have been written differently had he not been Swiss, though the basic preoccupations would have been the same.

Nevertheless, he reacts with a certain degree of irritation to the question of national, cultural or class identity. A favourite concept is that of simultaneity: 'Wir sind eben gleichzeitig immer in einem nationalen, einem übernationalen, einem kulturellen, religiösen Verein. Das weitet sich unentwegt aus. Also, Identität ist für mich eine Frage des Friedhofes – da ist man total identisch. Aber das bedingt natürlich, daß man eigentlich Spannungen leben kann, und das ist nicht leicht.' Such tensions are particularly manifest in multicultural societies or those strongly influenced by another culture. 'Ein Südamerikaner in Buenos Aires ist mehr Europäer als einer in Lima . . . Identität führt ja zur Abkapselung.' There is always an immense diversity of other possibilities. It is impossible to experience them all, for one is to some extent inextricably conditioned: 'Aber kulturell, intellektuell kann ich ausweiten, und das finde ich spannend.' It is a modern humanism 'wo der Mensch im Zentrum des Denkens steht'. Simultaneity implies the opposite of introversion: 'die Möglichkeit, das Andere, das Fremde zu erleben' (C 89).[6] This basic optimistic stance leaves little room for sympathy for fashionable identity crises, including that of Max Frisch, whose 'merkwürdig subjektive Ich-Bezogenheit' disturbs Loetscher 'weil er die intellektuelle Diskussion mit Stichwörtern beschäftigt'. At the same time he acknowledges Frisch's contribution as an influential 'Vater einer sehr introvertierten Literatur' (C 89). Thus with the possible exception of the sewage inspector in the early novel *Abwässer* (1963), Loetscher's characters are more concerned with basic survival or expanding what they already are than with finding themselves.

Artistically, Loetscher feels closer to Dürrenmatt, whose intellectual self-control coupled with immense imagination, whose sense of the grotesque and eccentric humour are all characteristics to be found in his own writings. Loetscher claims, for example, that the 'Helvetisches Zwischenspiel' in Dürrenmatt's *Monstervortrag über Gerechtigkeit und Recht* (1969) strikes the right balance: 'So radikal seine Kritik sein kann . . . sie hat nie an provinziellen Phantomleiden gelitten, daran, daß die Schweiz ein kleines Land sei und so gar nicht schicksalsträchtig wie andere. Eine Muse von schweizerischer Tüchtigkeit hat ihn nie geküßt, die des Ressentiments.'[7] Thus Hugo Loetscher does not suffer from the 'Kleinstaat' syndrome, nor the provincial sense of 'Enge' any more than Dürrenmatt did. For him, such clichés are not confined to Switzerland, but represent a general human situation: 'Ich habe unter der Kleinheit des Landes nie mehr gelitten als andere unter der Größe des ihren'; fortunately, a small country cannot play at power politics, but 'Verzicht auf Größe ist nicht unbedingt auch schon Bescheidenheit . . . Finanziell und wirtschaftlich ist die Schweiz eine mittlere Macht und der Schweizer Franken alles andere als eine Klein-Währung' (PS 68). Rejecting the feeling of a stifling 'Enge' which Paul Nizon, for example, diagnosed as specifically Swiss,[8] Loetscher points to its roots in 'ein persönliches Problem von Stoffmangel . . . Man muß aufhören. Es gilt, sich von dieser "Opfer-Theorie" zu lösen' (PS 76f.) Clinging to such ideas may have been understandable during the years 1933–45, but his own generation (b.1929) experienced a post-war process of emancipation. The need to escape from the uneventfulness or the insignificance of Switzerland is not as prevalent nor even justified as is often maintained. Switzerland may not be 'der Atem des Schicksals der Weltgeschichte,' but nor was Dublin, and yet it produced Joyce's *Ulysses*. 'Es käme mir nicht in den Sinn zu sagen: in Zürich nichts, in Paris das Wahre . . . Im Moment, wo man das ausspielt, fängt man an zu ideologisieren, und dann fängt man auch an, zu verfälschen' (C 89).

Loetscher travels widely, then, not because of a feeling of uneasiness or restlessness associated with living in a 'Kleinstaat', but because of a basic 'Erlebnishunger' for the immense variety of human experience in which, however, he constantly finds 'Grundsituationen des Menschseins' (C 89). The characters in his novels are thus representative metaphors, not symbolic abstractions, for these basic situations; they become individuals, 'Figuren', with fully documented private and social lives. More than in his journalistic and essayistic writing, where Loetscher concerns himself primarily with current sociopolitical problems, 'in der Literatur geht es mir . . . um die totale Kritik'.[9] To write a novel about a specific problem would result in that novel becoming superfluous once the problem was solved. Loetscher deplores the fashionable literary concept of 'ein notwendiges Buch'; the discussion of a social problem may be necessary, but 'die Literatur ist ihre eigene Notwendigkeit' (C 89); it should not be confined to a single ideological position.

Literature, for Loetscher, is a matter of patient ordering and formulation, of searching for the right words, which eschews the expediency of short cuts. At the same time, he is aware of the inadequacy of language: he realises 'daß Worte die Wirklichkeit nie abdecken, daß die Sprache immer defizitär ist, und daß das Schreiben nichts anderes als der oft verzweifelte Versuch darstellt, der Realität mit Worten beizukommen'.[10] From his first novel *Abwässer* to the more recent collection of satirical animal stories, *Die Fliege und die Suppe und 33 andere Tiere in 33 anderen Situationen* (1989), the realities which he struggles to express concern human beings as social and political beings. It is not so much the traditional theme of the individual versus society but of man as inescapably a social being by his very nature. And even in a humane society, all too often conflicts, clashes of wills, oppression and exploitation arise. Loetscher does not share what he calls a naive socialist vision of a classless and conflictless society; for without any forms of tension, such a society would be dead. Loetscher can thus be considered a highly political writer, though not in the normally accepted, narrowly ideological sense. All his characters and their lives are dominated by the social and political, and therefore economic, structures of their environment. Inevitably these impinge on their attitudes and activities, so that each individual's fate reflects the social forces which conditioned it. The eponymous protagonist of *Der Immune*, for example, 'richtete sich in der Gesellschaft ein, die er vorfand, und machte mit, was man den sozialen Aufstieg nannte' (I 263), despite the crucial perception: 'die Gesellschaft war darauf aus, einen von der eigenen Person zu heilen' (I 274).

In his first two novels, *Abwässer* and *Die Kranzflechterin* (1964), Loetscher understandably therefore took his landscape and imagery not from any idyllic alpine countryside but from the town or city ('Stadtschaft' as Kurt Marti called it), where the problematical complexities of social cohesion are more clearly marked. These novels, though similar, are in some ways counterparts to each other. Neither of the main characters are rebels, and they resist only in order to survive. They are contained within their own world, but are not imprisoned by it. Their concern is, respectively, the construction of a sewage system and canalisation to dispose of man's unwanted, yet inevitable waste products; and the provision of a ritualistic full stop for another inevitability, death – a wreath, to which everyone is in dignity entitled. Both books are narrated from the single perspective of the protagonist's occupation. The imagery emanates from the central metaphor and its associations; the concepts of waste, dirt and the wreath are real enough, but point to wider and manifold associations: the reject side of life, the negative, death. We have 'auf der einen Seite der Mann, der mit einer Welt rechnet, in der es den Dreck gibt, auf der anderen Seite die Frau, die das Leben auf der extremsten Seite, auf der des Todes, feiert' (SSG 85f.). The episodes, comments and observations provide the interplay and tension, a dialectic between concept and metaphor.

In *Abwässer. Ein Gutachten* a sewage inspector, emerging from his weekly routine inspection of the underground sewers, finds that a revolution has taken place. He is at first arrested on suspicion of trying to hide, then released and commissioned by his new masters, with the promise of promotion, to write them a report on his job and responsibilities and the qualities required by his successor. The opening sentence suggests humble respect, yet also the self-assurance of someone aware of his importance, expertise and acknowledged dedication. The inspector's prose is initially precise, dry, undecorative, yet with a strong tone of officialdom and a slight colouring of indignation; but a more personal note soon intrudes, though not too obtrusively; the inspector anticipates and excuses such personal references as being only 'beispielweise'. Here we have the dominant motif of the representativeness of the individual. Here it is not a question of pure individualism or collectivism, but of realising through one's qualities and inclinations one's appropriate place in society, at the same time as realising one's replaceability. Thus the novel ends with the inspector's own statement of the central idea and its consequence for him: 'Ich glaube nicht an das Individuum, aber daran, daß es einen ihm entsprechenden Platz einnehmen kann, den möchte ich nicht verlieren. Darf ich um meine eigene Nachfolge bewerben? Ich stelle mich zur Verfügung' (A 224). The ironic tone of self-assured humility returns.

The novel could not have been presented merely as a factual report on the sewage system. To give it the anti–ideological and sceptical anti–utopian social perspective, the representative figure of the inspector had to be created, with episodes and attitudes centred around one character. The general theme, however, led the author to present an anonymous town without national or regional characteristics. The universal implication of the metaphor is clearly stated by the inspector himself: 'Ein Strom von Dreck und Schmutz, von Krankheit und Verbrechen, von Leiden und Not, von Untat und Bedürftigkeit, und dieser Strom werde nach gutem Wissen und Können geklärt, im Spital und dem Sprechzimmer, in der Schule und bei Gericht, in der Kirche und in Büchern' (A 50). Thus Loetscher challenges traditional value judgements and the snobbish hierarchy of social roles.

In many respects *Die Kranzflechterin* provides a counterpart. Though death is a universal fate, ways of dying, however dehumanised, are much more personalised. Thus the eponymous heroine becomes convinced that it is her allotted professional duty to provide a wreath, the most representative image of death, for everyone who has died. 'Jeder soll zu seinem Kranz kommen' is the first sentence and runs like a refrain throughout the novel. In this case, Loetscher felt the need for an individual with a biography and a regional though not provincial background. Anna, like Loetscher's own grandmother, has Swabian origins and emigrates to Zurich. Like the Inspector, she is both individual and representative; she should not be seen mythically as one of the fates, nor as purely a personality. Loetscher's concern is for her social integration and function: through her work, he declares, she 'ermöglicht den Einblick in die Eingeweiden der Gesellschaft' (SSG 90). Anna celebrates death and develops her 'Todesperspektive' in weaving the wreaths for her time and society. 'Vivat! . . . Die Toten!' one of her friends exclaims after a particularly successful day. 'Sterbliche aller Länder, vereinigt euch,' she cries herself. In the process she becomes politically aware and sensitive to national and international events, all of which affect her lifestyle. She informs her daughter Else '. . . daß die Politiker die großen Helfer der Kranzflechterinnen seien' (K 86). The interplay between metaphor and reality is created through her professional failures as they impinge on her own life: the wedding wreath she destroyed after the bridegroom failed to appear in church; the one for her lodger and lover Barga, a foreign worker who dies after an accident on his building site, which she felt unable to complete; the one for a Jewish refugee suicide whose religion, unknown to her, forbade flowers; and the one she made for her niece, who died during an abortion, which she threw into the river when the girl's mother refused to accept it. Here metaphor and reality merge in language which is more vivid and resonant than in *Abwässer*.

Loetscher's next novel, *Noah. Roman einer Konjunktur* (1967) retains much of the satirical realism of the previous two, but the perspective is that of a detached, all-knowing observer. References to Turkish foreign workers, military service and the development of insurance firms place the story firmly in the context of a modern affluent society, and the exploitative economy described clearly takes Switzerland as its model. Noah ruins himself financially, whilst others enrich themselves on his obsession with the Ark. The condemnation of this acquisitive society is absolute; Noah reflects: 'Ich habe mir die Gesellschaft angeschaut, da fiel mir nur eins ein: regnen lassen' (N 27). Significantly, the religious implications of the story have been removed; in the absence of God's voice, Noah draws his own conclusions. The 'Stellvertreter' motif is again prominent when Noah eventually comes to realise that he is merely the representative of a social phenomenon: when he tries to auction the Ark he can only knock it down to himself. As there are no other bidders, Noah takes his place on the Ark, trusting that his exemplary decision will point the way to a collective solution in which the individual will not be sacrificed.

When Noah consults a psychoanalyst, he is asked to act out the flood; he reaches out for a sunbeam, crumbles it in his hand, imagining it to be a rainbow, and remarks: 'Das ist die Rolle, die ich spielen möchte: davonkommen; und das ist mein größter Auftritt: fester Boden unter den Füßen' (N 60). The last phrase recalls the moment in *Abwässer* where the inspector defends his occupation with the apparently paradoxical claim that only by creating his underground network 'macht er, daß der Boden unter den Füßen der anderen fest, tragfähig und verläßlich ist' (A 220), and inhabitants and the habitation can survive. For Loetscher, of course, it is language itself which provides the firm ground on which to pursue reality.

In *Wunderwelt. Eine brasilianische Begegnung* (1979) a Swiss traveller ('der Fremde') visits the impoverished north-eastern region of Brazil and observes a family photograph being taken with the coffin of a five-year-old girl. In his imagination and often from her own perspective and that of those around her, he talks to the girl of the life she would have had to lead, with all its suffering, hopes and frustrations. The traveller completely enters the mentality of the other culture and social class. The ironically used metaphor 'Wunder' has two aspects: that of the religious miracles presented to brighten the lives of the poor, but also that of the economic miracle in which these people have no share. The first is epitomised by a series of pictures in the church (Ex Votos), and the second by the advertisements that line the streets. It is a moving example of Loetscher's concern for suffering and poverty translated not into a journalistic report, but a work of literature.

By contrast, in *Herbst in der großen Orange* (1982) the narrator visits a particularly sunny and prosperous Los Angeles. He comes as a delegate to a conference on 'Gutachten', but finds himself staying on well beyond the duration of the conference. He is significantly called H., which confirms the more personal note of self-reflection in this book. H. interweaves the autumn of his own life with that of Los Angeles. His fears that certain symptoms might signify a terminal illness prove false; nevertheless the feeling of possibly facing extinction makes him sensitive to signs of decay and decline in Los Angeles, where borderlines between the real and the artificial become obscured (for example, the green lawns of the seafront and the fabricated ones of the film studios, or the prostitute who proves to be a transvestite). Experiences are often presented at second hand, history in 'realistically' constructed museums. The genuine and the real become the imitation and vice versa, as reflected in the film industry. The concept of 'Grenze' is an important motif; the possibility of death placing a borderline on the expansion of experience is also a powerful factor. As the narrator contemplates the Pacific and thus the immensity of what has not been experienced he remarks: 'In ihrem Rücken hatte die Große Orange die "Neue Welt", es war die alt-bekannte amerikanische. Vor Augen aber, wenn auch nicht in Sichtweite, so doch in Jetnähe, lagen am andern Ufer des Ozeans Neue Welten, die sehr alt waren' (HGO 62). Beyond this border the west becomes the east. Running through the Pacific there is another border: the international dateline, but 'bei Datumsgrenze dachte er an eine Grenze, hinter der es nutzlos wird, die Daten zu zählen' (HGO 165). The survival motif from *Der Immune* recurs: 'Manchmal war H., als übe auch er das Davonkommen . . .', for it, too, underpins this novel.

Der Immune (revised and reissued, 1985) and *Die Papiere des Immunen* (1986) are Loetscher's most significant, substantial and far-reaching works. To be or become 'immune' means 'davonkommen', that is to survive, to escape more or less intact though not without often intense involvement and personal commitment. The knack is to gain a sufficient modicum of detachment to withstand the immense pressures of living whilst maintaining an intellectual and emotional awareness of the heterogeneous world around one, with all its hypocrisies and horrors, and so avoid an emotional or mental breakdown. For the 'Immune' the critical question is an existential one: 'Nicht daß es ihn gab, überraschte ihn, sondern daß er ein Leben lang am Leben geblieben war. Deswegen fragte er sich gelegentlich: "Wie hast du das eigentlich gemacht?"' (I 40). This is echoed in the last words of the book: 'Wie es mir geht? Danke, ich komme davon, ich bin ein Leben lang am Leben geblieben. Das wundert mich in diesem Moment von neuem. Ich frage mich manchmal: Wie haben das die anderen gemacht?' (I 446). The reader is confronted with different possible answers to these questions. Loetscher made his own view clear in his Munich lectures: 'Und die Antworten sollten ein so breites Spektrum wie möglich abdecken: Vom Trick bis zur Verzweiflung, vom Sichfügen bis zur Rebellion, vom Fast-nicht-mehr-Davonkommen bis zum Trotz-allem-Davonkommen' (VE 98). *Der Immune* is constructed in narrative blocks of three or four episodes, each block held together by key words or themes, such as theatre, family, country, love. These blocks are linked by more personal and reflective commentaries often anticipating the next stage of development; together they form a complex picture of the protagonist's behaviour and mental attitudes. Yet *Der Immune* is in no way a *Bildungsroman*; for there is no chronological progression towards immunity, nor is the process concluded; for both socially and existentially, 'immunisation' inevitably remains incomplete.

The reader is thus no longer confronted with the coherence of a single enclosed world, but with a heterogeneous one, containing infinite possibilities of experiencing living (and surviving). The 'Immune' is aware 'daß er nicht aus Recht am Leben blieb, sondern dank besonderer Umstände' (I 39). The 'circumstances' relate to being a native of a country which was spared the ravages of war and which achieved unparalleled prosperity in the economic boom of the post-war years, in other words, Switzerland. But Loetscher does not confine his sharp social and cultural criticism to Switzerland (where, he comments bitterly, 'viele fanden die Verhältnisse idyllisch und paradiesisch', I 40), but he has his 'Immune' wander, like a melancholy mirror, through Zurich, Paris and South America. To capture the diverse aspects of two continents demands a wide range of narrative techniques and linguistic styles, especially when viewing oneself or one's country from the perspective of others. Thus the chapter 'Im Dorf der Väter' is a parody of a school textbook on *Heimatkunde*, 'Proletarier Sightseeing' is a pastiche of the tourist-guide style. The frequently quoted chapter 'Die Entdeckung der Schweiz' is a delightfully satirical response to South American school children's question on how Switzerland was discovered: a group of discoverers sailed up the river on rumours that somewhere a group of gnomes were guarding a hidden hoard of gold. Among the many other registers used are those of incantation, fairy tale, discursive monologue, historical narrative. As Loetscher himself put it: 'Der Leser fragt nicht: was passiert jetzt? sondern: was für eine Sprache passiert jetzt?' (VE 83). And it is this versatile and ironic use of language which is the main means of temporary 'immunisation' against the overwhelming pressure to which the individual is exposed.

At the end of the 1985 revised version of *Der Immune* two detectives arrive to arrest the protagonist, but leave empty-handed, ignoring a bundle of harmless-looking papers. The evidence contained in them about the existence of the 'Immune' is presented as a sequel to the earlier novel. *Die Papiere des Immunen*, however, is no straightforward continuation of the earlier work, despite its similar episodic structure. Loetscher now begins to question the whole strategy of his bizarre invention. The 'Immune' now finds himself incarcerated 'am schrecklichsten Ort der Welt' (PI 445): the brain of his begetter. The adventures he relates, which range freely through different historical times and cultures – often with marvellously satirical effects – are now conceived more in the nature of sceptical arguments with an unreliable *alter ego*. The very notion of 'immunisation' is sharply relativised, intellectual detachment seen as a debilitating fear of commitment. The humour, so characteristic of *Der Immune*, is as rich and intensive as ever, but in *Die Papiere* it has taken on a more sombre tone, its occasional grotesqueness strongly reminiscent of Dürrenmatt.

During work on his most recent book, *Die Fliege und die Suppe* (1989), Loetscher came across a ninth-century book of Arabian stories and observations on animals; its author had observed that every chapter required its own differentiated style and genre. This is clearly echoed in Loetscher's own *comédie animale*, significantly subtitled 'und 33 andere Tiere in 33 anderen Situationen'. The linguistic styles and narrative techniques are as varied as the animals themselves. These are not fables in the manner of La Fontaine; the animals behave as animals with the consciousness of their species, but in a world dominated by human beings, their language and activities. This creates a subtle tension and interplay between the two worlds. The fly is killed not by man, but by her irresistible attraction to the edible, in this case made by man: 'Ihren Tod aber fand sie in einer Beutelsuppe, die mit Streuwürze verfeinert worden war' (FS 84). 'Das Maultier im Militärdienst' is a parody of a military manual on using donkeys for carrying heavy loads. Even in this delightful volume we meet Loetscher's serious concerns: 'Perspektivenwechsel', simultaneity, 'Andersheiten' (here expanded into the animal world). *Die Fliege und die Suppe* is a *tour de force* of literary virtuosity, of sympathy and empathy, laced with an often farcical sense of humour.

Hugo Loetscher is never a one-sided writer: he is universal and cosmopolitan, yet an awareness of being Swiss pervades his writings. He is acutely conscious of the limitations of living, yet constantly reaches outwards; he knows of death, yet the dominant mood is that of an immense zest for living. All this is coupled with a healthy sense of amusement at the paradoxes that inevitably arise in any human enterprise. A favourite concept of his is 'Behaftbarkeit', the ability to be consistent and to be able to stand by one's life's work and attitudes. 'Für mich ist . . . moralisches Verhalten nicht so sehr eine Frage von einem Kodex und dem Einhalten von einem Kodex, sondern der Konsequenz, mit der einer lebt, was er sagt, oder predigt . . . und da würde ich ihn darauf behaften' (C 89).

Notes

1. References to Loetscher's work are to the following editions: I = *Der Immune*, revised edition, Zurich, 1985; W = *Der Waschküchenschlüssel und andere Helvetica*, Zurich, 1983; HLL = *Das Hugo Loetscher Lesebuch*, Zurich, 1984; VE = *Vom Erzählen erzählen. Münchner Poetikvorlesungen*, Zurich, 1988; A = *Abwässer. Ein Gutachten*, Zurich, 1963; K = *Die Kranzflechterin*, Zurich, 1964; N = *Noah. Roman einer Konjunktur*, Zurich, 1967; PI – *Die Papiere des Immunen*, Zurich, 1986; HGO = *Herbst in der Großen Orange*, Zurich, 1982; FS = *Die Fliege und die Suppe*, Zurich, 1989.

2. B. Cantieni, *Schweizer Schriftsteller persönlich*, Frauenfeld and Stuttgart, 1983, pp. 173–89; here p. 173.

3. Recorded conversation with the author, 31 August 1989. Future references = C 89.

4. Hugo Loetscher, 'Konrad Farner – Ungewöhnliche Stichwörter zu einem ungewöhnlichen Marxisten', *Tages-Anzeiger-Magazin*, no. 28, 14 July 1973. Reprinted in HLL.

5. Hugo Loetscher, 'Varlin – der besessene Realist', reprinted in HLL.

6. This is a summary taken from my conversation with Loetscher (see note 3). However, these ideas recur frequently; see, for example, the interview 'Die Schweiz ist kein Sonderfall' in *Perspektive Schweiz. Gespräche mit Zeitgenossen*, ed. Jürg Altweg and Aurel Schmidt, Zurich, 1986, pp. 63–84. Further references to this interview = PS.

7. Hugo Loetscher, 'Friedrich Dürrenmatt – Gedankendramaturg'. This speech was delivered on 10 January 1981 in the Zurich Schauspielhaus at the celebration of Dürrenmatt's sixtieth birthday. Reprinted in HLL.

8. Paul Nizon, *Diskurs in der Enge*, Bern, 1970.

9. Werner Bucher and Georges Ammann, *Schweizer Schriftsteller im Gespräch*, vol. 1, Basle, 1970, pp. 73–108; here p. 106. Further references to this interview = SSG.

10. Hugo Loetscher, 'Für eine Literatur deutscher Ausdrucksweise' in *Das Deutsch der Schweizer: Zur Sprach- und Literatursituation der Schweiz*, ed. Heiner Löffler, Aarau, 1986, p. 36.

8

Kurt Marti: 'Chaos in die Ordnung bringen'

Michael Butler

In one of the numerous post-1968 debates on the function of literature in capitalist society, Kurt Marti quoted approvingly Theodor Adorno's provocative statement, 'Aufgabe von Kunst heute ist es, Chaos in die Ordnung zu bringen'.[1] The immediate context was a controversy over the cultural and political role of the nonconformist writers of the *Gruppe Olten* in the deeply conservative society of contemporary Switzerland. Marti's support for the Group's social-democratic aims and his advocacy of the need to promote a strategic solidarity throw light on the paradoxical meaning he attached to the twin concepts of 'Chaos' and 'Ordnung'. For in Marti's view, the latter represents a spiritual and political sclerosis he feels to be widespread in Swiss society; 'Chaos', on the other hand, far from being the product of destructive anarchy, represents in fact the liberating, creative power of the imagination. And it is the crucial defence of the imagination as the key to the formation of a humane society which lies at the heart of Marti's work, not only as writer, but also as parish priest and citizen. This commitment to social and spiritual change (for him the same thing) helps to explain Marti's courageous support for unpopular and divisive causes, for example, the 'Autonome Jugendzentrum' during the Zurich 'Unruhen' of 1980 (against, in this case, his own Parish Council), the rights of conscientious objectors against a powerful military establishment, the women's movement, anti-nuclear protest and Green politics – all of which, in Switzerland at least, tend to be seen as subversive activities aimed against traditional values and the stability of the state.[2]

At first glance, Kurt Marti would seem an unlikely candidate for the role of critical, nonconformist intellectual. Born in 1921 (the same year as his fellow Bernese, Dürrenmatt), Marti enjoyed a secure childhood in a supportive and loving home, which gave him a firm existential base for his later ordination into the Lutheran ministry (RO 146).[3] His vocation and choice of career anchored him at the very centre of the Swiss social system with assured status as a member of an innately conservative *Beamtentum*. Yet it was precisely his day-to-day experience of the Protestant ministry, with its emphasis on preaching the Word, that gradually forced him to recognise the deficiencies of organised religion and the ossified language in which it was formulated. This theological predicament led him to search for a more convincing means of clarifying his sense of self, his relationship with God and with social reality. What he called 'ein Prozeß der Selbsterkenntnis'[4] turned him belatedly into a writer. Thus, whether Marti writes sermons, poetry, short stories or political diaries, his work reveals a persistent concern with locating an exact and more honest language for his experience. At the same time he is highly conscious of the slippery and treacherous nature of words: bombast, cliché, the polished lie provide a carapace behind which much social and political discourse hides its basic sterility. For the Lutheran Marti, it is the priests and theologians who have most conspicuously failed to keep the language alive so that the Church, with its dogmatism and ritualism, its characteristic avoidance of conflict, has become 'ein Rahmen ohne Leinwand, ohne Kreation und Bild, Selbstzweck also, und die Gefahr besteht tatsächlich, daß wir [= Christians] nur noch Marionetten dieses Selbstzwecks sind' (ZBB 93). This situation places a special responsibility on poets: 'Vielleicht hält Gott sich einige Dichter (ich sage mit Bedacht: Dichter!), damit das Reden von ihm jene heilige Unberechenbarkeit bewahre, die den Priestern und Theologen abhanden gekommen ist' (ZS 16). The typically humorous, self-dismissive note of this remark highlights the clear, if difficult, equation Marti establishes between religious faith, spontaneity and poetry. Literature for him, indeed, is an attack on, not a support for, complacency and spiritual sloth; it is a 'Gespräch mit Gott, das oft . . . den Charakter eines Streitgesprächs annimmt. Man könnte biblisch geradezu definieren: Wir, das heißt wir Menschen, *sind* ein Streitgespräch – mit Gott, deshalb auch miteinander' (GP 19f.).

Unlike Yeats, a poet he admires, the 'quarrel with each other' led Marti not to prose but initially to poetry. It is clearly the driving force of his first book, *republikanische gedichte* (1959), which overnight established his reputation. The controversy unleashed by this success has to be judged against a poetic tradition in Switzerland which was still largely dominated in the 1950s by lyrical inwardness – despite the eccentric power of such isolated individuals as Eugen Gomringer and the ill-fated Alexander Xaver Gwerder.[5] Combining the playful experimentation of Gomringer's concrete poetry with Brecht's concept of the poem as an accessible, socially orientated 'Gebrauchsgegenstand', poems like 'machtverhältnis' (SWH 6) were a breath of fresh air:

die ohne macht
machen
die mächtigen

was
machten
die mächtigen
machten
die ohne macht
nicht
was die mächtigen
machen?

mächtiger sind
als die mächtigen
die ohne macht

Not surprisingly, given the virulent Cold War attitudes in the Switzerland of the late 1950s and 1960s, Marti was promptly labelled a 'Nestbeschmutzer'; the socially critical poems of the collection – 'opposition in der schweiz', 'warnung', 'gutes tun an den opfern', 'die geldballade', in particular – were seized upon as examples of left-wing extremism, a crime all the more heinous for being perpetrated by an individual who by upbringing, training and profession was a member of the Swiss establishment.

A glance at the miniature cycle *heil-vetia* (1971) will stress the point. The seven short poems play with witty virtuosity on the Confederation's Latin name (helfetia / heil feezia / heul fetia / hehl fetzia / höll vetia / hell vetia / heil vetia) in a sustained attack on bourgeois complacency and self-importance, manifested in Switzerland in the particularly fatal conjunction of national identity with the army and the profit motive. At the same time, the fierce criticism is balanced by an angry affection for this 'mickey-mouse unter den völkern / disney-land der demokratie . . .' (VL 48). This ambivalence is most clearly illustrated in 'heil vetia 4' (VL 48), where the variations on the word 'heil' combine the twin possibilities of salvation and incipient fascism:

hehl fetzia
in deinen höhlen
    lagern die schätze der welt

bewacht
    von pünktlichen gnomen
beschützt
    von milizen und mirages
heilig heilig heilig: das asylrecht des geldes –
    und abends
erröten panoramisch die alpen
summen die wohnfabriken zuhauf
und dienstverweigerer meditieren
    friedlich in ihren zellen

The vulnerability of the individual is set against the ruthless materialism of the modern state; but the creative centre from which spiritual renewal must come is provocatively located in the 'modern' monk, that most un-Swiss and unsettling 'Nein-Sager', the conscientious objector.

Just as the spiritual protest of the *republikanische gedichte* and the *heil-vetia* poems cannot be detached from the political message, so too there is a strong political dimension to Marti's overtly religious poetry, *gedichte am rand* (1963), and the even more provocative *leichenreden* (1969). The *gedichte am rand*, as the title suggests, arose in the margins of the poet's reading of the Gospels and represent idiosyncratic footnotes, as it were, to Marti's ministry. Thus, for example, he meditates in 'weihnacht' (SWH 21), on the central mystery of John 1,14 ('Und das Wort ward Fleisch und wohnete unter uns'), where this 'chaotic' miracle of affirmation invades the rigidity of human unfreedom in an immediately recognisable, but haunting way:

damals

als gott
im schrei der geburt
die gottesbilder zerschlug

und

zwischen marias schenkeln
runzelig rot
das kind lag

Similarly, Matthew 16, 26 ('Was hülfe es dem Menschen, so er die ganze Welt gewönne, und nähme doch Schaden an seiner Seele?') leads to one of the most 'political' poems in the collection, 'heilsmaschinen' (SWH 31):

dies ist ein tüchtiges land
mit sauberen menschen
und heilsmaschinen
die peinlich exakt funktionieren

nach seiner geburt
wird jeder bürger
noch zappelnd
aufs fliessband gelegt
und automatisch
durch zeremonien gedreht
bis ihn die letzte
liebevoll ausspeit
in die elysischen felder

dies ist ein tüchtiges land
mit sauberen menschen
und heilsmaschinen
die peinlich exakt funktionieren

Politically subversive, these poems are also deeply Christian, but refreshingly free of sentimentality and traditional piety. The interdependence of secular and religious spheres is shown in negative form; the poems represent creative moments of chaos undermining a powerful, but inflexible order.

The *leichenreden* employ the same technique of understated linguistic iconoclasm. The thirty poems form a sustained antinecrologue which excoriates the humbug of conventional funeral orations. Puns, paradox and caustic wit dissolve ingrained linguistic habits. Each poem is preceded by eclectic quotations from philosophers, theologians, poets and – occasionally – mind-tugging graffiti observed on the walls of Paris in May 1968. In this way secular and spiritual concerns are set in a dialectical relationship which challenges the anaesthetising hypocrisies of everyday life. The resurrection of the dead, for example, is cast into doubt because the living ignore the need for 'resurrection' in their own lives ('ihr fragt'); the *Leistungsprinzip* is reduced to absurdity in 'sein leben war arbeit', where the departed achieves his life's ambition, 'das eigene heim', only 'in der urne aus ton' (L 57); a woman is seen as the victim of a harsh, moralising, patriarchal society ('als sie mit zwanzig'); death is greeted, shockingly, as a merciful release from the prison of a 'respectable' marriage ('es war eine gute ehe'). Other poems, however, celebrate the mystery of an old woman's contentment despite having been exploited throughout her life ('während 39 Jahren / war sie uns / eine zuverlässige mitarbeiterin',

L 55); or simply affirm the miracle of existence in 'es ist ein wunder', where, in a stanzaic form strongly reminiscent of the experimental work of August Stramm, Marti modulates passive and active verbs into a final triumphant 'es ist ein wunder / ist es ein wunder? / es ist' (L 7). Such poems strip away the pretentious veneer of ceremonies of consolation to reveal the triviality and emptiness beneath. The *leichenreden* continue to touch a highly sensitive nerve, for with twelve reprintings to date the volume remains Marti's most popular work.

This characteristic refusal to accept surface values and the ideological structures behind them also informs Marti's laconic short stories, *Dorfgeschichten* (1960) and *Bürgerliche Geschichten* (1981). Both collections trace tell-tale cracks in a smug, bourgeois society where eccentricity of any kind is swiftly marginalised. The very title of *Dorfgeschichten* ironically conjures up a Swiss nineteenth-century idyll and the edifying tales that underpinned it. But these 'village stories' owe more to the darker side of Keller and Gotthelf than to idealised perceptions of a sturdy Swiss reality. Marti's 'village' is already undermined by the encroaching town, and the 'heroes' in these prose cameos are frequently outsiders or foreigners whose presence in the community is perceived as a threat. Sometimes the danger is sexual vitality ('Dolce vita'), at other times political nonconformism, represented by an unwelcome peace poster in a block of flats ('Der Plakatmaler'). At a more existential level, an old man cannot communicate his sense of shrivelled opportunities to the younger generation; a bleak loneliness is the product of lost articulacy ('Der schrumpfende Raum'). Personal inadequacy, a sense of missed or suppressed opportunity, is caught in an unpretentious prose which avoids sententious moralising. Clearly based on Marti's pastoral experience, the *Dorfgeschichten* present a microcosm of defective social interaction which anticipates by four years the similar themes of Peter Bichsel's better known collection, *Eigentlich möchte Frau Blum den Milchmann kennenlernen* (1964).

The *Bürgerliche Geschichten*, by contrast, situate their protagonists in a more generalised, though still specifically bourgeois reality. A similar technique is employed: an anonymous narrator hears and notes down the strange stories that lie behind the outward ordinariness of other people's lives. The common theme is the eccentric who enters a superficially ordered existence, to be feared or uneasily tolerated – a mute symbol of imagination paralysed by social and political conformity. Against a background of affluence underpinned by the *Beamtentum*, the banking system and the army, with their insidious tentacles stretching into every corner of society, these brief tales set up little pockets of resistance. The revolt is sometimes seen, as so often in Marti's poetry, in negative form: the suicide of a fifty-year-old woman accountant whose real life was restricted to dreams while she lived in faithful conformity to bourgeois norms ('Flörli Lis'), or a man's recognition just before retirement of the triviality of a wasted existence ('Ein uninteressanter Mensch'). Elsewhere, the repressive ideology of the 'Leistungsgesellschaft' is unmasked: a schoolboy achieves momentary respite through truancy from the treadmill of a 'training for life' ('Charlie Mingus ist tot'), or a 52-year-old teacher suffers an abrupt collapse of identity: 'Und plötzlich also merkt man, wie man bei sich und zu Hause halt doch nicht ganz bei sich und nicht nur zu Hause ist' ('Eigenartige Beschädigungen', BG 146). It is in this story, in particular, that the narrator is most closely drawn into a 'Bruderschaft der Beschädigten' (BG 151), an empathy which reveals Marti's own solidarity with his defeated and unexceptional protagonists. The challenge represented by such individuals, damaged by the normative fictions of a 'heile Welt', is most sharply caught in the last story of the collection, 'Der Fürst'. During the celebration of Holy Communion, the narrator–priest is disturbed by the presence of a tramp-like stranger who quietly and with a touch of sovereign confidence demands bread and wine, not in neat, liturgical portions, but in quantity. Against a ceremony whose meaning has been eroded by constant repetition, the priest is suddenly confronted with a *genuine* hunger and thirst. The stranger departs as mysteriously as he arrived, leaving behind a persistent irritation in the narrator's mind – an imitation of the effect many of these *Bürgerliche Geschichten* have on the reader.

'Der Fürst' links up at many points with Marti's idiosyncratic 'diary', *Ruhe und Ordnung. Aufzeichnungen, Abschweifungen 1980–1983* (1984). In many ways modelled on Max Frisch's *Tagebücher*, these fragments, observations, and brief political commentaries argue for the dispossessed, the poor, the pacifists. The bourgeois concepts of 'Ruhe' and 'Ordnung' are relativised and undermined by a vision of an 'Urchristentum', a Christ-like church/society, which dispenses with the arrogance and aggression of a patriarchal system. In a final, witty vision Marti juxtaposes the creative anarchy of Julian Beck's Living Theatre with the Pope's melancholy imprisonment in the Vatican. But the attempt to introduce vitalising chaos into an instrumentalised order fails amidst papal incomprehension.

In one particular area, however, Kurt Marti has unquestionably achieved a major revitalisation: 'Mundartdichtung'. The previous revival of interest in dialect literature in the 1930s had taken place against the threatening background of European fascism; the patriotic proponents of 'geistige Landesverteidigung' had called on all writers and intellectuals to exclude the outside world and use their creative gifts to defend traditional Swiss values. Untrammelled by such ideological constraints, however, Marti's two volumes in Bernese dialect, *rosa loui* (1967) and *undereinisch* (1973), were able to bring dialect poetry into the modern age. What had previously been a deeply conservative action to hold on to old words and customs against a foreign and repugnant 'modernity', became in Marti's hands a tool with which he achieved a trenchant immediacy, matched only by the *leichenreden*. The fascination with the expressive possibilities of dialect was not an isolated phenomenon. Clearly, Marti drew inspiration not only from Gomringer, but also from the work of the Austrian poets H. C. Artmann, Friedrich Achleitner and other members of the *Wiener Gruppe* who had begun to explore the same rich vein in the late 1950s. There is, however, a major difference between the Austrian and Swiss exploitation of dialect. Unlike their Swiss colleagues, Austrian poets are not normally exposed to the linguistic tension set up between how they speak ('Mundart') and how they write ('Hochdeutsch'). The Austrians were drawn to 'Mundart' primarily for aesthetic reasons, attracted to the medium because of the fascinating sound qualities of dialect and the often brilliant 'alienation effects' that could be achieved by aleatory games with language. In German Switzerland, on the other hand, 'Mundart' is not a comparatively rare phenomenon restricted to rural areas or the working class, but the everyday means of oral communication for every stratum of the population. Thus Marti's dialect poems are not a series of intellectual games, but possess a natural sound and rhythm which increase their impact on his Swiss readership. Their matter-of-fact quality highlights, by contrast, the dishonest abstractions of much official propaganda couched in High German.[6]

What characterises Marti's 'Mundartdichtung' is, above all, his skill in dealing with political, existential and erotic themes in a way not previously attempted with any consistency. A good example of his forceful revision of the genre in political terms is 'früelig' (SWH 116):

hahnefuess und ankeballe
früelig trybt scho schtyf
liechti rägetropfe falle

radioaktiv

härzig öigt dr erscht salat o
wie ne gwunderfitz
aber warschaupakt und nato
näme kei notiz

The poem achieves its effect by the sudden deflation of conventional expectations initially aroused by the traditional title, rhythm and vocabulary. The miraculous promise of natural renewal is abruptly checked by man's more sinister 'miracle': the ultimate capacity to destroy all creation. Marti boldly thrusts the horrors of the contemporary world into the hitherto cosy arena of Swiss domesticity. In 'Wie geits?' (SWH 114) a playful use of language starts with banality and modulates into a gentle threnody on transience:

äs chunnt
äs geit

ganz zerscht
chunnt meh
als geit

doch gly
chunnts so
wies geit

und bald
geit meh
als chunnt

bis
alles geit
und nüt me chunnt

The gentleness as a necessary counterpart to pain, which is characteristic of so much of Kurt Marti's work, emerges particularly strongly in the love poems in these two collections, as in the title poem, 'rosa loui' (SWH 115):

so rosa
wie du rosa
bisch
so rosa
isch

kei loui süsch

o rosa loui
rosa lou
i wett
so rosa
wär ig ou

Startlingly direct and unsentimental, 'rosa loui' relates the magical iridescence of the Rosenloui Glacier in the Bernese Oberland both to the loved one ('rosa lou') and to an avalanche ('loui' = 'Lawine'). Natural beauty, love and risk are inextricably fused, but peril is checked in a moment of clarity which is the formal structure of the poem itself. Similarly, 'liebesgedicht' in *undereinisch* (SWH 131) reveals the overwhelming power of sexual love, for an experience of which no danger is too great:

wenn
e lawine
vo zärtlechkeit
für is z'begrabe
über is abe
geit

schtirben i
gärn e chly
wett i
nid grettet sy

Such poems owe their effect to the tension set up between the pithy speech patterns of dialect and such awkward High German concepts as 'Zärtlichkeit' which culminates in an imaginative shock effect.

In their range and flexibility, Marti's 'gedicht ir bärner umgangsschprach' are among the most impressive products of the mid-1960s revival of dialect poetry (usually termed 'modern mundart'), and together with Ernst Burren, Ernst Eggimann and the *chansonnier*, the late Mani Matter, he has ensured that dialect poetry can no longer be regarded as an uncomplicated refuge from modern society and all its ills.

Kurt Marti has always retained a capacity to surprise his readers. He is well aware that such labels as 'nonconformist' or 'left-wing intellectual' are control mechanisms of the 'Ordnung' which he so despises. *Abratzky oder Die kleine Brockhütte* (1971) is a further example of Marti's ability to employ wit to subvert such pressures. The subtitle of this slim volume – 'Nachträge zur weiteren Förderung unseres Wissens. Lexikon in einem Band' – gives the clue to the book's ironic strategy: with mock-humble Swiss modesty this 'kleine Brockhütte' challenges the monumental authority of Germany's multi-volume encyclopaedia, *Der Grosse Brockhaus*. Yet what is presented ostensibly as a scholarly mini-compendium rapidly undermines all positivistic faith in the reliability and coherence of 'facts'. Thus the 'Lexikon' looks backwards to Flaubert's absurdly complacent encyclopaedists, Bouvard and Pécuchet, and forwards to Max Frisch's Herr Geiser in *Der Mensch erscheint im Holozän*. Indeed, the book can be seen as a comic pendant to the darker theme of Frisch's story, whose protagonist has to suffer the final collapse of a once stable world guaranteed by memory and modern science. In a splendid parody of scholarly precision, the alphabetically arranged entries are kitted out with full bibliographical details and cross references which send readers on a wild-goose chase after 'truth'. Caught in a labyrinth of pseudo-certainties, they have to find their own way out. The mock-serious amalgam of fact and fantasy underlines once again the liberating function of the imagination in a world dominated by rigid systems and data banks.

Given such irreverence, it is hardly surprising that Marti is no stranger to controversy, fuelled in his case by his 'insider' position as priest and civil servant. But none of his creative work has stirred up more virulent criticism than his direct interventions in Swiss politics. The publication of his diary, *Zum Beispiel Bern 1972* (1973) marked a high point in Marti's conception of committed literature. His intention and method are clear: 'Diese Aufzeichnungen sind eine Art politischer Mikroskopie. Kleine Vorgänge in kleinen Verhältnissen durch das Vergrößerungsglas meiner Subjektivität beobachtet und spontan notiert' (ZBB 55). The loosely structured diary has two major strands: a self-defence against critics who dismiss him as a blinkered, closet 'Marxist', and a critique of the growth of reactionary forces gathered round the 'Nationale Aktion zum Schutz von Volk und Heimat'. In particular, he focuses on the activities of Major Ernst Cincera, who at the time was touring Switzerland with a particularly unpleasant brand of right-wing demagoguery. Marti's 'subjective microscope' reveals the insidious dangers of what he terms 'Cincerismus' – 'ein Helvetismus für McCarthyismus' (ZBB 28) – that misguided patriotism which blindly equates socialism with political subversion. He points to the irrational roots of the fear of 'Überfremdung', whipped up by the extreme right-wing Nationalrat, James Schwarzenbach, and his

'Republikanische Bewegung'. In an appendix, Marti (no pacifist himself) also documents his defence of a young conscientious objector against the bullying incomprehension of the legal and military authorities.[7]

A venomous response from the Right was predictable, but Marti was also attacked by the Left for what was considered to be an inadequate, because subjective, response to the objective constraints of modern Swiss society and for his overdue concentration on the plight of nonconformist intellectuals like himself. Though such critics had a point, they tended to see the book for what it was not. For *Zum Beispiel Bern 1972* makes no pretence to conduct a scientifically based sociopolitical analysis, but is presented – as the title indicates – as an ongoing *conversation* which aims to document the political issues of contemporary Switzerland and to define an individual's response to them. Marti himself was quite aware of the vulnerability of his subjective viewpoint: 'Bin ich nicht selber eine Figur, mit der gespielt wird?' – but he concludes defiantly: 'Nur dezidierte Subjektivität, die ihre Grenzen wenn nicht einfach kennt, so doch einkalkuliert, scheint mir genügend Aufschluß über politische Mikroprozesse versprechen zu können' (ZBB 105). The narrowing of focus implied by his subjective stance is thus not only a guarantee of authenticity, but simultaneously an appeal for solidarity. The book, indeed, forms a fascinating prose commentary on one of Marti's best-known early poems, 'opposition in der schweiz' (SWH 9):

noch op-
und doch schon
position

halb op halb po
regiert sie mit
meist wird das pro
mit contra quitt

position
und doch noch
op-

Marti's 'diary' registers a timely protest against an unthinking acceptance of Switzerland's famous *Konkordanzdemokratie*, the political system which all too often stifles opposition by seeking compromise before the issues are properly engaged.

If *Zum Beispiel Bern 1972* was an overt attempt to focus political attitudes and prejudices through a subjective lense, Marti's only novel, *Die Riesin* (1975), concentrates primarily on the labyrinthine nature of the psyche in its struggle for balance and creative expression. The eponymous and erotically omnivorous giantess, first glimpsed in an uneasy dream, is pursued through the text by the narrator as if she were a fictive reality rather than a hallucination. Technically, the novel is an uneasy compound of 'Bericht', mono- and duologue, lyrical description, mini-drama and explicatory letters addressed by the librarian–narrator to a friend. The central thrust of the story, however, clearly echoes Frisch's *Mein Name sei Gantenbein*, published a decade earlier: 'Stets zwingt man uns ein anderes Leben auf, als wir leben möchten, auch leben könnten. Was der freien Selbstentfaltung, der Menschwerdung des Menschen im Wege steht, sie verhindert, verbiegt, unterdrückt, wird als Riese erlebt, als übermächtig erfahren. Insofern wimmelt's in unserer Zivilisation von Riesen' (R 58). Although the lucidity of these words, uttered by the narrator's philosophically-minded colleague, is lightly ironised by the narratorial viewpoint, the statement sums up Marti's meaning. The 'Riesin' becomes a metaphor which encapsulates any social and psychological force which threatens to overwhelm and distort human life. In Freudian terms, she can assume the forbidding shape of a crushing 'Über-Ich' or remain an inchoate, erotic power lurking within the Unconscious. In the political context, the ogress is manifested in systems of right and left which are geared to crush individual growth and responsibility.

Within its narrow compass of 140 pages, the book raises urgent questions about the patriarchal culture of bourgeois society, a theme Marti is to develop in many of his essays and sermons during the 1980s. In particular, it points to the atrophying of the imagination as the root cause of our civilisation's malaise: 'Sind wir nicht Verstandeskrüppel? Gehen wir nicht zugrunde daran?' (R 129). The critique may not be startlingly original, but *Die Riesin* fits consistently into Marti's view of the common nature of poetry and theology: both seek to establish a balance of mind and feeling, intellect and imagination, through which the individual can flourish. Here sexual and political emancipation is posited as integral to a healthy psyche, and the sterility of Western hubris is countered by a suggestive hint that Eastern traditions could offer a viable antidote. The narrative's connection with Marti's poetry can be seen in the central notion of *play* as a method of restoring human vitality; for play releases tension and gives fresh scope for the unpredictable. Thus the narrator concludes his story: 'Wenn das Lachen aufhört, haben die Riesen gesiegt' (R 140). Nevertheless, despite the bravura manipulation of narrative modalities, the novel is ultimately weakened by a lack of memorable characters in which to embody the author's ideas. The poet's perception is not matched by the stamina required for sustaining longer prose narratives – a point conceded by Marti himself.[8]

Marti's later work remains true to his search for a creative balance between extremes. But in both the collection of poems, *abendland* (1980), and his most recent volume of short stories, *Nachtgeschichten* (1987), the darker tones are more in evidence. The religious poetry of *abendland* is closely linked to the explorative 'Notizen' of *Zärtlichkeit und Schmerz* (1981). The latter bring Marti very close to Heinrich Böll, for like Böll, his concern is to rediscover the Christian Word through rescuing the concept of 'Zärtlichkeit': 'Zärtlichkeit als intensivste Form der Aufmerksamkeit. Je vollkommener sie ist, desto sensibler, verletzbarer auch' (ZS 68). Echoing Böll's *Frankfurter Vorlesungen* (1966) and the central theme of *Gruppenbild mit Dame* (1971), Marti declares: 'Zärtlichkeit ist gleichermaßen Sinnlichkeit, die intelligent, wie Intelligenz, die sinnlich macht . . . Sie wird, die Anarchistin, erst herrschen, wo keine Herrschaft mehr ist' (ZS 66). The book argues for a 'feminisation' of the patriarchal system and for a recognition of the miraculous in everyday life. In particular, it articulates a persistent fear that the marginalisation of Christianity (a feature of both capitalist and Marxist societies), with the consequent reduction of the Church to a 'Dienstleistungsbetrieb' which enables the powerful to stabilise their power (ZS 124), will prove the end of our civilisation. The tone of these 'Notizen' is indeed sombre, but their very aphoristic structure retains precisely that anarchic energy which systems are designed to control. Only the rediscovery of 'Zärtlichkeit' can withstand the cold rigidity of 'Schmerz'. The writer/priest is thus faced with a sisyphean task, but he is spurred on by a central hope: 'daß Gott ein Tätigkeitswort werde' (ZS 135).

A similar movement from secular scepticism to religious hope characterises the poems of *abendland*. The book is carefully structured in three sections. The first contains poems which deal with betrayal, as in the title poem where Judas's individual act of treachery is set provocatively 'gegen die VIELEN / der christen der kirchen / die dich verfluchen' (A 18); or in a restatement of Christ's suffering in terms of the language of human cruelty, 'die passion des wortes GOTT' (A 11):

das blutet aus allen wunden

das wird vergewaltigt noch und noch
das ist verraten zertrampelt zerschossen geköpft
    gerädert gevierteilt gezehnteilt

. . .

und ALSO wurde das wort GOTT
    zum letzten der wörter
    zum ausgebeutesten aller begriffe
    zur geräumten metapher
    zum proleten der sprache

In a particularly telling poem, 'reich gottes in der schweiz?', a visitor from 'bobrowskiland' is shown a country where the spirit has been stifled by the profit motive and where God's word lives on only as 'ein glimmender docht / in den herzen den köpfen / von spinnern rebellen / und einiger stiller im lande' (A 32).

The second section develops the idea of rebels, individuals whose hopes are actively subversive in a world where dogma, authoritarianism, the institutionalised church and systems in general perpetuate Christ's crucifixion ('immerwährende kreuzigung', A 47). Taking up the feminist side of rebellion, Marti boldly rewrites the Lord's Prayer in radically trinitarian terms: 'unser vater / der du bist die mutter / die du bist der sohn / der kommt / um anzuzetteln / den himmel / auf erden . . . ('unser vater', A 50).

The final section turns the concept of hope into Yeatsian 'epiphanies', momentary flashes of insight, as in 'grosser gott klein' (A 82):

grosser gott:
uns näher
als haut
oder halsschlagader
kleiner
als herzmuskel
zwerchfell oft:
zu nahe
zu klein –
wozu
dich suchen?

wir:
deine verstecke

The concentrated simplicity of this delicately crafted poem is immediately followed by the longest and technically most surprising item in the book, 'frau mann liebe', a loosely flowing, erotically charged collage of fragments from over fifty sources, ranging from Rabelais to the American Beats, from William Blake to Ingeborg Bachmann, from Novalis to Pablo Neruda, from the Mahanirvana Tantra to Paul Eluard. The result is an astonishing paean of praise to sexual love. Seen in dialectical relationship to 'grosser gott klein', it places the richness of human experience firmly in a divine context, as a simultaneous emancipation of spirit and body.

The *Nachtgeschichten*, for the most part, continue the themes of the earlier stories. Night is central, for it is at such a time that dreams and hallucinations arrive to challenge the norms of everyday reality. The contours of bourgeois existence are blurred and hidden truths begin to emerge. Thus these stories are accounts of individuals who have lost touch with their true identities or of eccentrics who do not fit into acceptable patterns of social behaviour. For example, a woman dying of cancer conducts a faintly belligerent conversation with a silent crucifix ('Bruder der Nacht'); an old man at the end of his life spins out words to keep the reality of death at bay ('Das schwarze Kamel'). In a story strongly reminiscent of Frisch a lawyer disappears without trace, leaving behind a slightly envious narrator ('Die Kunst des spurlosen Verschwindens'). Another tale recounts the disorientation of a middle-aged novelist when confronted with the unpredictable vitality of a group of young 'Spontis' who have occupied a decrepit villa and live out the wild violence that he can only enjoy in his imagination. The final eight narratives concentrate on the problem of sexual fulfilment, where the pale protagonists are never quite sure what is real and what dream. The stories ironically turn against the anonymous narrator as he dimly perceives his own reality reflected in the tales he relates.

In his more recent poems, *Mein barfüßig Lob* (1987), Marti repeats the external structure of *abendland*. However, here the three sections are clearly entitled 'Klage', 'Lob' and 'Sabbat'. Thus the Christian frame of reference is overtly established and the poems presented as a kind of linguistic pilgrimage. In the nine poems of 'Klage' there are echoes, both in rhythm and image, of the Romantic 'Lied', the melodious melancholy of Georg Trakl and the sombre vision of Paul Celan. But a tired scepticism threatens to overwhelm the poet and his sense of belonging to *any* tradition, either of affirmation or spiritual revolt, as in the third section of 'schwarze frühling' (MBL 16):

wär
noch etwas
zu sagen?

mich wandelt
die lust an
niemand zu sein

unbeirrt
bleiben die kapitäne
auf untergangskurs

die welt:
eine träne – in wessen
erblindetem aug?

Nevertheless, this contemporary Job is swiftly rescued from the depths of negativity; the poems of the central section offer a prompt antidote to apocalyptic despair: the key is love and an intense awareness of the pleasure of ordinariness ('gedeckter tisch: / die teller die gläser / feldblumen / im krug' ('heheda endzeitgenossen', MBL 35)). In an imitation of Easter Saturday, that strange hiatus between Golgotha and Resurrection, these poems of praise act as a counterweight to the fashionable attractions of nihilism: 'eiszeit! doch mit / dir im arm / fühl ich wieder / wütend mich und warm' ('karsamstag', MBL 25). The sense of imminent renewal is palpable: 'heilige unwissenheit / blüht / der unaussprechlichkeit gottes / entgegen' ('cusanische strophen', MBL 52).

The final section celebrates the restored vibrancy of faith, which Easter Sunday brings, with eleven poems of pared down simplicity. Marti's characteristic love of linguistic play and parody is linked to the traditional notion of Sabbath rest where love can exact its gentle demands, for example, in 'mailid' (MBL 70):

eros
ion
mai
ner
ruh
du –

wie beteert
mich hach
dein lid
ohne worte

Neither *abendland* nor *Mein barfüßig Lob* mark any radical break from Marti's early work. What is new in these collections is the careful shaping of each volume and a sharper delineation of the religious roots of his inspiration. The clearest expression of this dual commitment to literature and spiritual reality was supplied by Marti himself in his essay, 'Versuch einer theologischen Definition der Literatur' (1963):[9] 'Nur im Wort Gottes sind Sprachprozeß und Weltprozeß, sind Wort und Wirklichkeit unmittelbar zueinander: das Wort Gottes ist Tat-Wort, Schöpfungs-Wort' (GP 111). And later in the same essay he sums up his personal credo: 'Literatur ist Lob der Sprache. Moderne Literatur ist im besonderen: Lob der Sprache vor dem Horizont der Sprachlosigkeit' (GP 117). It is this fundamental commitment to language that gives the writer his status and makes conflict with ruling ideologies inevitable. To refuse to challenge the status quo is, for Marti, to accept the grotesquely diminished, merely decorative role of 'literarische Gartenzwerge'.[10]

Whether as poet, theologian or politically active citizen, Marti is concerned with the central issue of 'Menschwerdung', that is, the process of the imagination freeing itself to grasp the miracle of the Word made flesh. It is through the creative use of language that we explore and locate most accurately our true selves. For this reason literature cannot be divorced from politics any more than religion can be divorced from society without a disastrous diminution of humanity. Against the possibility of a final anonymous holocaust, whether atomic or ecological, Kurt Marti affirms the inalienable value of the awkward individual and rejects the comfortable complicity of smoothly functioning systems: 'Wenigstens nicht einverstanden gewesen sein: das ist nicht zuletzt ein Ausdruck meines Dankes für dieses Leben' (GP 153).

Notes

1. 'Ein Gerücht im Supermarkt – die Gruppe Olten', *drehpunkt*, vol. 10, nos. 40/41, 1978, p. 23.

2. For an example of Marti's fearless attitude towards Swiss taboos, see his conversation with Switzerland's leading Marxist intellectual: Kurt Marti/Konrad Farner, *Dialog Christ–Marxist. Ein Gespräch*, Zurich, 1972. Marti was also the instigator (with Otto F. Walter) of the 'Aufruf' in March 1962 to ban atomic weapons in Switzerland. This was the first common action undertaken by progressive Swiss intellectuals since the Second World War. The text, signed amongst others

by Karl Barth, Max Bill, Friedrich Dürrenmatt and Hermann Hesse, is reprinted in Otto F. Walter, *Gegenwort. Aufsätze, Reden, Begegnungen*, Zurich, 1988, p. 130.

3. References to Marti's work are as follows: RO = *Ruhe und Ordnung. Aufzeichnungen, Abschweifungen 1980–1983*, Darmstadt and Neuwied, 1984; page references to paperback edition, Darmstadt and Neuwied, 1986; ZBB = *Zum Beispiel Bern 1972*, Darmstadt and Neuwied, 1973; ZS = *Zärtlichkeit und Schmerz. Notizen*, Darmstadt and Neuwied, 1981; GP = *Der Gottesplanet. Aufsätze und Predigten*, Darmstadt and Neuwied, 1988; SWH = *Schon wieder heute. Ausgewählte Gedichte 1959–1980*, Darmstadt and Neuwied, 1982; VL = *Der Vorsprung Leben. Ausgewählte Gedichte 1959–1987*, Frankfurt am Main, 1989; L = *leichenreden*, Darmstadt and Neuwied, 1969; page references to paperback edition, Darmstadt and Neuwied, 1976; BG = *Bürgerliche Geschichten*, Darmstadt and Neuwied, 1981; R = *Die Riesin. Ein Bericht*, Darmstadt and Neuwied, 1975; A = *abendland. gedichte*, Darmstadt and Neuwied, 1980; MBL = *Mein barfüßig Lob. Gedichte*, Darmstadt and Neuwied, 1987.

4. *Der Schriftsteller in unserer Zeit. Schweizer Schriftsteller bestimmen ihre Rolle in der Gesellschaft*, ed. P. A. Bloch *et.al.*, Bern, 1972, p. 87. See also the interview with Werner Bucher in Werner Bucher and Georges Ammann, *Schweizer Schriftsteller im Gespräch*, vol. 2, Basle, 1971, p. 128.

5. Marti was attracted to the internationalism of concrete poetry against the unadventurous nature of much contemporary Swiss poetry. Gomringer represented 'innerschweizerisch die radikalste Gegenposition zu Heimatstil und Heimatmystik'. *Die Schweiz und ihre Schriftsteller – die Schriftsteller und ihre Schweiz*, Zurich, 1966, p. 59.

6. For Marti the change from dialect to High German involves 'einen Verlust an Beweglichkeit und Spontaneität'. *Der Schriftsteller und sein Verhältnis zur Sprache*, ed. P. A. Bloch, Bern and Munich, 1971, p. 248.

7. It was such deeply resented activities that presumably led the cantonal authorities in 1972 to block a proposal that Marti be appointed to a Chair in theology at the University of Bern. However, the University defiantly awarded Marti an honorary doctorate in 1977. A brief biographical sketch of Kurt Marti can be found in *Kurt Marti. Texte, Daten, Bilder*, ed. Christof Mauch, Frankfurt am Main, 1991, pp. 53–7. See also Ernst Rudolf Rinke, *Der Weg kommt, in dem wir gehen. Theologie und Poesie der Zärtlichkeit bei Kurt Marti*, Stuttgart, 1990, and Christof Mauch, *Kurt Marti: Mundart–Theologie–Politik*, Tübingen, 1991.

8. The point was accepted by Marti himself: 'Auch habe ich den Verdacht, daß ich den langen Atem nicht hätte.' *Schweizer Schriftsteller im Gespräch*, p. 136.

9. In: Kurt Marti/Kurt Lüthi/Kurt von Fischer, *Moderne Literatur, Malerei und Musik. Drei Entwürfe zu einer Begegnung zwischen Glaube und Kunst*, Zurich and Stuttgart, 1963, pp. 146–65. Reprinted in *Gottesplanet* (GP 109–31).

10. *Die Schweiz und ihre Schriftsteller*, p. 16.

IV

Widening Perspectives

9

E. Y. Meyer: The Construction of History through Literature

Wilfried van der Will

To be saddled with the name Meyer in Switzerland is to be marked with a label of ordinariness. Small spelling variations of the name, far from holding out any possible hope of distinctiveness, merely point to further proliferations of banality. However, in a country which cultivates the fiction of democratic egalitarianism with conspicuous pride it is perhaps fitting to have a commonplace name. After all, its ubiquitous appearance could, together with other commonplace names, be said to bear witness to a largely anti-aristocratic, republican middle class which exacts conformity from its members and ensures a consensus of social conservatism. Yet it would be preposterous to suggest that E. Y. Meyer belongs amongst the watchdogs of conformity, opposed to tolerating the manifestations of plural society. On the contrary, Meyer's concern is that conformity and conservatism, far from preserving Switzerland's continued prosperity, are actually endangering it. He is an anti-modernist dissenter, but burdened by a name that denies him readily recognisable distinction. If it is fair to assume that the name undermines the sense of individuality of even ordinary men and women, how much more must it weigh down on the developed self-image of a writer and thinker? The self-awareness of modern artists, while rarely devoid of narcissistic and élitist traits, can encompass an understanding of exemplary individuality at any level of society. Meyer hints at this in one of his speeches: 'Der Einzelne, der der Künstler par excellence ist . . .'[1] It is clear from the context of this speech at a conference on 'Das freie Wort zwischen Ideologie und Kommerz', that Meyer's defence of the artist's freedom is meant as a defence of the liberty of individual expression generally. The artist is seen as an archetypical case of modern existence:

Und der Künstler, in diesem Experiment- oder Modell-Land im besonderen und in der Welt im allgemeinen, ist dann auch nicht mehr bloß ein außenseiterischer Sonderfall . . . sondern er wird zum Prototyp des 'modernen' Helden schlechthin, des Einzelnen, der immer, wenn das soziale Gefüge des Unbewußten aufgelöst wird, eine heroische Reise unternehmen muß, um neue Formen ausfindig zu machen. (SM.HDF 94f.)[2]

The artist's commonplace name can now be read as an emblem of Everyman in the contemporary world. Art must strive to embody what is 'exemplarisch für die Situation des heutigen Menschen' (SM.HDF 95). Meyer has contented himself by adopting the diphthong of his surname as his initials to give himself some distinction both from his namesakes in the annals of Swiss literature and from those crowding the German-Swiss telephone books.

The fear of submersion in the anonymity of modern mass existence and the struggle for individual distinction, or rather, typicality, is a constant theme in Meyer's writings. So is the threat issuing from modern civilisation to the survival of life in general and human culture in particular. Neither theme is particularly original in German literature, with the former arising in the literature and thought before and after the turn of the century (Nietzsche, Rilke, Hofmannsthal, among others) and the latter going back as far as the writings of German classicism (for example Goethe's *Faust II* and his poem 'Der Zauberlehrling'). Both are well-worn topics within contemporary intellectual circles in Europe and have become stock-in-trade features of the literary review pages and even of the political news. Ecologists of many varieties are engaged in the analysis of a culture which seems hell-bent on its own destruction, and subcultural cells committed to alternative lifestyles are springing up everywhere in advanced industrial societies. Coincidentally, Meyer's first book, a collection of surrealist short stories entitled *Ein Reisender in Sachen Umsturz* – showing individuals in various situations of disorientation – was published in the same year (1972) in which the Club of Rome brought out its famous *Limits to Growth*. In other words the thematic content of Meyer's writings is about as original as his name.

Yet it would be wrong to assume that because his themes are well within the critical mainstream of contemporary intellectual debates Meyer's work is redundant. On the contrary, Meyer uses fiction in order to help reinforce a change in social and historical consciousness by displaying a range of narrative situations encapsulating discussions and deliberations in which old philosophical tenets can be critically explored and alternative thinking developed. The achievement of Meyer's prose therefore hinges on its realistic portrayal of wide-ranging sociological, philosophical, psychological, anthropological and many other types of reflection as the lived experience of contemporary human beings. Meyer justifies the fact that these are usually Swiss by arguing, or having his fictional characters argue, that Switzerland is a prototype of modernity:

> Die kleine Alpenrepublik wird, *so gesehen*, dann zu dem Land, das in seiner Ganzheit auf dem materialistischen Weg des technisch-industriellen Fortschritts auf diesem Planeten bis jetzt vielleicht am weitesten gegangen und auf diese Weise nicht nur zu einem führenden internationalen Finanzplatz, sondern auch zu einem der *materiell reichsten Länder der Welt* geworden ist, und erhält dadurch für die Welt, in positiver oder negativer Hinsicht, Experiment- oder Modell-Charakter. (SM.HDF 94)

Narration (in the form of the novel, but also in that of drama)[3] is the device used to translate into modern myth a version of the past which explains our present predicament and at the same time opens up the future as a complement of new possibilities in which none is dogmatically privileged.

The narrator in Meyer's first novel, *In Trubschachen* (1973), is flatly referred to as 'man'. This is done with such ruthless consistency that we never learn more about this figure than a few fragments of his biography: he is male and still a student at university, trying to complete a short thesis which is part of his final examinations. It is for this reason that he has withdrawn for a short holiday from the distractions of town life into the seclusion of Trubschachen. This is not a fictional place but one that really exists, and the book starts with a detailed description of all the stops from Biel (Bienne) via Bern (Berne) and then through various valleys in a slow train to the Emmental, where Trubschachen is to be found about twenty miles due east from the Swiss capital. The narrator's painstaking representation of the railway connections and the timetable appear designed to lure the reader into the deepest provinciality of alpine cowherds and local cheese making. But we soon learn that the gaze of this narrator is that of an alert and sophisticated contemporary observer. Trubschachen gradually attains paradigmatic character. Initially it appears only as a little place where the immediacy of human relations, the warmth of small-scale community, the carefully (and narrow-mindedly) guarded limits of moral, religious and ideological tolerance have not yet vanished. However, if this trip into a lower alpine valley bears some of the hallmarks of a nostalgic flight to an island of the past which is preserved within an alien present, it is made perfectly clear towards the end of the novel that modern town life will swamp this idyll very soon. The almost anonymous narrator, who is given to speculations in the subjunctive, brutally conjures up the moment when the ripeness of the Emmental cheese will be analysed by X-ray machines, when much of the land and many farmsteads will have been bought up by townspeople as second homes, when multi-storey buildings will have replaced the low family dwellings of the farmers and dairy workers and the two family-run hotels will have become anonymous catering establishments (T 217). It is obvious that this narrator acts not only as a historian and critic of modernity but also as an active post-modern analyst and politician. He constantly points to the inherent reasons for these develop-ments: the spirit of competitiveness for its own sake, the Kantian sense of duty and thrift by which the individual in bourgeois industrial society was, and to a large extent still is, driven. *Pflicht* is seen as the ideal that has pervaded the existence of the hard-working peasantry of the Emmental. It is the reason for its present-day affluence, but eventually traps it in the luxury of consumerism, which is destined to end in the dubious pleasures of stereotyped lives in concrete tower blocks. The latter – 'riesige, seine Bewohner vollkommen anonym haltende Wohnblocks' (T 50) – are seen as the architectural denunciation of individuality and identity by modern society. In his 'Rede an Architekten' (May 1981), published in *Plädoyer* (1982), Meyer later let fly against 'den sich krebsartig ausbreitenden baulichen Monotonie-Gigantismus' (P 97) which, he avers, was initially created by the desire for security. While in the novel the reasons for the seemingly unstopp-able encroachment of Modernism as an architectural style and a way of life are located in the ethic of industrialism, i.e. the restless Kantian striving for the fulfilment of duty, the later essay blames contemporary society's limitless desire for financial insurance of every kind. It is the millions of premiums and bank deposits which drive the office blocks skyward.

Feeling his individuality to be constantly undermined by the modern world in which he moves, the narrator finds little comfort in Trubschachen. Of course he enjoys the pleasures of eating and drinking and faithfully records the copious menus and the many bottles he tackles. But he is symptomatically debarred from con-ceiving of himself in the first person and hence remains tied to a self-reference ('man') which presents his existence as that of a generalised third person, a latter-day 'thinking thing' (*res cogitans*), rather than a doubting or affirming 'Ich'. The narrator is never allowed to develop a proper consciousness of self. Typically, his first sensation after arriving at the hotel is both cerebral and suggestive of his fears for the security of his own identity. He is reminded of his erstwhile philosophy teacher, who could not bear the thought of just using hotel rooms without leaving the slightest personal mark on them. Death in such an environment would be the final act of annihilation in the average mass. This reminiscence is conveyed in one sentence, lending it a special, relentless intensity:

Dann, nachdem man sich gewaschen hat, erinnert man sich – wie fast jedesmal, wenn man sich anschickt, in einem neubezogenen Hotelzimmer zu übernachten – wieder an einen seiner Lehrer und daran, wie er einmal, in einem Wintersemester, in einer Vorlesung über Tod und Leben – 'Der Tod als philosophisches Problem' – erzählt hat, daß er jedesmal, wenn er in einem Hotelzimmer übernachtete, daran denken müsse, daß er in dieser ihm völlig fremden, nichtssagenden – nichts über ihn aussagenden –, für einen nichtexistierenden Durchschnittsgeschmack eingerichteten, von soundso vielen Menschen – ohne daß sie auch nur eine einzige Spur ihrer persönlichen Anwesenheit hinterlassen *hätten* – vor ihm von soundso vielen Menschen – ohne daß sie auch nur eine einzige Spur ihrer persönlichen Anwesenheit hinterlassen *würden* – nach ihm benutzten (nicht bewohnten) Umgebung, zu der er keinerlei, aber auch überhaupt keine Beziehung habe – und das sei ein ihm unerträglicher Gedanke – *sterben* könnte . . . (T 19)

This quotation illustrates a major feature of Meyer's style in his first novel. The depersonalisation of the narrator implicitly contradicts the specific moments of the narrated story and translates them into paradigms of general experience. True, an intensely personal experience appears to be narrated and it is illustrated by an individual reminiscence. The gradual act of recovering his memory in ever more precise detail is stylistically represented by the narrator in a long paratactic construction, interrupted by encapsulated clauses and rhetorical repetitions leading to further extensions. The reader is obviously meant to be made aware of the narrator's hard labour in trying to achieve precision of communication. Yet, what emerges is a narrative style overdetermined by the message it carries and consciously designed to slip away from any individual characters to whom it may be assigned as a speaking or thinking part in dialogue, indirect speech or interior monologue. The effect of adhering to the depersonalised 'man' is to lift the story as a whole and all its individual sections separately into a supra-provincial dimension, closer to philosophical and sociological generalisation.

Not least by creating a field of reference with the names of Kant, Camus, Gotthelf, Thomas Bernhard, Hegel, Marx, Moritz Schlick and Tolstoy, the novel becomes an exercise in intellectual history. It is a critical reflection of the contemporary European present rather than a tale within the random limits of a narrowly defined here and now. While it is clear that the narrator–protagonist is a fairly self-indulgent kind of person, something of a glutton and given to excesses of drinking, the novel is sparing in its psychological characterisation. The language of this narrator is not therefore indubitably his, it plainly lacks idiosyncrasies. The nearest that the diction comes to displaying these is when certain Swiss lexical items or deviations from High German are strewn into the prose.

Such peculiarities are hardly sufficient to mark out any one of the characters mentioned as psychologically distinct. True, their ideological profiles are sketched in: the liberal schoolteacher and the cautiously progressive parson, the staunchly conservative military officer and the critically observant narrator. But at the same time the author appears unwilling to submit to conventions of individual characterisation. This is not because he is unfamiliar with psychological portrayal. Examples of it appear in his earlier book, *Ein Reisender in Sachen Umsturz*. The characters are deliberately kept within the indistinctness of average existence. The author appears to move within the strict parameters of a fundamental ontology of modern life in which the individual subject never gains sharp definition. Meyer's conception of his characters in *In Trubschachen* brings to mind Heidegger's acute analysis of 'das Man' in *Sein und Zeit*:

Das Dasein steht als alltägliches Miteinandersein in der *Botmäßigkeit* der Anderen. Nicht es selbst *ist*, die Anderen haben ihm das Sein abgenommen . . . In der Benutzung öffentlicher Verkehrsmittel, in der Verwendung des Nachrichtenwesens (Zeitung) ist jeder Andere wie der Andere. Dieses Miteinandersein löst das eigene Dasein völlig in die Seinsart 'der Anderen' auf, so zwar, daß die Anderen in ihrer Unterschiedlichkeit und Ausdrücklichkeit noch mehr verschwinden. In dieser Unauffälligkeit und Nichtfeststellbarkeit entfaltet das Man seine eigentliche Diktatur . . . Jeder ist der Andere und Keiner er selbst.[4]

The narratorial 'man' and the averageness of the other characters in Meyer's novel illustrate the historical threat to individuality by the same modernity which, at its inception in the eighteenth century, had staked everything on the creative, economic and moral emancipation of the individual. This is why the central point of reference

in the novel is Immanuel Kant who, as a herald of the Enlightenment and legitimator of natural science, is seen as a pivotal figure in
the inauguration of the modern world. Conventionally speaking,
the explosion of the productive forces over the last couple of
centuries has given human beings both the freedom from the
exigencies of nature and the power to destroy it, in its entirety or
piecemeal. Meyer paints a scenario where, irrespective of its divisions into social classes, contemporary society has become en-
slaved by the very principles which brought about its unchecked
expansion.

In the author's view, this social hypertrophy was and still is
predicated on a work ethic whose theoretical elaboration is to be
found in the *Critique of Practical Reason*. Meyer's *In Trubschachen* is
nothing less than an attempt, in narrative form, to reconstruct the
history of modernity and to open up critical distances to it in order
to escape its built-in fatality. In other words, Meyer's view of the
role of the writer in contemporary society is astonishingly positive.
Not only does he seem to believe, in whatever ironically refracted
ways, that writing can be employed to reconstruct the path of
intellectual history, he is also suggesting a distinct message to his
contemporary readers: reform your lives, your view of the world,
and, in particular, abandon your naive belief in the possibility of
unlimited technological progress and economic growth. It falls to
the 'teacher' during a discussion in the pub to formulate the overall
parameters not only of this particular exchange of views but of the
task of contemporary mankind, namely 'daß es doch in erster Linie
darum gehe, einen vernünftigen, den menschlichen Möglichkeiten
entsprechenden – und zwar den menschlichen Möglichkeiten im
Menschen entsprechenden – Ausweg aus den, vor allem in den
Städten immer häufiger anzutreffenden, *abstumpfenden, überfor-
dernden, menschenfeindlichen Lebensbedingungen* zu finden' (T 158).
The subjunctive, which is the grammatical mood of much of the
novel, is the stylistic device with which Meyer constitutes the
narrative as an exploration of the possibility for a turn from one age
to another. Symbolically, the narrated time is set at the turn of the
decade, from 27 December 1969 to 3 January 1970. Meyer's *oeuvre*,
too, is set on a divide, as he himself observes: ' . . . am Ende einer
Zeit, die wir bisher DIE MODERNE nannten, und am Beginn
einer neu anbrechenden Zeit, für die in einer noch relativ hilflosen
Weise erst einmal der Begriff DIE NACHMODERNE gebraucht
wird' (SM.HDF 95). Modernity, which has determined the past
two hundred years, may yet prevent a post-modern age from dawning. Janus is a two-faced God. The novel as reconceptualisation of

history becomes a condition of the possibility of exploring and disseminating new consciousness. Kant's philosophy is made the object of a vehement attack in order to help put the old age, that of modernity, to rest. The criticism of Kant is evident in the implied sympathy for Edward VIII, who had to choose between the perceived duty of the king and the inclination of the lover and who, as the text reminds us, opted for the latter by abdicating on 10 December 1936 (actually 11 December), with Winston Churchill the only voice pleading with the British nation for tolerance (T 118). Despite the complex picture that is drawn of Kant – his anti–militarism (T 94), his chivalrous manners (he is called an 'äußerlich wie innerlich vollendeter Kavalier des ancien régime', T 95), the clarity of his prose (T 96) – the basis of his ethic, namely the ideal of unadulterated duty, is dismissed as fatally flawed (see especially T 171–2 and 181). The narrator prefers a hedonistic ethic.

Both the technique and the content of the narrative never leave any doubt that Meyer is a writer with a considerable erudition in literary history, literary theory and literary technique, influenced stylistically by Heinrich von Kleist, Adalbert Stifter, whose imprint is particularly recognisable in *Die Rückfahrt* (1977), Robert Walser, Franz Kafka and Thomas Bernhard. The last is mentioned by name in *In Trubschachen*, for Bernhard's novel, *Watten* (1969), is the book that the narrator avidly turns to on his first night in the hotel 'Zum Hirschen' (T 33). The reviewers have rightly pointed out that Bernhard's influence on Meyer cannot be overlooked. They share the same publishing house (Suhrkamp Verlag), whose head (Siegfried Unseld) saw to it that the blurb of Meyer's first book encouraged the comparison. It was not just sales promotion. There are, indeed, many overt and covert references to the Austrian's work. *In Trubschachen* has a narrative framework which, based on a person withdrawing to a quiet spot to write a treatise, imitates Bernhard's in *Das Kalkwerk* (1970). It is a narrative pattern first tried by Bernhard in *Verstörung* (1967) and elaborated later in his *Beton* (1982). Not a single word of the thesis is written by the end of the narrated time either in *Das Kalkwerk* or *In Trubschachen*. Certain details of the narrative content also remind one of Bernhard. Not only are Bernhard's tales set within provincial mountainous environments (Bernhard's Ungenach[5] is Meyer's Trubschachen), the social psychology of the mass of the people in the Steiermark seems to have inspired the way that those in the Emmental are described. While, for example, the people of the former are said to be a mixture of brutal excesses and helpless sentimentality, particularly as far as the treatment of women is concerned,[6] the communities of the Emmental are said to be given to sexual deviance (inbreeding) and a violent temper (T 84–6). Aspects of the overall intellectual orientation of Bernhard's narrative strategies, for example his persistent questioning of the scientific conception of life and matter, the alienation of human beings from nature and their concomitant alienation from self, modern science as a fatal historical error, have all left their mark on Meyer. Many more points of contact between the two writers could be cited. However, the interpretative value of such parallels is questionable, for they inevitably lead one to concentrate on the similarities between the two authors, crucially blinding oneself to their differences. While Bernhard's narrative world is a worst-case scenario, headed towards disintegration, catastrophe and the isolation of the individual, Meyer's is a struggle for persuasive discourse, supported by a basic optimism that possibilities for genuine progress might exist as long as the history of the false progress, the promise of the 'false paradise' (see SM.HDF 96) can be analysed. The practice of philosophical reasoning remains a vital part of Meyer's fictional prose and, together with his essays, *Die Hälfte der Erfahrung* (1980) and *Plädoyer*, makes up his contribution to a New Enlightenment. The essentially up-beat nature of Meyer's intellectual effort is positively indicated by the explicatory subtitle of *Plädoyer*: 'Für die Erhaltung der Vielfalt der Natur beziehungsweise für deren Verteidigung gegen die ihr drohende Vernichtung durch die Einfalt des Menschen.'

Meyer's novel invites other comparisons. There is, first of all, the play on the genre of the *Bildungsroman*. In the later *Die Rückfahrt*, Stifter's *Der Nachsommer* provides the narrative matrix that is overtly and covertly alluded to in the text, whereas in *In Trubschachen* the references are to Thomas Mann's *Der Zauberberg*. Such references, however, are rather indirect, if not obscure. For example, *In Trubschachen* might appear like a compressed version of Mann's novel. Hans Castorp spends seven years in the 'Berghof' sanatorium, whilst Meyer's narrator spends seven days in the hotel 'Zum Hirschen'. If in this case even the informed reader is left wondering what to make of the compression of years into days (is life in the last third of the century that much faster?), there can be little doubt that Meyer provokes comparison with Mann when he has his protagonist walk into the deep snow. But his existential experience there is hardly congruent with that of Hans Castorp. The comparison is nevertheless telling on account of the differences in the intellectual orientation of the respective authors. Castorp's most daring excursion away from the comforts of civilisation into the alpine wilderness is described in a famous chapter when the protagonist, engulfed by a snowstorm, struggles to regain consciousness and the world of human habitation. The distinctions between dream and reality, hallucination and empirical observation, become blurred. Reflection reaches a new, supra-rational dimension, revealing as mere 'prattle' the multicultural discourses of Western Europe in the 'Berghof', particularly as represented by Settembrini and Naphta. All things human – culture, the state and the individual – are seen to hold a median position between 'mystic community and windy individualism'. The essence of humanity is defined as 'aristocratic', i.e. above ideological opposition.[7] Meyer's protagonist shares with Hans Castorp the struggle against exhaustion within the seductively soft embraces of the snow. But in Meyer the hallucinogenic situations are those preceding and following the walk through the snow. In the first, the protagonist, hung-over from a heavy bout of drinking, has a dream of a primaeval landscape which antedates all human history or has been deserted by man and beast (T 190); in the second situation the protagonist, recovering in a hot bath from his exhausting walk, loses the sense of distinction between himself and the surrounding world, thinks of how easy it would be to cut an artery and see the blood run out, but pulls himself together by therapeutically remembering Kant's essays on psychology (T 207–8). While Thomas Mann highlights the possibility of conquering the lures of the death drive (Freud's *Thanatos*), Meyer concentrates on images showing the whole of human history as episodic and that of the individual as incidental. This comparison illustrates the point that whenever similarities with other authors are suggested by Meyer, they turn out to be vague approximations at best or positively misleading at worst. His purpose appears to be the provocation of thought by the suggestion of *Eine entfernte Ähnlichkeit*,[8] the title he gave, significantly, to one of his short stories.

This is not generally true, however, of the references to Kafka which colour Meyer's second novel, *Die Rückfahrt*. Early on in this lengthy text the protagonist, Albin Berger, has a fantasy about a watermark on the ceiling of the room in which he is lying. It reminds him of a beetle or a squid with a face and a head that is attached to a body shaped like a small breadloaf and which, the anonymous narrator tells us, could be called Gregor Samsa. Such literary references express the indebtedness of the author as much as giving him possibilities for ironic pastiche. More seriously, Meyer has one of the characters in *Die Rückfahrt*, the psychiatrist Dr Santschi, reflect on Kafka's position in modern culture. The

Czech writer is said to inaugurate a new historical awareness of the limitation of human possibilities in an age of advanced industrialisation. Science and technology are pressing human beings into conformity, stifling individual creativity. Writing gains special importance in that it may provide a way of escaping the seemingly inevitable conformity of mass civilisation. It is significant that writing, as the least material and the least technologically elaborate form of creativity, but, by implication, the most reflexive, is given priority even over 'drawing', 'sculpting' and 'gardening' (R 85), all of which are highly regarded activities not only by Santschi but also by its author. Meyer's references to Kafka are of a different order from the similarities of his writings to Bernhard. Kafka clearly serves as a resource for classical images of modernity, of the predicaments which face society and the individual once the process of secularisation, the loss of metaphysical certainties and religious faith, has become the most crucially determining factor of human life.

There are hints in Meyer's work that Kafka is understood as an artist who transcended the absurdity and the negativity of what he wrote by the act of writing itself. Kafka is seen as one who was traumatised by the modernist shift towards an intensified period of alienation from self and from nature. Yet he demonstrated at the same time that, however negative the implications of this shift may be, it need not lead to intellectual paralysis. In other words, the literary images of the disorientation, the enfetterment, the brutality and violence of modern existence articulate human life and thus make it part of a potentially liberating social discourse. For Berger, creative writing might not only replace his regular psychoanalysis; it is the only meaningful activity within a nihilistic environment: 'Schreiben [war] ja das einzige geblieben, in dem er für sich noch einen Sinn sah, und an dem es sich für ihn nötigenfalls auch zu scheitern lohnen würde' (R 51). Kafka becomes Berger's role model. Reference to his writings provides Berger with a vital compass for his intellectual orientation which, at the same time, is offered to the reader. One of the most crucial images which is recalled from Kafka's *œuvre* is that of the 'Kleine Fabel'. In it a mouse complains that its world, endlessly wide at first, had gradually narrowed and become hemmed in between walls which, as the mouse went on running, were fast approaching each other, inevitably leading towards the trap. 'Du mußt nur die Laufrichtung ändern, sagt daraufhin die Katze zu der Maus und frißt sie auf' (R 85).[9] The story's teaching is threefold: first, that in the course of an individual's life and in that of human history there is an accelerating loss of possibilities ('Die möglichen Möglichkeiten . . . nehmen immer mehr ab', R 85); second, that it is foolish to complain to a superior power which delights in one's own destruction; and third, that an alternative course to what appears to be our inexorable destinity is always possible. Meyer's position as an author in relation both to his characters and to his readers is that he is the bearer of the cat's message without subsequently devouring his addressees. There is a reference in the author's 'Rede an Architekten' which can serve as a simple explanation of the novel's title: 'Wir haben erkannt, daß . . . wenn wir die Selbstvernichtung nicht wollen, nur *ein* Weg übrig bleibt: den der Umkehr, oder wenn Sie so wollen, der *Rückfahrt*' (P 100).

While Kafka's writings are exploited as a quarry to provide images for the devastation which modernity has wrought on the individual and society, his very existence as an artist can serve as some kind of pointer to the possibility of a transcendence of the industrial–bureaucratic phase of that modernity. Kafka certainly has a special position in Meyer's work, but it is important not to overestimate it, for Meyer draws on the entire literary and philosophical heritage available in the twentieth century to gain analytical leverage for a better understanding of contemporary life. Many names from the history of literature and thought crop up in Meyer's writings. In his position as author he acts as a polymath. In *Die Rückfahrt* the reflections of Berger, his discussions with Santschi and later those with the curator Effinger are such that the whole span of human history and civilisation and even of the cosmological dimensions of space and time are made the subject of discussion and critical commentary. The range of literary and philosophical reference is therefore extremely large. In the first book alone there are references to and observations on the work of the following: Hugo Ball, Samuel Beckett, Martin Buber, Sidney H. Courtier, Oliver Cromwell, Albert Einstein, Knut Hamsun, Hermann Hesse (Hermann Haller), Horace, Ernst Jünger, Immanuel Kant, Franz Kafka, Gottfried Keller, Friedrich Nietzsche, Adalbert Stifter, Jonathan Swift and Richard Wagner. It is not necessary in this context to evaluate their relative importance within the novel, for they are merely listed here to show the syncretistic procedure with which Meyer builds up his narrative scope and the method he uses to give it intellectual depth. History is not conceived as a simple linear continuum, but in perpendicular fashion, as periods of time swinging back and forth. In other words, historical time is capable of repetition, return and reversal through the intervention of human beings. This was once a conscious social practice which, the curator tells us in the novel, could still be observed amongst 'primitive' peoples. It is not without irony for him, and no doubt for his author, that these peoples 'am Rande des Weltgeschehens' (R 69) have preserved the art, 'geschichtliche Wendepunkte zu setzen, das heiße, die Zeit anzuhalten, umzudrehen und *rückwärts wieder laufen zu lassen*' (R 69).

Meyer is both a *poeta doctus* and a *poeta docens*. Apart from playing games of literary allusion with the reader and impressing on him or her the fact that the author is working consciously within the broad tradition of European–American literature and thought, there is a constant, if not always consistent, attempt at interpreting that tradition in a particular way. The discussion of the literary–philosophical heritage may sometimes appear like an erudite play with the encyclopaedia of European intellectual history. It may sometimes cause the same boredom as the speeches and deliberations of the Freiherr von Risach in Adalbert Stifter's *Der Nachsommer*, but, like these, there is an overall design to the erudite material woven into the narrative. While in *In Trubschachen* the intellectual universe is still rather narrow and, as in the essay 'Das Zerbrechen der Welt' (1975),[10] predicated on Kant as a major point of orientation, *Die Rückfahrt* has a greater epistemological scope; like the ambitiously wide-ranging 'Rede an Architekten', it seeks to regain philosophical positions from before philosophy became the history of metaphysics. To this extent, Meyer implicitly corrects his earlier view that it was Kant who broke the world in half. The fracture of being into physics and metaphysics, phenomena and noumena, the world of sense perceptions and those of ideas, goes back as far as Plato and Aristotle. The narrative as the authorial structuration of history in its philosophical aspect becomes part of a contemporary argument for the return to a partnership between man and nature. Not only must pre-Socratic notions of the world be retrieved, as both Nietzsche and Heidegger held; the naive, innocent and clean world of the Houyhnhnms in *Gulliver's Travels*, so frequently referred to in the novel, and that of magic practice must serve as a utopian goal in the formulation of contemporary culture and politics. To the obvious question, whether such ideas do not lead to dangerous irrationality, Meyer would no doubt reply that, on the contrary, his work is part of the 'Dialectic of Enlightenment'.

As far as one can judge from the excerpts published to date, Meyer's third novel, *Das Naturtheater*, further advances this intellectual project within the terms of fictional narrative. The title contains an allusion to Kafka's tantalisingly mysterious 'Das Naturtheater von Oklahoma', the fragmentary chapter which ends the unfinished novel *Amerika* (published posthumously in 1927). The 'Naturtheater' of Meyer's novel is a gigantic musical happening conceived, planned and organised by the German composer Walter Altdorfer. The narrator of the novel is his friend, Max Matter, a Swiss writer who, after the death of his wife, is invited to join Altdorfer in Munich as a literary consultant. The project is to reconcile, in musical terms, art and nature. A site near Trieste, significantly a town mediating between Eastern and Western thought, has been chosen for the performance. The novel, which encompasses the whole of European culture and history, rehearses a discourse, substantially within the creative élites of the contemporary culture industry, in which new contemporary awareness is being forged. The overall intention is 'unsere weltweite Bedrohung sowie mögliche neue Überlebensstrategien aufzuzeigen'[11] The narrative text is extensively interspersed with dialogue, allowing the representation of many characters' points of view. These can amount to mini-essays, for example on the corruptness and morbidity of the Austrians,[12] or the crucial role of the nobility in providing continuity and leadership in the past and having the potential today to muster forces of resistance against the surreptitious destruction of the world by science and technology.[13] Character portrayal in *Das Naturtheater* is much more graphic than in the author's previous books.

Meyer's struggle to retrieve individuality from the debris of mass existence is documented in his two novels and in the project of the third by the progression in narrative perspective from the generalised anonymity of the third person to first-person narration. In the first novel the narrator–protagonist remains unnamed because, as we have shown, his anonymity is part of the story about the outcome of contemporary history which is to be told. In the second novel there appears to be an anonymous third-person narrator, but on closer inspection his knowledge and his way of seeing things implies the named protagonist's point of view (Berger's), which in fact dominates the narrative. In contradistinction to *In Trubschachen*, the techniques of the psychological novel are fully deployed, giving detail and depth to the more individualised background of the story. The author clearly now works on the assumption that, by focusing on a protagonist who sets out to retrieve his own past and takes part in reflections on European history and the prehistory of mankind, the necessity for the fundamental reorientation of society will emerge from the intimate biography of an individual. Exemplariness is no longer achieved by showing an anonymous *res cogitans* in a narratorial position but by letting an individual embark on an autobiographical journey. In the third novel the author has chosen first-person narrative, opting for the affirmation of the reasoning self. It is as if by a bold step the alienation effected by modernity is traversed in order that self-confident individuals, at least as artists, may anticipate a post-modern project of reconciliation between human civilisation and nature. It remains to be seen whether such an ambitious undertaking can succeed or whether decadence and decay, Trieste as 'ein Sinnbild für den Untergang des Alten Europa und unsere Unfähigkeit, ein Neues Europa zu errichten',[14] will triumph in the last resort.

Notes

1. E. Y. Meyer, 'Das freie Wort', speech delivered at an international conference of the Austrian PEN Club in April 1989, printed in *Schweizer Monatshefte*, July/August, 1989, vol. 69, p. 552.

2. SM.HDF refers to E. Y. Meyer's 'Nachwort' in *Sunday Morning. Theaterstück*, Hochdeutsche Fassung, Kreuzlingen and Bern, 1987. Other references to Meyer's work are as follows: T = *In Trubschachen*, Frankfurt am Main, 1973, page references to paperback edition, 1979; R = *Die Rückfahrt*, Frankfurt am Main, 1977; page references to paperback edition, 1980; P = *Plädoyer*, Frankfurt am Main, 1982.

3. See Meyer's *Sundaymorning* (1984), in Swiss German; *Sunday Morning* (1987), in High German; and *Das System* (1983. Unpublished).

4. Martin Heidegger, *Sein und Zeit*, Tübingen, 1953 (7th edn, 1st edn 1927), pp. 126-8.

5. Thomas Bernhard, *Ungenach*, Frankfurt am Main, 1968.

6. See Thomas Bernhard, *Verstörung*, Frankfurt am Main, 1980, pp. 15ff.

7. See Thomas Mann, *The Magic Mountain*, trans. H. T. Lowe-Porter, Harmondsworth, 1960, p. 496; *Der Zauberberg*, Frankfurt am Main and Hamburg, 1970, vol. 2, p. 523.

8. E. Y. Meyer, *Eine entfernte Ähnlichkeit. Erzählungen*, Frankfurt am Main, 1975. The title story appears to be based on the biography of Robert Walser, but, like the other two stories in this collection, 'Die Erhebung der Romanfiguren' and 'Groß-Papa ist wieder da', actually explores experiences based on the author's own autobiographical material.

9. Cf. Franz Kafka, *Sämtliche Erzählungen*, ed. Paul Raabe, Fischer Taschenbuch 1078, Frankfurt am Main, 1984, p. 320.

10. Reprinted in *Die Hälfte der Erfahrung. Essays und Reden*, Frankfurt am Main, 1980, pp. 33–51.

11. E. Y. Meyer, '"Das Naturversöhnungsprojekt". Aus dem Roman *Das Naturtheater*', *Schweizer Monatshefte*, vol. 67, 1987, pp. 831–4 (p. 831).

12. See E. Y. Meyer, 'Die Fahrt durch das Land der Nekrophilen' (excerpt from *Das Naturtheater*), *Der Bund*, Bern, 11 April 1987.

13. See E. Y. Meyer, '"Reservat im Schloß". Aus dem Romanmanuskript *Das Naturtheater*', *Neue Zürcher Zeitung*, 21/22 February 1987, p. 69.

14. E. Y. Meyer, 'Das Naturtheater', *drehpunkt. Die Schweizer Literaturzeitschrift*, no. 71/2, 1988 (Jubiläumsnummer), p. 152.

10
Christoph Geiser: The 'literarische Ich' as Vantage-point
Malcolm Pender

In his speech of acceptance on being elected to the West German *Akademie für Sprache und Dichtung* in 1985, Christoph Geiser describes how his 'literarische Ich' gradually took shape in his work as the 'Verkörperung des Außenseiters . . ., als Verweigerer wider Willen, Spielverderber aus Ungeschicklichkeit'; the process was like 'die Geburt eines Ungeheuers, allerdings, für schweizerisches Selbstverständnis'.[1] It would certainly be difficult to imagine a figure more at odds with Swiss orthodoxies than the first-person narrator in Geiser's major prose works – the short story *Zimmer mit Frühstück* (1975) and the novels *Grünsee* (1978), *Brachland* (1980), *Wüstenfahrt* (1984) and *Das geheime Fieber* (1987). For it emerges in the course of these works that the narrator, raised in a *großbürgerlich* environment in Basle, has been to prison for refusing to serve in the Swiss army, earns his living from writing, journalism and selling advertising space, has left-wing political views and is homosexual. The sensational nature of these divergences from the behaviour patterns of his class is countered by the sobriety and strictly controlled formal structure of their presentation. Moreover, the 'literarische Ich', from his marginal position, succeeds in imbuing his narratives with a significant measure of much wider validity.

In the life of Christoph Geiser (born 1949), which has parallels to that of his 'literarische Ich', two dates are important in the present context. In 1967 his cousin committed suicide, an event which provoked a strategy for Geiser's own survival: 'Ich mußte dem Selbstmord eine Alternative entgegenstellen, eine andere Form der Verweigerung und des Ausbruchs' and he sought to breach 'die Mauern aus Diskretion und Tabus', which had created the pressures fatal to his cousin, by committing to paper 'eine Geschichte, die in all ihren Zusammenhängen zu erzählen war'.[2] If this family tragedy provided the initial impetus towards writing, the public events of 1968 were to impart direction. At the time of the protest movement Geiser, together with the writer Werner Schmidli, established the journal *drehpunkt*, a radical forum for literary and political discussion. Subsequently, Geiser refused to do military service,[3] and became involved with the Communist 'Partei der Arbeit' and its publication *Vorwärts*. He was later to describe his political activity as the 'archimedischen Punkt, von dem aus ich . . . meine Welt, die Welt meiner Herkunft, aus den Angeln heben konnte'; but, although this activity is a tool to understanding, it need not, in Geiser's view, itself figure in the work of the writer since it is already in the public domain; instead, the writer applies his political understanding to the private sphere since it is a function of literature 'die Spielregeln der Gesellschaft dort bloß-zulegen, wo sie am unsichtbarsten sind . . .: im privatesten . . . Bereich'.[4] Thus an examination of the particular and specific yields conclusions which have more general application.

Progress towards the creation of the 'literarische Ich' was not easy. On the one hand, the failure of the 1968 movement must have heightened Geiser's feeling of personal isolation which necessarily arose from his break with his background. On the other hand, it proved difficult to impart literary shape to his story. The poems and short stories of the early 1970s tackled the problem without providing a solution. A fresh approach in 1974 to the material of the family background encountered difficulties, and while seeking to overcome these, Geiser wrote *Zimmer mit Frühstück*, the first longer text in which he was able to give coherence to the first person narrator.[5]

Zimmer mit Frühstück is the story of a short stay in Corsica. Everyday arrangements, before and during the holiday, are detailed in a manner which suggests that the narrator is seeking reassurance from their orderly execution. As a single guest he experiences the tyranny of social norms at the hotel, which is geared for couples. Despite his initial resolve to seek a holiday resort which has 'nichts, was mich an Vertrautes erinnert' (Z 26),[6] he writes from Ajaccio to most of the names in his address book; yet he addresses in French a mother and son whom he has just heard speaking Bern dialect. And, running like a *leitmotif* through his other considerations, there is the figure of the young adolescent, constantly glimpsed near the beach and in the town. Personal habits tautly ordered as if against constant threat, failure to fit socially approved patterns, the desire for escape coupled with the desire for contact – these are all features which are to recur in later works. The presentation of death at the close of *Zimmer mit Frühstück* is, however, exceptional. With the same fastidious care expended in planning his holiday, the narrator prepares his own death – 'gar nicht so schwierig' (Z 142) –

swallowing pills and swimming out to sea. Only the final line of the *Erzählung* shows the reader that this is in fact an imagined suicide, later described by Geiser as a liberation which helped him to establish that he was himself 'ein Überlebender'.[7]

Having discovered not only 'die Familie als Thema', but also 'die Familie als latenten Erreger der Krankheit zum Tod'[8] in the course of his work on *Zimmer mit Frühstück*, Geiser moves, in his first novel *Grünsee*, towards creating for the first-person narrator the family and social background which was absent from the *Erzählung*. Initially, however, the approach is oblique: the narrator, from the perspective of the present in 1976, seeks to reconstruct an account of the 1963 typhus outbreak in Zermatt where his grandmother, the head of the family, had rented a house from the early 1950s until 1972 during the ski season. His intention is to combine what he has extracted from records such as newspaper files with what he knows of his grandmother, who, it emerges, is now unable to go to Zermatt. The novel is structured round the account of four days he spends there, thirteen years after the epidemic, as a member of his brother's house party.

If the public event provides an approach to the family background which is not too emotive, a second dimension of distance to the topic is created by the narrator's discussion of the difficulties which face him as he arranges his material: he has to present in his narrative people whom he knows well: he is undecided as to the extent to which he can adjust reality; for example, he would like, contrary to the facts, to keep his grandmother and his father (a doctor) in Zermatt during the period of the epidemic; but he would not, on the other hand, like to follow the pattern of other literary models such as Camus's *La Peste*. Thus the problem of writing in general and of fashioning autobiographical material in particular is, as with Max Frisch's *Montauk* (1975), one of the central themes of *Grünsee*.

The framework is provided by the narrator's memories, as he walks in and around Zermatt, of his grandmother's annual migration there for the months of February and March. A powerful matriarchal figure, she travelled from Bern, with two servants and an abundance of luggage, including family silver, in a manner which suggests a temporary displacement of family headquarters. From his first visit in 1954, the narrator observed the social and family rituals which dominated the two months and to which his parents and other members of the family were as docilely subservient as he was.

Gradually emerging as the central recollection against this background, however, is the story of Pingger, a cousin three years older than the narrator, who is portrayed as a high-spirited, imaginative youngster. His parents, always 'tief enttäuscht' at his misdeeds, are in the habit of separating him from the family as a punishment 'damit er selber zur Einsicht komme, mit schlechtem Gewissen und leerem Magen in seinem verdunkelten Zimmer' (G 109). Later, he resists all pressure to settle to a career, and the news of his suicide at the age of twenty-two in Sicily in 1967 during the ritual family visit to Zermatt has a profound effect, especially on the narrator. Pingger's father, searching for an explanation for the death, 'legte sich und seinen Zuhörern eine Geschichte zurecht, die ohne Gründe und Motive auskam' (G 132). The opposite extreme is provided by the glib confidence of the mass-circulation Swiss daily *Blick*, which, under the headline 'Schweizer Student von Ratten getötet' (the body had lain undiscovered for several days), makes 'eine rührende Geschichte' (G 140) out of the tragedy. The narrator recalls how, without success, he probed further at the time: 'Nachts . . . suchte ich, über mein Tagebuch auf dem Tisch gebeugt, nach Gründen' (G 135). The inadequate narratives of the uncle and of the newspaper are part of the unresolved past and, significantly, the narrator closes his main discussion of Pingger with a description of a physical reaction in the present: 'Ich würge, ich erbreche fast nichts, und möchte alles herauskotzen können' (G 146). Yet the committal to paper of these painful memories has helped the narrator to see his way: he abandons the device of approaching the family background through a public event: 'Was soll ich noch damit, mit dem Notspital, dem typhuskranken Bergbauern und dem Fieberdelirium . . .?' (G 150). He can now approach the topic more directly, and can structure his narrative in a way which can perhaps suggest connections and render motives less opaque.

The juxtaposition of recollections of the past with descriptions of the present gradually yields a picture of change: for differing reasons, family members feel less bound to appear in Zermatt, disasters such as Pingger's suicide disrupt the fragile continuity and latterly only the narrator and his brother still visit the old lady, herself plagued increasingly by physical and mental manifestations of age, until, in 1972, she decides not to return the following year. Against this depiction of a gradually disintegrating centre, a metaphor for which in Bern is the 'Garten meiner Großmutter, der allmählich verwildert' (G 156), attempts to maintain a façade look ridiculous. Pingger's father, for example, now divorced from Pingger's mother, and about to marry his mistress, 'eine Bauerntochter', gives her 'Sprachunterricht, brachte ihr das Berndeutsch der Oberklasse und die korrekte französische Aussprache bei' (G 157).

The development of the narrator himself emerges in parallel with the decline of the grandmother. If the Pingger tragedy had built up within an apparently intact structure of family cohesion, the narrator's loneliness, for example, amongst the friends of his brother in the present, is a feature of its gradual collapse. The muted indications of earlier interest in young men – 'schon damals fing es an, daß ich ihnen nachschaute' (G 135), he records in the year of Pingger's suicide – culminate in the description of his agitated excitement as he passes the homosexual meeting place beside the Swiss Federal Parliament in Bern; arrived at his home nearby, he admits: 'Ich schlucke Schlaftabletten, aber der Lichtschein des hell erleuchteten Bundeshauses, auf dem Hügel vor meinem Fenster, hindert mich jeden Abend am Einschlafen' (G 189).

If memories have helped the narrator gradually to shape his story, they have also brought pain – he wishes he had not come back to Zermatt – and a sense of helplessness at the immutability of the past: 'Erinnern heißt wiederholen, was sich nicht wiederholen läßt' (G 177). The cost of looking at the past is almost too great, but the narrator is impelled by a sense of duty towards life. In this spirit, he determines, before he returns to Bern, on a final attempt at contact with his brother and friends over a meal at the restaurant called Grünsee: 'Ich *will* . . . aus Neugier, Langeweile, Wut, Trauer oder Angst, ohne Überzeugung – alles versucht haben' (G 204). His gesture towards maintaining contact with his fellows could not be more qualified. If one result of his 'Ich-Erforschung' yields a picture of 'eine bürgerliche Schweizer Kindheit um 1960, stellvertretend: exemplarisch',[9] another circumscribes in no less exemplary fashion the limitations of the narrator's response to life now.

Like *Zimmer mit Frühstück* and *Grünsee*, *Brachland* opens in Bern. The narrator, reading his mail in the bathing establishment on the banks of the River Aare on his twenty-ninth birthday in high summer, discovers an invitation from his father. The latter has brought a small property in Alsace for his retirement and invites his son to visit him. The garden has lain untended for three years and the narrator reflects: 'Ich könnte ihm helfen; gemeinsam . . . würden wir das Brachland roden', but immediately he foresees a problem; 'Ich wüßte nicht, worüber reden. Ich habe ihm nie etwas erzählt und er mir auch nicht' (B 17–18). The ensuing narrative, which covers the period to the end of the same year in Bern, Alsace and in the family home in Basle, evokes their relationship against its central characteristic: the narrator writes 'nicht gegen das Vergessen, sondern gegen das Schweigen und Verschweigen . . ., jenes oberstes Gebot seiner Kindheit'.[10]

Significantly, one of the first memories evoked by the family house and its adjacent surgery is associated with pain inflicted by the father: the narrator as a child, about to be given an injection, sits in the waiting room 'und darauf wartete, daß er mir weh tat' (B 23). The dictates of the father dominate the daily routines of childhood and adolescence, and his membership 'der liberalen Bürgerpartei und einer Vereinigung besonders standesbewußter Ärzte' provides him with 'ein klar umrissenes Weltbild' (B 124). Yet it is part of the narrator's purpose that the figure of the father should not be demonised as was the case in several of the many 'Väter-Bücher' published in German in the late 1970s and early 1980s. For, prior to the depiction of the domestic martinet and political conservative, the narrative shows the fears and worries of the ageing doctor at the innovations made in the practice by his younger partner. The figure of the father is thus relativised by the structure of his portrayal.

This other perspective also shows the father in the role of son. The narrator's grandmother, a Russian medical student in Basle, was divorced by the husband she met there. A very harrowing period followed for the two sons of the marriage – interventions by the father in their visiting rights to the mother, her suicide attempt, her incarceration for ten years on the grounds of schizophrenia. Such was the trauma for the narrator's father that 'Grandmama russe' – who died in the infancy of the narrator – became a taboo subject. Yet he himself, as a father, adopts unfeeling, authoritarian attitudes which, in turn, create trauma and suffering in the following generation – his experience as a son has a negative influence on his role as father. Significantly, it is on the 'neutrales Territorium'[11] of Alsace during the narrator's first visit that the father, for the first time, mentions 'Grandmama russe' (B 138). It is here too that the father and the narrator move towards some kind of rapprochement, as they cook and wash up, as the father thrice admits to fears, expressed in the direct medium of his Basle dialect (B 158, 181, 184). But the limits to communication are indicated too: the narrator asks his father not to switch off a radio programme on homosexuality, but when, at the end of the broadcast, his father has not understood the significance of the request, the narrator admits: 'Da konnte ich schon nichts mehr sagen' (B 269). As his mother has remarked earlier in Alsace: 'Ein Garten, der so lange brachgelegen hat, wächst nicht in einem Sommer' (B 193).

In the case of the narrator's mother, to whom his relationship is warmer and more open, silence is again shown to ensure continuity for harmful and inappropriate attitudes. She and her brother, brought up in a *großbürgerlich* house of long tradition, were subjected to a reign of terror by a nanny who knew of their mother's adultery. On the surface, they were 'dressierte Äffchen' (B 228) for social display, whilst behind the scenes they were subjected to indignities and torments until such time as the nanny over-reached herself. Despite these indelible memories, however, the mother is never once shown to intervene benevolently in directing the lives of her sons, since this is regarded as the province of her husband. Once again, childhood experience acts as a negative force on parental attitudes. Another parallel to the father is provided when the narrator's tentative attempt to broach the subject of homosexuality in the presence of his mother (B 195) is vitiated by the same inability to express himself as she had evinced about sex instruction (B 192).

Whereas *Zimmer mit Frühstück* ignores family circumstances, and *Grünsee* concentrates essentially on the less immediate, extended family, *Brachland* deals with central family relationships. This development is paralleled by the fact that Switzerland acquires an increasingly important dimension in the three texts. In *Zimmer mit Frühstück*, the scenery on the journey between Bern and Geneva is described. *Grünsee* features a historical case of public health mismanagement in an international resort on the periphery of Switzerland and also sketches in aspects of family life in and near Bern. In *Brachland*, however, both the main setting and the historical aspects of the novel relate to wider Swiss dimensions. On the one hand, the narrator's family home in Basle, together with the other properties previously introduced in *Grünsee*, provide the basis for the depiction of a representative *großbürgerlich* lifestyle. On the other hand, the involvement in public life in the 1930s and 1940s of both sides of the narrator's family shows attitudes which cannot have been untypical of the Switzerland of the period. Had the Nazis invaded, his father's mother, a Russian Jewess, would have fallen victim to the virulent anti-Semitism of the small Swiss town where she had settled with her husband: 'Grandmama russe wäre aus mindestens zwei, wahrscheinlich sogar aus drei Gründen vergast worden' (B 189). His mother's father, on the other hand, Swiss ambassador to Berlin from 1938 to 1945, is defended by her against charges of Nazism and anti-Semitism, but her very defence makes her realise that, since he wanted the post and since he was accepted in it over such a long period, the reality could not have been quite so straightforward. Thus, in *Brachland*, the 'literarische Ich' presents not only a gradually emerging picture of 'die Familie als latenten Erreger der Krankheit zum Tod', but also, with the wider historical dimension of the novel, 'die Familiengeschichte in ihrer Verflochtenheit mit der Zeitgeschichte'.[12]

At the start of *Brachland*, the narrator had observed the male bodies in the bathing place and had reflected on 'Jäger und Wild, Abwehr und Spiel', on the rituals which take place 'in markierten Revieren und nach Einbruch der Dämmerung' (B 11). Again, as in *Grünsee*, there is the same fevered excitement as he passes the meeting place at the Bundeshaus and the strong urge, once home, to go out again. Again, too, confrontation with the past brings fresh pain. Similarly, there is a highly qualified sign of hope at the close: as they part, the narrator and his father shake hands, a form of communication akin to the 'späte Versöhnung' (B 183) which the father had with his mother. In one sense, the representative value of *Brachland* might lie in making clear the extent of the damage done within the family, since this permits the very limited scope for reconstruction to become visible. This achievement acquires an ironic dimension from the reputed reaction of Geiser's own father to the novel: 'Die ganze Tragödie gut erfaßt – aber müssen das alle Leute wissen?'[13]

Wüstenfahrt, like the three previous prose texts, begins in Bern, where the narrator has lived for the past seven years and where he now reviews a central feature of his life during this period, his homosexual affair with a married, successful and influential lawyer. For reasons which are examined in the course of the novel, the relationship, the strains within which have been sharply highlighted by a recent holiday spent by the two men in the United States, has reached a point of crisis. Whereas the minimal contours of the 'literarische Ich' in the neutral setting of *Zimmer mit Frühstück* had been followed by the painful establishment of identity in *Grünsee* and *Brachland*, *Wüstenfahrt* takes place in a very precisely defined wider social setting and brings up-to-date the examination of the narrator's past.

The committal to paper is for the narrator a necessary act of self-assertion against the ascendancy of the other man in the relationship, ironically, a motivation not dissimilar from the reasons for writing about his family. As he flies back alone to Switzerland across the American continent, he resumes work on the account begun prior to the holiday which was dominated by the behaviour of the other: 'Ich mußte, allmählich, in *meinen* Text zurückfinden' (W 59). Back at his desk in Bern, the narrator recognises his psychological need to distance himself by writing, and also his emotional need of the relationship: 'Ich kämpfte . . . um meinen *eigenen* Zusammenhang – notierend, ein pausenloses Selbstgespräch: mit dir' (W 141). *Wüstenfahrt* shows the cost to the narrator of living with these two contrary and irreconcilable needs.

Unlike Alsace in *Brachland*, the United States in *Wüstenfahrt* does not provide neutral territory for tentative reconciliation. Instead, the foreign setting becomes the 'Projektionsraum innerer Konflikte und Sehnsüchte'[14] in the relationship, into which the reader is introduced without preliminaries as the novel opens. This initial lack of framework focuses attention on the emotional fluctuations in the narrator as he reacts to the behaviour of the other in the United States. With an age difference which makes them look like 'Vater und Sohn' (W 29), and a difference in physical appearance which makes of them 'ein unmögliches Paar' (W 51), the couple follow a pattern of tourist activity which, apart from the desert itself, impinges little on the narrator because of his preoccupations. Untouched nature such as the desert is part of 'das andere Amerika', as, in another sense, is Stevy, who, like countless others, has been rendered 'vollkommen chancenlos' by 'die Effizienz der Wenigen' (W 112) and prostitutes himself to rich homosexuals such as the narrator's partner.[15] For in California the impossible couple becomes an even more impossible threesome, with the passive, monosyllabic Stevy acting in relation to the two others as 'die Schablone für die Sprachlosigkeit der beiden, nicht etwa den Katalysator'.[16]

Not the least of the strains on the relationship is the guilt experienced by the narrator at the casual manner in which Stevy was cast aside when the couple went into the Arizona desert, and this points to an essential difference between the two Swiss. Whereas the narrator has come to perceive himself as a social outsider, his lover is very much part of *bürgerlich* society. On the return to Bern, more details of their differing lifestyles emerge. The double life of the partner is symbolised by the 'Altstadtbeiz', the front part of which is frequented by the professions, the back part by 'das *andere* Bern' (W 59); in both he has a role: in the one, as a successful lawyer, in the other, as a powerful philanthropist where his business is 'solche kleine freaks wie mich gratis zu verteidigen' (W 13) (he acted for the narrator when the latter refused to do military service). The sexual aspect of the lawyer's contact with 'das andere Bern' is firmly hidden behind a *bürgerlich* façade: a career, a wife and family, a large house and garden, an immutable daily schedule. But his homosexuality is also shown to be a form of rebellion against this façade, against the pressures, 'eingezwängt zu sein in diese grauenhaften, immer zu engen Kleidungsstücke, Umgangsformen, Rollenzwänge, Machtspielchen' (W 157). Since the lawyer is dedicated, however, to preserving the constraints against which he is rebelling – 'Willst du meine Familie zerstören? Meine Existenz ruinieren?' (W 191) he asks the narrator rhetorically – he is, though in a different fashion from the narrator, in an irreconcilable situation. He is also aware that, ironically, his power in both spheres of his life is dependent on the maintenance of the façade and so, outwardly confident, he is in constant fear of discovery. His lifestyle reflects the mendacity of *bürgerlich* society.

For the narrator, the irony of their relationship is much more bitter. Having very painfully come to terms with the manner in which he has freed himself from his social background, and having constructed a correspondingly marginal lifestyle, he is now involved with a man who represents and reinforces the social contradictions with which he has broken. Whereas the comportment of the lawyer reflects the manner in which the power structures of an exactly depicted society are maintained, the anguish of the narrator symbolises the fact that the individual who has acquired some measure of personal emancipation is nevertheless obliged to continue to live in a society which itself remains unrestructured. In that sense, *Wüstenfahrt* constitutes a much darker sequel to the not unhopeful close of both *Grünsee* and *Brachland*, since change in society is shown to require dimensions of time which ignore the brevity of the individual's lifespan.

The title of *Wüstenfahrt* relates in the first instance to the journey through the desert, where, at the wheel of their car, the narrator experienced a feeling of identity with his own existence – 'nahtlos fließende Zeit, Gegenwart' (W 13) – which he never again acquires. His partner senses that the narrator is in his element, characterising him as a 'Wüstentier' (W 120). In Bern, on the other hand, the narrator's perception is constantly assailed by luxuriant greenery, at his window, in gardens close at hand, above all in the garden of his partner, the upkeep of which is the responsibility of his partner's wife. Clearly, this ubiquitous burgeoning plant life has associations of fecundity, but also of constraints and hindrances not present in the desert. In the case of the lawyer, it is also symbolic of the contradictions of his situation – he is afraid 'zugewuchert zu werden' (W 212). The close of *Wüstenfahrt* inverts the situation of its opening: the intermittent sense of fleeting liberation in the desert is replaced, in the grounds and at the lake of the lawyer's property, by a sense that vegetation is ineluctably closing in on the doomed couple. In the final analysis, the title relates to the existential situation of the narrator, who, excluded from the cycle of growth by his sexual nature and yet unable to spend his life alone in the desert, is condemned to arid lack of fulfilment in the ambiguously proliferating vegetation of *bürgerlich* society.

Das geheime Fieber examines this existential dilemma from a different perspective. In a Berlin gallery, Caravaggio's *Amor als Sieger über irdische Macht, Kunst und Wissenschaft*, in which the nude youth, grinning knowingly at the spectator from a position of supremacy over the symbols of the forces which he has vanquished, absorbs the attention of the narrator, both as a realistic and as a symbolic representation. The main section of the novel is set in Rome, where the narrator, in a series of associative passages describing some of Caravaggio's pictures and evoking aspects of his life, displays his own affinity with the emotional turbulence which he takes to characterise the life of the painter four hundred years ago. The close of *Das geheime Fieber* describes reflections and incidents connected with a visit to a Caravaggio exhibition in Naples. Alternating between past and present, between art and reality, *Das geheime Fieber* does not present a narrative so much as a portrayal of the irreconcilable forces at work within an individual consciousness.

The narrator is, on the one hand, a 'Schriftsteller . . . bemüht um Aussagen' as he seeks to impart meaning by language. He is also, on the other hand, a spectator who recognises that the pictures in the gallery stand beyond language: 'Bilder sind stumm; keine Antwort; nichts darf man erwarten' (GF 10). The contrast between the urge to verbalise and the inadequacy of verbalisation has existed since childhood. Then, for 'ein entsetztes Kind . . . im Nachtraum', language had an incantatory function: 'rhythmisch aneinandergereihte Wörter' sought to hold at bay an undefined catastrophe which the child sensed was about to engulf him and his perceived world; the threat could have been eliminated had the unknown acquired features: 'Ein Bild wäre die Erlösung', but simultaneously the child applies the trivialising assessment of his social environment: 'Doch Bilder sind bloß Kunstgegenstände, Erbstücke' (GF 90). The adult, however, is aware that the picture for which the child longed would have ordered and given shape to the inchoate, and in this respect the picture has, ironically, a function similar to that of language. But this similarity simply emphasises once again the difference between the two modes, and the writer–narrator concludes: 'Ich fürchte Bilder' (GF 12).

Another reason for his fear of pictures derives from their impact. Excited by the lifelike nature of the male statues in the Capitoline

Museum in Rome, the narrator had discovered that they lacked genital organs and had fled 'aus diesem Horrorkabinett der Anatomie' (GF 39) to a picture: 'Ein Bild, nach all den Statuen, ist wie die Rückkehr ins Leben' (GF 40), and the effect is all the stronger since the painting depicts a nude youth as Amor – 'der Bub macht mich geil' (GF 41). But, of course, the painting has one dimension less than the statue. Driven in both cases by his obsessive attraction to the male body, the narrator attributes the qualities of life to art. In both cases, the limits of art remind him also of the inadequacies of his life, which lacks the kind of union which he was tempted to seek in art.

The narrator imagines a not dissimilar process occurring in Caravaggio as the latter paints light falling on the human body – 'ein Leib aus nichts als Licht im dunklen Nachtraum'; as the painter reaches out to touch the light, he encounters only the glass of the mirrors with which he has surrounded himself – 'hier ist nur er selber, klein, verwachsen, mit angewidertem Gesicht, ins Unendliche vervielfacht sein eigener Ekel' (GF 116). Intensity of feeling causes the individual to cross a threshold, only to be thrust all the more rudely back into the unstructured reality of life. But, ironically, it is a desire for involvement in life which is suggested by the immobility of the work of art. The narrator, as he looks at a statue, imagines the body imprisoned in the stone seeking to escape 'in die vierte Dimension, in die Bewegung, in die Zeit und zu den Menschen, die ihn bloß von fern bewundern. Das wäre die Erlösung' (GF 86). In both these imaginary situations, the creator denied contact with his creation, and the creation seeking entry to the dimension where it was created, the narrator sees models of the limitations and contradictions of his own situation.

The figure of the Italian painter acts as a vehicle, not only for reflections on the genesis and character of art, but also for the exploration of the narrator's own nature. As Caravaggio sought with each picture to create a vantage-point, 'dieses nachträgliche Fenster in eine andere Wirklichkeit' (GF 67), the narrator seeks to observe, through the figure of the artist, 'die Fremdheit des Ichs mit seiner ganzen Widersprüchlichkeit und Abgründigkeit'.[17] The narrator perceives an affinity of attitude, in that Caravaggio rejected the then prevalent mannerist style and is now regarded as 'der erste Naturalist der Kunstgeschichte' (GF 16); he mounted an assault on established values and perceptions by using models from the margins of society for the great allegorical and religious themes of his paintings, and the unflinching realism of his depiction contrasts with the visual stylisations of his contemporaries.

The evocation of Caravaggio also gives the narrator access to a dimension of religious awareness no longer available in modern life. Caravaggio is racked by self-torment and by the desperate desire for release from the pain of the conflicting forces within him: 'Die Auflösung der Form wäre die Erlösung', he reflects, only to reject this as 'eine undenkbare Lösung'. An amelioration of the common lot likewise holds little comfort: 'Was nützt ihm die Erregung einer neuen Zeit, die Hoffnung auf die gemeinsame Erlösung, wenn er seine eigene nicht findet'; and the task is rendered doubly impossible in that he seeks redemption both as an artist and as a human being: 'Das Licht der Erlösung müßte am eigenen Leib spürbar sein' (GF 125f.). The narrator makes the relationship to the present clear when he transposes the imagined discussion about Caravaggio between his brother, a monk, and the cardinal who was his patron, into the framework of the modern world, where the cardinal, in the guise of 'einer dieser Dirigenten des industriellen Zeitalters' (GF 161), claims: 'Behandeln wir ihn nun wie irgendeinen gewöhnlichen psychisch Kranken, so nehmen wir ihm die Spannung, aus der er schöpft' (GF 163). If, four hundred years ago, the artist was dependent on the protection of rich and powerful clergy, in a normative, post-religious age, the artist is saved from being degraded 'zu einem trostlosen Sozialfall' (GF 163) only if his work can be commercially exploited (the pictures on the wall by Francis Bacon and David Hockney are 'unbezahlbar', GF 162).

In *Das geheime Fieber* the 'literarische Ich' seeks to express the internal intensity of the dilemma which he had shown within the framework of a social context in his previous texts, most clearly in *Wüstenfahrt*: namely, that he cannot find the fulfilment towards which his nature drives him. Like Caravaggio, he is reminded, when it seems possible that he can transcend himself, of the fact that he is surrounded by mirrors.[18] The existential insufficiency of a world which only reflects the self is agonisingly and darkly rendered in the portrayal of the barriers by which the self is constantly blocked as it attempts to express itself. *Sieghafter Amor* symbolises an attraction which, infinitely seductive, destroys. The drives and limitations of homosexuality acquire wider validity as an emblem of the desire to go beyond the confines of the personality. The last image is of 'ein im Entsetzen geöffneter Mund, der keine Luft mehr bekommt, um zu schreien' (GF 214).

The figure of Christoph Geiser provides a good indication of the extent of change in the German-Swiss literary scene in recent years. A professional writer with a committed political stance, he regards literature as a 'Freiraum für die Verweigerung',[19] but in keeping with his view that literature can reveal social attitude at work in the private realm, his concept of 'Verweigerung' goes far beyond the immediately political. In his speech of acceptance on the award to him of the 'Literaturpreis der Stadt Bern' in 1982, he addresses his fellow writers: 'Wir verweigern uns permanent dem verheerenden Zwang nach Glück und schreiben an gegen die bemerkenswerte Unfähigkeit zu leiden.'[20] It is noteworthy that, in a Swiss society whose ethos is epitomised by consumer achievement, Geiser's stress on pain as an ineradicable element of the human condition derives not only from his own experience, but also from social observation: 'Ich selber bin, bis jetzt, in meiner Literatur kein Ankläger, weil ich ringsum nur Opfer sehe.'[21] Arguably, commitment allied to sympathetic tolerance would have been much more difficult to sustain in the more restricted 1950s and 1960s.

Geiser has been concerned to show how social attitudes are created, and in this his earlier work relates to a body of German-Swiss texts of the 1970s, such as, amongst others, Werner Schmidli's *Fundplätze* (1974), Adolf Muschg's *Albissers Grund* (1974), Gertrud Leutenegger's *Vorabend* (1975) and Hansjörg Schneider's *Lieber Leo* (1980). Another major theme examines how an individual consciousness comes to terms with the emotional, social and existential consequences of homosexuality, and this also relates to a body of writing, for example to Guido Bachmann's *Gilgamesch* trilogy (1966–82).[22] But it is the unique achievement of Geiser that, through the device of his 'literarische Ich', he succeeds in imparting a general validity to both these themes, in the first demonstrating how restrictive social values are transmitted by the family, in the second showing how homosexuality is a metaphor both for general human limitation and for the longing to transcend limitation.

Notes

1. See *Deutsche Akademie für Sprache und Dichtung. Jahrbuch 1985*, Heidelberg, 1986, pp. 194–5.
2. Klaus Pezold, 'Gespräch mit Christoph Geiser', *Weimarer Beiträge*, vol. 29, 1983, pp. 1604–17 (p. 1606). For his literary distillation of this material, Geiser rejects the term 'autobiographisch', which he restricts to books 'mit dem Anspruch auf faktentreue Wahrheit': 'Mich selber gebe ich, soweit ich mich überhaupt preisgebe, nicht mit meiner eigenen Geschichte preis – sondern auf Umwegen, mit Zitaten eben, in Beobachtungen, Bildern, Metaphern, Projektionen, in bestimmten

szenischen Situationen': letter dated 6 November 1983, quoted in Martin Schellenberg, *Stoffe – Motive – Formen im Werk Christoph Geisers*, unpublished PhD thesis, University of Zurich, 1987, pp. 120–1.

3. See Marc Haring and Max Gmür (eds), *Soldat in Zivil?*, Zurich, 1970, p. 48, where Geiser characterises the Swiss army as 'ein rein im Emotionalen wurzelndes Tabu'; for a chilling description of what a military 'Divisionsgericht' dealing with 'Dienstverweigerer' was like in 1972, see Kurt Marti, *Zum Beispiel Bern 1972*, Darmstadt and Neuwied, 1973, pp. 17ff.

4. Pezold, 'Gespräch', p. 1608, p. 1614.

5. Pezold, 'Gespräch', pp. 1608–9; see also 'Ich wehre mich schreibend', *Kulturmagazin*, vol. 27, June/July 1981, pp. 33–7 (p. 33).

6. The following abbreviations are used in the body of the text: Z = *Zimmer mit Frühstück*, Basle, 1976; G = *Grünsee*, Zurich and Cologne, 1978; B = *Brachland*, Zurich and Cologne, 1980; W = *Wüstenfahrt*, Zurich, 1984; GF = *Das geheime Fieber*, Zurich, 1987.

7. Christoph Geiser, 'Sprechen aber heißt Grenzen verletzen', *Basler Zeitung*, 17 December 1983.

8. Ibid.

9. Dieter Bachmann, 'Das langsame Finden des Ich zwischen den Andern', *Tages-Anzeiger-Magazin*, 31 October 1981, pp. 52–5 (p. 53).

10. m.v. (= reviewer), 'Kindheit in Erinnerungsbildern', *Neue Zürcher Zeitung*, 5 September 1980.

11. Manfred Gsteiger, 'Verweigerung und Identität: Die Figur des Vaters bei Cherpillod und Geiser', in Peter Grotzer (ed.), *Aspekte der Verweigerung in der neueren Literatur aus der Schweiz*, Zurich, 1988, pp. 185-96 (p. 192).

12. Klaus Pezold, 'Zum literarischen Schaffen Christoph Geisers', *Weimarer Beiträge*, vol. 29, 1983, pp. 1618–34 (p. 1631).

13. Dusan Simko, 'Das Schweigen einer Familie', *Deutsches Allgemeines Sonntagsblatt*, 7 June 1981.

14. Gabriele Wettberg, *Das Amerika-Bild und seine negativen Konstanten in der deutschen Nachkriegsliteratur*, Heidelberg, 1987, p. 130.

15. See Schellenberg, *Stoffe – Motive – Formen*, p. 148.

16. Wettberg, *Amerika-Bild*, p. 140.

17. Ingrid Pohl, 'Christoph Geiser: Das geheime Fieber', *Neue Deutsche Hefte*, vol. 35, 1988, pp. 134–6 (p. 134).

18. See also Christoph Geiser, 'Der letzte Mensch': 'Leider, dachte Adam, genügt mir mein Spiegelbild nicht', in Renate Nagel (ed.), *Das helle und das dunkle Zimmer. Schweizer Schriftstellerinnen und Schriftsteller schreiben von der Angst*, Zurich, 1988, pp. 114–32 (p. 120).

19. Pezold, 'Gespräch', p. 1617.

20. Christoph Geiser, 'Literatur – die Spitze eines Eisbergs', *Der Bund*, 17 June 1982.

21. Geiser, 'Sprechen aber heißt Grenzen verletzen'.

22. Compare Schellenberg, *Stoffe – Motive – Formen*, pp. 166–7; see also Hansruedi Fritschi, 'Das langsame Auftauchen einer Figur. Der Homosexuelle in der Schweizer Literatur', *Tages-Anzeiger*, 27 August 1983.

11

Margrit Schriber: Women and Fiction in Switzerland

Mary E. Stewart

Margrit Schriber, born in 1939 in Lucerne, began her literary career in her late thirties with the novel *Aussicht gerahmt* (1976).[1] Since then she has frequently been praised in reviews for her keen observation of everyday lives, especially women's, and for her precision of language. To see her as a 'Swiss realist' is indeed tempting; she has first-hand knowledge of the everyday commercial world, having herself worked in advertising, banking and modelling, and all her novels and stories contain moments of acutely observed gesture, behaviour and interactional psychology in very normal and recognisably Swiss contexts. Others, notably Marianne Burkhard,[2] have seen her Swissness at a deeper level, noting the repeated motifs of enclosure – houses, framed windows, interiors – which she interprets convincingly as metaphors for gender-specific role patterns exacerbated by the nature of Swiss society and women's traditional place within it. Nobody has however as yet given detailed attention to the full quality and complexity of Margrit Schriber's writing, which seems to me to integrate images of Switzerland and women's lives into feminist writing at a deeper level still; this indeed also situates it in a broader European literary context, for its concerns are also with fictionality and the problem of attribution of meaning. It is entirely characteristic that her very first novel is set in a small semi-rural community and opens with an outside male *Fremder* who observes, and is observed by, the female narrative persona within a house, and that both are engaged in forms of writing. Images of isolation, perspective and interpretation are all thus immediately interwoven, but with an inherent ambiguity about the nature and scope of 'enclosure'. What is implied by terms such as 'freedom' and 'confinement', 'reality' and 'writing', and what is their relationship to each other, where gender, conventional social structures and the act of recording/ narration are all in play?

The denseness and subtlety of Margrit Schriber's writing is

perhaps best illustrated initially by looking at one small example in detail rather than a whole text in outline. In the story 'Apriko-senbäume am kreuzenden Geleise' (1977) there occurs the line 'Sich vorzustellen, daß es den Mann des Lebens gibt!' (LW 41). To interpret this apparently simple line accurately is inordinately difficult; it seems at first reading a piece of straightforward interior monologue within a poignant but unsentimental and sharply observed tale of brief romantic encounter, a what-might-have-been situation. Yet on closer attention it is an extraordinarilly complex utterance of utterly ambiguous syntax, tone and function.

On the simplest level of narrative interpretation it might indicate elegiac regret, and thus would touch on the very dominant motif of problematic male–female relationships in Margrit Schriber's plots; but its syntactical form could equally well represent joy, a real capacity for intensity of experience, a belief in *Leben*, a belief in life and hope, albeit not actually fulfilled in this story – and there are surprisingly many motifs of vitality, nature, rebirth in these texts too, which would seem perhaps to relativise disappointment. Yet such joy could also be read as selfconscious irony, especially within a story whose 'plot' reflects women's complex emotional dependence on men, and in many of Margrit Schriber's texts the motifs of nature and 'reality' or intensity of experience attach to men, not women, whose failure to realise themselves is defined by the absence or distance of such motifs. The very last line of this story, for instance, describes apricot tress glimpsed from a train window as the narrator moves between two equally unsatisfactory encounters with men. But if we are dealing with the self-irony of the narrator, does it indicate a mocking acceptance of inevitably problematic male–female relations, with echoes of deeper cultural debate such as Schiller's naive/sentimental opposition? Or is the irony directed rather at the very attempt to define women's identity by reference to men – a particularly biting irony in the context of Swiss social and political history? What kind of cultural context is being evoked here, with what range of reference?

That question in itself then highlights further problems about the status of the line in the text, not just its tone. It follows on from a piece of 'traditional' first-person narration of a conversation, picking up some of the words used there; but is our quotation a thought or comment by the same narrator, that is reflecting two 'voices' of one narrator, or is there a second narrative voice? If construed in this way, then the line draws particular attention by its dual perspective to the act of imagination in the verb *sich vorzustellen*, so that narration/writing itself becomes an issue – and one might move full circle, as it were, and relate that back to the male–female theme with which we first started: women's lives as 'written' by men, or women and 'narrative distance' as both problem and protective mechanism. Does *Vorstellung* get in the way of *Leben*? But whose imagination and whose life? Do men restrict women by their Frischean 'images', or do women limit themselves by their dreams while men simply 'live'? Does society 'write' us all? Or is it the act of standing contemplatively aside from life and male 'activity' which gives women their only possibility of freedom? Might one even construe Margrit Schriber's elements of 'realism' as a reassertion of power over reality? All of these themes and concerns are adumbrated in this one exclamation, which does not allow us to resolve which aspect is dominant either: and that irreducibility too is both characteristic of and essential to the nature of Margrit Schriber's texts.

How is all this exemplified in the wider context of her writing? Her focus may initially seem very narrow, her material anecdotal, her style 'simply' realistic: yet even at this level there is – as critics have seen – a sharpness of observation which lingers provocatively in the mind of the reader. Her interest centres on men and women in interaction, within both marriage and the family and the world of offices and banks, but also on women with other women, often mothers and daughters. The novel *Muschelgarten* (1984), for instance, delicately evokes a triangle situation – husband/sister/wife – where all three are locked in a painful struggle for emotional dominance or freedom but none can 'win' because each depends on the others in unavowed, insidious ways. The novel *Kartenhaus* (1978) focuses on another kind of family relationship: that between parents and child, showing the painful attempts of an older woman in a small village to define herself anew after divorce within a social and mental 'landscape' of traditional Swiss values and role models; but the 'house of cards' of the title refers also to the daughter's attempt to find emotional security in memories of her childhood. Both women's lives are shown to be fraught with complex defence mechanisms against male dominance, where self-protection and self-evasion are deeply entangled. Another novel, which is perhaps the most obviously 'Swiss' on the surface – *Tresorschatten* (1987) – focuses on a woman's subordinate role in the male world of a bank, sharply counterpointing the security of the context with the insecurity of institutional and emotional exploitation, which often go hand in hand. This is a theme she touched on in fact much earlier too, in stories of the 1970s like 'Hinter der Trennscheibe' (AS 63–70) or 'Montag' (AS 100–8), which capture with painful accuracy the problems of older women trying to adapt to modern office technology, and the hierarchical structures of office life. And no less painful are the brief aperçus of women in family rather than office interaction: the struggle of mothers to let daughters go, and of daughters to realise freedom. 'Rücksichtslos wäre ich freier' says one daughter in 'Moment über dieser Sandkastenlandschaft' (LW 9–15), encapsulating with memorable incisiveness the problematic tension between longing and conditioning so many women recognise in themselves. There are other stories which are painful in another sense: in their unmasking of female connivance at the competitive values of the male world, such as the biting satire on the *Kaffeenachmittag* in 'Samstag' (AS 145–51). At the level of *Erlebnisliteratur* – depiction of women's lives – Margrit Schriber has eye-opening observations and subtle, often disturbing insights in plenty. Yet her full quality emerges, as already indicated, with 'deconstruction' of the apparently simple male/female opposition which structures many of her plots.

If we look at the images surrounding this opposition we can detect repeated motifs which take us further. Men are often shown as 'naive', unquestioningly at home in their physical world and often associated with natural imagery: the father in *Kartenhaus*, who hunts and fills the house with his trophies, the husband in *Muschelgarten* who runs the 'Lion Bar'. They fully occupy their own 'space': 'Da liegt Arnold auf der anderen Seite des Ehebetts und füllt den Raum mit seinem Atem' (MG 39). Women on the other hand have problems over asserting their physical presence to the same degree: 'Es gibt Augenblicke, da halte ich mich für eine Erfindung' (VF 180); or another comments of her reflection: 'In der Nachtscheibe versuche ich ein Lebewesen zu entdecken. Ich sehe nur mein Gesicht' (AG 130). The woman who compliantly accepts her role in a male world loses her 'shape': 'Die Aushilfe gehört schon fast zur Ausstattung der Bar' (MG 45); others feel interchangeable – 'er ist früher mit jemand anderem an diesem Tisch gesessen. Ich bin am Platz dieser anderen Person' (LW 53). The image of the 'invisible' woman then becomes the dominant motif in *Tresorschatten*: in the underground world of a bank's security vaults the narrator is 'stillgelegt' (TS 16). These images of 'absence' connect with another complex, where men are shown as active, as 'doers' constantly in movement, and women as passively waiting and watching, like Sleeping Beauty (MG 80), never outside in the world but always indoors, framed by windows, focused on others for meaning and direction. Marianne Burkhard has highlighted many variants on the house motif,[3] which seems to define women's severely circumscribed existential space – and often in Margrit Schriber's work it occurs within recognisably Swiss landscapes, thus emphasising the long-term exclusion of women from Swiss public and political life: something she glimpses that they have in common with other 'non-contributors' to a prosperous society, such as the sick, the impoverished and elderly, who are also enclosed in institutions paradoxically called 'homes', particularly in the stories of the significantly entitled collection *Ausser Saison*.

The house motif is also shown as dominant in women's minds, it is the shape of dreams for the lonely female pianist at a fashion show in Margrit Schriber's one radio play, *Ein Platz am Seitenpodest* (1978). She envies both the marketable beauty of the younger models and the family life of an older one – both motifs of relative security. In other words, the house motif shades again and again into mental confinement, and leads us onto a further, deeper level of Margrit Schriber's investigation of male–female interaction, where men are perceived as givers not just of stifling security but of meaning; they are shown often specifically as controllers of language, with women as recipients, though this is an aspect of her work which has received little attention. In the story 'Grenzen eines Flugs' (LW 16–22), the text begins with the female narrator receiving a telegram from a man with whom she has had a casual affair, announcing that he will be sending no further letters. She lies in the bath with it balanced on the foam: 'Zwischen den gespreizten Knien thront es auf einer weißen Säule. Ein Anspruch auf Bedeutung, der übertrieben ist' (LW 16). The written word here very clearly links with sexual possession: both are seen as control mechanisms, and the text of the story reveals very subtly how the initial seduction is enacted through language – not literally the language of overt sexuality, but by the man's total control of language, his uninhibited use of it to conjure up quite arbitrary 'realistic' pictures of a potential life together which have no possible counterpart in actuality. It is a tool for the exercise of power, not the creation of shared meaning, its falseness evident in the self-important gesture of the telegram and the assumed significance to the recipient of the letters now to cease. A similar normal point is made in *Muschelgarten*, with the clichés of parting: 'Was er antworten soll, fragt Anton. Was möchtest du hören? Sie wüßte ohnehin alles. Daß er nichts lieber als. Aber daß. Wenigstens im Moment. Kurze Zeit noch. Abwarten. Verständnis haben' (MG 219). In the most intimate of situations the words do not communicate personal emotion and hence equality, but a demeaning, because ready-made, prescription for convenient behaviour, an often enacted male–female ritual which makes another female figure in the same novel see silence as a minimal freedom: 'Nicht antworten müssen jetzt. Nie im Leben mehr den Mund aufmachen' (MG 241). Women are the objects, not the sharers of meaning: 'Es stört den Wirt nicht, wenn sie, während er mit seiner Schwester telephoniert, im selben Raum Servietten faltet. Wenn sie mithört, was er über sie erzählt' (MG 17). And in another of many vivid pictures, Margrit Schriber captures precisely this link between language and control: 'Die Damen lauschten der Stimme, den Worten, ihre Fingerspitzen auf der Perlenschnur, die der Geliebte in ihrem Nacken schloß . . . Sie glaubten, solche Sätze seien für sie erfunden' (TS 12–13). The singular 'lover', though grammatically normal in German, certainly emphasises the interchangeability of the speech event, and the manipulative sub-text contained in the significantly unspecified words is enacted in the physical gesture, whose control aspect is rendered more obvious by the echoes of phrases like *jemandem den Nacken beugen*.

Yet these instances of linguistic control lead us further still, to a level where women are not just manipulated but in a sense created by language, not just used as characters *in* fiction but shown *as* fiction. When one of the female figures sees herself as Sleeping Beauty (MG 80), she is not day-dreaming but expressing two fundamental perceptions, about her powerless waiting role in a man's life and about the derivativeness – the 'fictionality' – to which it condemns her on the level of identity. Another image is that of female 'friendship' forged only through male mediation and embodying the man's vision, not personal commitment: 'Wir sind keine Freundinnen. Wir stehen demselben Mann nahe und müssen uns darum vertragen. Er erwartet es so . . . Wir sind dieses umrankte Bild. Die Schwägerinnen unter dem Rosenspalier' (MG 43). Again and again the word 'Geschichte' is used in *Tresorschatten* to indicate hopelessly episodic love affairs – stories, female roles and thus identities, written by men: ironically, of course, taking up a motif well established in Swiss literature by a man, Max Frisch. More significantly, the narrative complexity of the texts themselves and the constant foregrounding of 'Vorstellung' reflects how women's lives are others' creations. The narrative voice of *Muschelgarten*, for instance, is an unidentified and quite arbitrary observer who imagines what might be going on with the figures he sees: 'Und jemand, irgend jemand, denkt sich das alles aus' (MG 186). The ensuing text is highly persuasive in its psychological accuracy, but highly ironic by the same token. 'Real' lives are as fictional as fictional ones seem 'real'. Again in *Tresorschatten* a similar point is made; the narrator Magda Vogt writes both as herself and of herself as a separate figure, and it is never clear to whom the narrative is addressed – to an implied reader, yes, but is that reader separate from or identical with the narrator? Thus the self who writes as well as the one who is written about may be construed as fictional – just as in *Vogel flieg!* the female narrator both imagines and participates in the lives of the people she watches. And with wry irony, precisely the most honest of her reactions to others are written down on picture postcards and never sent, thus becoming – like their writer – a mere fantasy, image rather than actuality.

This last example, however, also draws attention to the possibility that women 'write' their own lives as much as they are written by men, by their need for security or their fear of change and adventure. Talking of the lion on the inn sign, the owner's wife comments: 'Er schlägt mit seiner Goldpranke nach mir, das ist der Preis, den ich für meine Sicherheit bezahle' (MG 51). The female narrator in *Aussicht gerahmt* has chosen to leave an office job for freelance writing, but one kind of security is traded for another, the picture window that gives her panoramic vision of the world outside guarantees also a 'Sicherheitsabstand' (AG 69). Of course this need to feel safe is created in large measure by women's lack of practice in freedom, painfully evidenced by the story 'Moment über diesem Sandkastenlandschaft' (LW 9–15), where an anxious, conventional mother tries to hide her anxiety and live up to her supposedly emancipated daughter, and the daughter attempts to fulfil that image without betraying her own fear. However, security is also shown as a particularly Swiss disease, fostered not only by women's historical social role – defined by enclosure – but also by prosperity. In 'Das Zwischenland' (LW 23–33), the female narrator's reply to an invitation to drop everything and fly away interweaves both elements: 'Ich habe aber Termine. Und dann der Hund, die Wohnung, das Geld. Und wer weiß, ob jetzt überhaupt auch Charterflüge, und darum aus der Schweiz die herzlichsten Grüße . . .' (LW 24). Later in the same volume, when a similar invitation is issued to 'be spontaneous' and leave a 'desk in Switzerland' for France, the acceptance is disastrous as much because of bad conscience as because of male manipulation ('Spielfeld', LW 106–20).

In her later works, Margrit Schriber seems to be seeing women's lives as a general representative image of Swissness rather than as specifically shaped by Switzerland. The same kind of language begins to attach to both: 'Unsere Stadt ist klein, von Hügeln umfaßt . . .' (TS 21), and both the subservient role of women and the Swiss fixation on security are embodied in the figure of Magda

Vogt. Her name links the notions of 'maid' and 'guardian', just as her job as clerk in a bank vault combines both the lowest, most exploited rank of the hierarchy and a kind of priestly ritual. Women's 'guarding' of men's self-image coalesces with the guardianship of money: 'Ein Platz, ein Stockwerk unter dem Boden im Panzerraum einer Schweizer Bank, dem Tresorkunden zu Diensten' (TS 6). In fact *Tresorschatten* represents an extraordinarily subtle and sustained interweaving of many of the images and thematic levels we have already outlined. Magda, the abandoned mistress, lacks any social or personal substance, she is the 'shadow' of the novel's title, given shape and presence only by her endless reflection in the shiny walls of the vault to which she has been banished to avoid her ex-lover's further embarrassment. But this ultimate image of women's imprisonment and 'unreality' is also the image of what lies at the heart of Swiss life. The womb-like, enclosed space of the vault is where the solemn rituals of a pseudo-religion based on money are enacted, the closeting of a client with his secret deposit box in an inspection cabinet is an image both of anxious hoarding and of the possessive love nest. Discretion, caution, order – these are the mottos of a way of life that embraces both bank and clients: '. . . die sanfte Musik aus den Deckenlautsprechern, die Kunden für unsere Dienste empfänglich macht und abgestimmt ist auf die Leistungskurve der Angestellten' (TS 51). Yet although the cult of money, of security, is the powerhouse of social life, it engenders a profoundly unreal existence from which there is no way back into the immediacy of existence, 'Einmal im Jahr bucht er Abenteuerferien' (TS 76) we read of one high official, the very formulation negating the purpose: even 'escape' is integrated wholly into order. The bank's stress on hyper-security is both symbolic and absurd, because the whole of life is already circumscribed, lacking essence. Two images in particular highlight this. The townscape is captured beautifully in calendar photos and again in a prize-winning drawing displayed with pride at the bank and ironically entitled 'eine Stadt zum Leben' (TS 21); and – with wicked humour – the official 'voice' of the bank, issuing investment advice to clients, is a fictional figure named Sebastian Clever. The bank is but an image of a general fear and search for safety which issues in routine, stereotyped lives: 'Aber was ist zu gewinnen? Eine Erfahrung und noch eine Erfahrung . . . Der Schatz im Tresor ist ein Trost' (TS 66–7). There is bitter irony in the Swiss crowds' unmasking of a fakir as a 'fake' outside the bank: 'Der Fakir blutet, ist verwundbar, ist wie du und ich . . . Mit uns nicht, Bürschchen!' (TS 89). Freedom, intensity exist only as 'Vorstellung', imagination (TS 62, 70, and *passim*), and life is eternally 'Schuld' (TS 135–6). One can hardly avoid the symbolic association of this Swiss vault with Hades or with Plato's Cave Allegory.

Margrit Schriber's work moves, then, more and more towards a general rather than a merely feminist symbolism, though the perspective almost always remains that of a female narrator. This combination is in fact a vital aspect of her writing, for precisely the classical allusions are both general and specific in reference, being well-established self-referential metaphors in women's writing.[4] Women as writers is a further thematic concern of these works, quite directly addressed in texts such as *Aussicht gerahmt*, and it has a dual aspect. On the one hand, as we have seen, the apparent withdrawal from male-dominated society into observation may be as much a product of fear and dependence as of objectivity, a transference of inhibition rather than an overcoming of it – a 'rewriting' of self that is as restrictive as men's creation of women's lives. One narrator comments perceptively of any alternative to her chosen solitude: 'Besessen, wie ich sein kann, würde ich in allem nur den einen entdecken' (LW 12). Yet that is not the end of women's 'story'. Separation, isolation, writing consciously *as* a woman may be the only positive hope of renewal. Men's lives are, after all, as circumscribed as women's, their freedom – as expressed so often in natural imagery – perhaps less a state of unfettered naivety, envied by women doubly bound by their entrapment and their consciousness of it, than another kind of unreality, a sort of narcissistic *Präexistenz* betokened by their unconcern over words. Any attempt by women to live like men is therefore a blind alley, it simply reinforces the dichotomy from which they suffer, and there is a highly amusing satire on the aggressive 'masculine' feminist who mistakes negation for resistance in the story 'Eine Ebene mit Pappelbogen' (LW 56–70). Even writing *about* women's lives simply and directly is a trap, for it implies a simple assumption of authenticity that is itself highly suspect, a participation in male forms of discourse.

What is needed is some other form of writing, and it is striking how many images of flight and movement, travel, there are in these texts, intimating a longing for a way of being that is not contaminated by the oppositions and tensions the texts also illustrate so effectively, 'schwerelos dahinziehen' (LW 143). The story 'Moment über dieser Sandkastenlandschaft' (LW 9–15), for example, deals with the pleasures of flight as unrelated 'space', as something that is neither parting nor arrival, and the title makes implicit links with childhood: the world below has the scale of a child's sand-pit toys, so that freedom is divorced in a sense from adult experience, as it is in Magda Vogt's images of happy childhood (TS 79–80). Again, the title *Vogel flieg!* enshrines an image of ideal escape; yet these images subvert themselves, the flight can only ever be temporary by definition – or terrifyingly final, as for the woman who opts out of time by killing herself at the railway station in 'Zwischen zwei Zügen' (AS 82–90). In the case of *Luftwurzeln*, 'Luft' is as easily associated with 'Wurzeln' as it is with un-connectedness. Equally, the image of childhood as ideally happy is ambivalent: it is as much a house of cards as the mother's respectable marriage in *Kartenhaus*. And travel too is associated with as many negative connotations as it is positive: restless unrootedness, running away, even dependence itself in 'Unüberschaubare Landschaft' and 'Spielfeld' (LW 82–95, 106–20). Escape, it seems, *is* only possible in images, or in ironic literary quotation: there are for instance strong echoes of the superficially positive ending of Max Frisch's *Mein Name sei Gantenbein*[5] which redouble its original irony (TS 172), and quite direct quotation from Heine on love and illusion: 'Das war im Monat Mai' (TS 60).

Yet it is precisely in images, in the conscious use of writing to re-gain control over language, that hope resides. There is no escape through pure fantasy: 'du lügst', says a child with uncomfortable directness to an imagined and arbitrary change of scene (AG 126). Yet another child offers an alternative, in resisting instruction to paint only what he actually sees and adding what he personally feels to be right and appropriate (VF 215–16). Magda Vogt's endlessly reflected figure in the shiny walls of the vault is at least a reflection that is not through a man's eyes (TS 13), and the almost relentlessly maintained female perspective, the largely first-person narrative stance in all these texts, is not a counsel of despair but in some senses a use of self-reflection as a positive step forward. The act of 'zerlegen' (LW 44), of distancing, is indeed a problem but also an act of resistance that takes many forms. Talking as *ich*, I, has both aspects – that of isolation and of confidence, a confidence that is not that of 'naive' self-narration but is enacted in the associative structure and supple, variable focus (comment, thought, narrative) of these texts, and above all in their multiple self-irony. The figures view their own fears and bondage with dismay but also clarity; they see the 'fictionality' of their lives within the power of men as 'writers', but they are also all using precisely fictionality – viewing their own actions as observers rather than simply relating – as a means of self-understanding. The same is of course true for Margrit Schriber herself. There is in her texts a quite delightful play on her own name, as also on the genre of autobiography: many details of the texts quite clearly relate to aspects of her own non-literary experience, especially childhood, but they are 'given' to fictional personae, who are in their turn, of course, the author's fictions. Such subversive games betoken a highly refined literary awareness which resists and offers a challenge to male categorisation, not least in their mocking of a well-established male preoccupation with *Identitätskrisen*. One might also draw attention again here to the many literary and mythological references in the texts. While on the one hand they underline the inauthenticity of all writing, its derivativeness – and thus are doubly suitable images for women's lives – on the other hand they represent an act of confidence, a conscious rather than a defensive reclaiming of ancient themes.

Margrit Schriber never contemplates defiance, an aggressive anti-male stance, nor does she move more than briefly outside specifically or at least recognisably Swiss settings: the understated delicacy of her touch is perhaps one reason why she has been perceived as having a rather narrow range. However, her reaction to the problems of women's lives and of life within Switzerland is nonetheless provocative. What is needed, it seems, is a consciousness that is neither male/assertive nor yet pliantly submissive. Magda Vogt's vanishing act leaves the values that oppress her untouched, as do the battle cries of Françoise the feminist (LW 61). What Margrit Schriber offers us is not a simplistic escape from Swiss/female conditioning in either direction, but a rewriting from within. She does not narrate either women's lives or Swiss actuality with continuous immediacy, though there are many passing pictures that force the reader to instant recognition and simple narrative recuperation: thus she resists the temptation of creating an alternative (narrative) security to those that she unmasks. Nor, however, does she accord Swiss conventionality or male manipulation the complicit 'honour' of out-and-out aggressive attack or blatant nonconformism, either in subject or narrative style. She is asserting a new position of ruthless honesty, a questioning of self as woman and self as Swiss, but without any false assumption of omniscience or externality, for that too would be to assume a 'male' voice.[6] Instead she finds a third way, as it were, by exhaustively exploring her own experience, filling out the contours of the known, and she then 'deconstructs' each level of understanding from within female experience, by the subtle interplay of image and metaphor. Of course there is no final conclusion to be drawn, for that would fall into the trap of logocentricity once more. What we have instead is a highly fluid and ambiguous mode of writing, one that refuses to allow us to situate thematic 'guilt' and 'innocence' clearly, one that refuses to let us separate out what is 'important' from what is 'trivial' narratively either, or to distinguish clearly between specifically Swiss and more general cultural problems. Indeed one might also say that the question of genre is fluid too: the novels have barely detectable plot structures and extremely elusive time frameworks, while the collections of stories often display a shared focus both in themes and motifs. Yet precisely this extraordinary fluidity is the strength of these texts. It may not be a radical new language à la Kristeva or Verena Stefan, but it is certainly a way of writing that represents a subversion of all neat categorisation – whether rooted in gender or nationality.

It is interesting that it is this same subverting fluidity which strikingly characterises Margrit Schriber's latest novel *AugenWeiden* (1990), which also begins to move away from a primarily female focus to a more overt concern with the interplay of constrictions between men and women, young and old, and thus perhaps marks a new level of confidence in her writing. The setting is again recognisably a small community in Switzerland, but the deeper preoccupations are more general. The title – as always – has multiple meaning, with its obvious echoes of both 'Augenblicke' and 'Trauerweiden': it hints at the fixation of ageing provincial couples on their observation (and disapproval) of figures around them as a source not only of interest but also of vicarious meaning, even self-identification, in otherwise empty lives; at the sensual attraction held by young girls for older men, the unadmitted desperation to hold time still which renders them both tragic and absurd; at the desire to shape the world around into the realisation of one's dreams – something to 'feast the eyes on' – which can become ruthlessness in the hopeful young, and sad self-deception in the need for hope of the ageing; at the way that the ageing view their own past and use that image both elegiacally and defensively. Yet nowhere is authorial judgement given, the narrative voice is more fluid and ambiguous than in any of Margrit Schriber's earlier texts, for the novel is in a sense precisely about the existential need for, as well as the dangers of judgmental attitudes. Its fluidity in a sense betokens an authorial refusal to make the figures themselves into simple 'Augenweiden'. Fundamental questions are raised: how do the principles of stasis and movement relate in modern lives? Is the couples' still centre of observation somehow 'better' or more 'real' than the closely observed but despised cars rushing by on the distant autobahn? Is it acquired wisdom to find pleasure in small things – 'Wir sind tatsächlich Lebenskünstler' (AW 183) – or is this quiet calm essentially unreal in its careful circumscription in both time and space – 'ihren Traum vom Leben für das Leben halten' (AW 143): a petrification in fear of loss? The interplay of perspectives is constant, the reader rarely absolutely sure of the narrative voice and so inescapably confronted with the central ambiguity of terms like 'reality' and 'image'.

As one of Margrit Schriber's many narrators says: 'Das Vertraute durch mein Bemerken ungewöhnlich werden lassen, das wäre schon viel' (VF 99). This is what Margrit Schriber herself has achieved, and her thematic range is constantly expanding. Moreover her consistently ambivalent discourse gives her writing a 'sentimental' vitality (including overt sensuality) which is quite equal to male 'naive' energy on the level of gender – echoing that joy which we found as one reading of our first quotation. Yet it is not only in the context of gender that Margrit Schriber has found her own voice: her writing may draw on her Swiss context, but there is here too a sophistication which quite clearly places her Swiss narrative within mainstream European writing.

Notes

1. References are as follows: AG = *Aussicht gerahmt*, Frauenfeld, 1976; AS = *Ausser Saison*, Frauenfeld, 1977; K = *Kartenhaus*, Frauenfeld, 1978; VF = *Vogel flieg!*, Frauenfeld, 1980; LW = *Luftwurzeln*, Frauenfeld, 1981, page references to paperback edition, Frankfurt am Main, Berlin and Vienna, 1985; MG = *Muschelgarten*, Zurich, 1984, page references to paperback edition, Frankfurt am Main, 1987; TS = *Tresorschatten*, Zurich, 1987; AW = *AugenWeiden*, Zurich, 1990.

2. Marianne Burkhard, 'Gauging Existential Space: The Emergence of Women Writers in Switzerland', *World Literature Today*, vol. 55, 1981, pp. 607–12; and 'Diskurs in der Enge. Ein Beitrag zur Phänomenologie der Schweizer Literatur' in A. Schöne (ed.), *Akten des VII. Internationalen Germanisten-Kongresses Göttingen 1985*, vol. 10, Tübingen, 1986, pp. 52–62.

3. See note 2.

4. Sandra M. Gilbert and Susan Gubar, *The Madwoman in the Attic*, Yale, 1979.

5. Max Frisch, *Mein Name sei Gantenbein*, Frankfurt am Main, 1964, p. 496.

6. Sigrid Weigel, *Die Stimme der Medusa*, Dülmen-Hiddingsel, 1987; reference to paperback edition, Reinbek bei Hamburg, 1989, p. 8.

12

Hermann Burger: 'Die allmähliche Verfertigung des Todes beim Schreiben'

John J. White

The inexorable 'Konsequenz' of Hermann Burger's death by his own hand on 28 February 1989 can hardly have escaped those who had been following his literary activities over the preceding two or more decades. Viewed from the vantage-point of such a final act, his writings, his life even, now seem to possess a distinct teleology. That is to say: they appear to find their logical culmination, not in the contrived 'Stechlinsche Heiterkeit' of most of the posthumously published *Brunsleben*, the first novel of Burger's planned *Brenner* tetralogy, but in the often engagingly presented, albeit remorselessly self-destructive, philosophy of the *Tractatus logico-suicidalis* of 1988 – a treatise evidently formulated with an eye to its becoming monumental in more senses than one.

The last three sentences of Burger's *Tractatus* read:

1044 Ich sterbe, also bin ich.
1045 Was zu beweisen war.
1046 Finis.

The measured nature of such a conclusion serves to emphasise the calculation with which one of Switzerland's most promising contemporary writers had, like some latterday Hanno Buddenbrook, drawn a definitive line at the end of his literary life still some time before his planned suicide. (The imperfect tense of 'Was zu beweisen war' was doubtless preferred since it was destined to be an apt temporal perspective by the time most readers came to the *Tractatus*.) The subsequent appearance of the on the whole more relaxed *Brunsleben*, which only collapses into depressive outpourings during the course of its final 50 pages, scarcely detracts from the generally unswerving nature of Burger's literary path since his first collection of poems, *Rauchsignale* (1967). For the greater part of his work has had as its hallmark a profound sense of morbidity and endogenous depression, accompanied by – and sometimes partially compensated for by – the search for an alternative reality to the contemporary Swiss world so frequently evoked and lampooned in it. And, with an increasing incessance, Burger's writings have tended to display the symptoms of a pronounced death-wish, or at least an increasingly franctic urge to escape from the anguish evoked in them. His modern fairytale, the *Eismärchen* 'Der Puck' (in the collection *Blankenburg*), is instructive in this respect. It is about a bullied boy desperately anxious, in spite of his antiquated skates, to join in a game of ice hockey with his schoolmates; he is callously spurned by them, only to find eventual solace in a magic realm at the bottom of the skaters' frozen lake, where he is duly transformed into an inanimate puck. Here, Burger has presented us with a work that can be read as emblematic of a dominant theme in much of his fiction: that of the quest for self-extinction through fantasy. For if death is one of the central phenomena in Burger's fiction, then retreat into fantasy, as the somewhat arch play on Puck the sprite and the ice-hockey puck implies, is the other. The one mode – of overtly death-fixated writing – is epitomised by his finest novel, *Schilten* (1976). The best-known examples of the alternative – fantastic – register are to be found in the three *Diabelli* stories and in *Die Künstliche Mutter*. It is between these two poles that most of Burger's other writing, both prose and poetry, moves.

'Erdbestattung', part of a whole complex of poems thematically related to *Schilten*, is Burger's personal 'Elegy written in a Country Churchyard'. It records the impressions of a 'Zaungast . . . des Todesbetriebs', witnessing a long-deceased body being exhumed to make room for a new grave:

> Ecce homo - nach drei Jahrzehnten -, der Anblick ist lehrreich,
>   Zeitig soll man den Tod aus der Nähe besehn,
> Sind wir doch samt und sonders Todes-Analphabeten,
>   Klammern das Sterben aus, sondern die Leichname ab.
>
> (KI 15)[1]

This work (concluding with the seemingly relieved words 'mir galt es diesmal noch nicht', although with Burger one can never be too sure) offers a useful introduction to the author's private, quasi-mythological 'Thanatos-Reich' (KI 37) set in the Aargau. It figures as part of the cycle *Kirchberger Idyllen*, one of Burger's more impressive attempts at countering what is here diagnosed as modern man's 'Todes-Analphabetentum'. Yet the underlying conception of death as the great educator, most prolifically and

John J. White

memorably presented in the eccentric ramblings that gradually usurp the narrator's sanity in *Schilten*, is peculiar neither to this idiosyncratic figure nor to the adjacent *Kirchberger Idyllen*. For death in one form or another haunts the pages of most of Burger's other works, as well; and not without good cause, for in the final analysis, as Grazio Diabelli puts it, 'das Leben ist eine Dissertation über den Tod' (D 72).

In 'Die Ermordung eines Privatdozenten', the first section of Hermann Burger's second novel *Die Künstliche Mutter*, Wolfram Schöllkopf of the fictive ETU Zurich ('dieser Höchsten aller Schweizerischen Hochschulen') learns with anguish of his dismissal: 'die Erdrosselung seines Lehrauftrags'. In an inaugural as Lecturer in the twin disciplines of Germanistik and Glaciology he had, for his sins, drawn attention to the fact that Switzerland's glaciers, ostensibly of such strategic defensive importance to the entire nation, had become a topic of contemporary literary interest: 'Die militärwissenschaftliche Hälfte der Abteilung [für Geistes- und Militärwissenschaften] sah es ungern, daß die Gletscher als topographische Bestandteile des Réduit-Verteidigungskonzeptes der Schweizer Armee von der jüngsten Literatur dieses Landes vereinnahmt und damit in ihrer erdgeschichtlich-strategischen Lage quasi ans Ausland, also den Feind verraten wurden' (KM 9f.). So, in the ensuing satirical scenario, Schöllkopf becomes the university's (and Switzerland's) scapegoat; the messenger is blamed for the message. His initial reaction to his sacking is melodramatic: 'Es gab zwei Möglichkeiten: diesen Schädelin [the man behind his treatment] standrechtlich abzuknallen oder auf den grießgrauen Fliesen der Gullschen Ehrenhalle zu zerschellen' (KM 11). Schöllkopf not uncharacteristically opts for the latter course of action, but is quickly thwarted in the enterprise by an ill-timed heart attack (later described as 'ein Selbstmordversuch seines Herzens', KM 112). Nevertheless, he is not one to give up easily: further remedies are always suggesting themselves, e.g. 'an einer Überdosis Kokain gestorben macht sich immer gut in einer Biographie' (KM 20). Eventually, in the final, phantasmagorical part of the novel, as a postscript to what can at best be called a caricature of a cure at the hands of the Artificial Mother (an eccentric sanatorium programme offering an elaborate form of subterranean sexual therapy as an antidote to his loveless childhood and sexual starvation in later years), Schöllkopf is metaphorically 'begraben im San Gottardo . . . liquidiert, sein Privatdozenten- und Privatpatiententum' (KM 243), only to be synthetically resurrected and split into two figures, 'Armando uno' and 'Armando due'. These siblings eventually – shades of the boy in 'Der Puck'! – transform themselves into twin inanimate objects: 'achsialsymmetrische Amphoren oder Porzellanreiterstatuetten. Wir können . . . zum Gegenstand eines Dinggedichts gemacht werden' (KM 259). In retrospect, Burger was to interpret his hero's artificial cloning as a form of 'Ersatz-Ich' solution – 'überhebliche Verdoppelung und tödliche Neutralisierung des Ichs zugleich' – and to see in the way in which Schöllkopf's deep-seated depression gives way to the Armandos' manic euphoria 'eine Art Gesundheit, aber keine, die zum Leben paßt' (AV 93ff.). In fact, this final section of *Die Künstliche Mutter* is aptly entitled 'Tod in Lugano'.

Such an obsession with extinction and with various forms of self-annihilating escape into the surreal is common enough in Burger's writings, and it usually appears to be motivated by the catalogue of childhood deprivations and emotionally impoverished later years that afflict his main characters, from Armin Schöllkopf to Hermann Arbogast Brenner. If Schöllkopf can declare 'mein Gepäck waren vor allem die Depressionen' (KM 40), so too could the majority of the later protagonists – and their creator, also. And while *Die Künstliche Mutter's* self-styled 'Penispatient' and 'Männerwrack aus dem Unterland' (KM 63) may have the effrontery to parade some contrived metaphors for his emotional deprivation ('von einer Eismutter aufgezogen' (KM 71), a case of sexual 'Lumbalvergletscherung' (KM 147), 'als Frustronaut vom weiblichen Planeten ins All geschossen' (KM 151)), what he is diagnosing turns out to be at root a common malaise among Burger's figures. As a consequence, a yearning for the love they did not have, either from their mothers or from later women in their lives, is often accompanied by thoughts of ending it all. Ambros Umberer (of *Der Schuß auf die Kanzel*) always lives with a cyanide capsule at the ready. Hermann Arbogast Brenner, the hero of *Brunsleben*, having valiantly tried for well over two hundred pages to stop his mask of late-Fontanesque serenity from slipping, likewise eventually admits that he is living on borrowed time, 'jede Seite . . . kann die letzte sein' (B 289f.). From here on, his so-called 'Tabakblätter' turn to thoughts of suicide, with repeated complaints that EXIT's brochure 'Wie bringe ich mich am zweckmäßigsten um' is callously withheld from those suffering from extreme depression. In other words he is, as he admits at one point, 'am Ende seiner Tage' (B 296). It is difficult to conceive that a novel whose material is starting to swirl down the plug-hole of clinical depression at this dizzy rate could have ever given rise to a full-fledged tetralogy. In the words of another character from this period of Burger's writing: 'Tödlich ist es, wenn ein Roman in der Tintenunendlich-keit steckenbleibt' (SK 169).[2]

Both death itself and various surrogate modes of 'tödliche Neu-tralisierung des Ichs' are Hermann Burger's stock-in-trade. In addition, the imagery of death is often exploited for its metaphor-ical potential, as when, at the moment of his calamitous 'Hokuspo-kuskrise', the great 'Prestidigitateur' Grazio Diabelli, describing himself as being both professionally and existentially 'vernichtet', declares: '[ich] geisterte . . . schon längst nur noch als scheintoter Artist durch die Varietés Europas. . . . Meine Devise kann . . . nur heißen: perire et delectare' (D 32f.). Burger's final creation, the cigar manufacturer and bon viveur Hermann Arbogast Brenner, shares Diabelli's interest in magic, and in particular in Houdini, and for equally fragile reasons: 'Nur derjenige nimmt zum Illusionis-mus Zuflucht, der an der Realität mit ihren physikalischen und juristischen Gesetzen restlos verzweifelt' (B 305). However, during the course of the novel his despair, far from being sublimated by such interests, gradually develops into an extreme depression, a state of mind which he equates with spiritual death. In the wake of thoughts about Flavia Soguel, the lost love and mother-substitute who is a recurrent motif in so many of Burger's works, he defines his depression as 'ein umfassendes Schirmeinziehen . . . ein Tot-stellungsreflex ebenso wie eine Demonstration in äußerster Not, die Transmitter hören auf zu springen, weil der Kranke eine Meta-pher braucht, die nach außen schreit: Seht, so hundsmiserabel geht es mir!' (B 327). But such a living death has at least one redeeming feature: it is not death itself. 'Der endogen Depressive ist der Ausgestoßene der Schöpfung, [aber] . . . es fehlt ihm die Kraft, Hand an sich zu legen, irgendwie wäre es auch nicht logisch, denn für die Hinterbliebenen ist er bereits gestorben' (B 330).

Elsewhere, on a more literal plane, Burger's characters' thoughts spiral obsessively around the subjects of 'Tod' and 'Scheintod'; in particular, the nightmarish predicament of coming round to find oneself buried alive within the claustrophobic confines of a coffin. Whole sections of *Schilten* and its 'Satyrstück', the 1988 story *Der Schuß auf die Kanzel*, are concerned with the possibility of 'Schein-tod'. The latter not only contains a lengthy discussion of Gottfried Keller's lugubrious cycle of poems 'Lebendig begraben', but in-cludes a description of how the narrator of *Schilten* allowed himself to be buried in a coffin for a brief period, just to experience at first hand what it would be like. Referring to Christoph Wilhelm Hufeland's classic work on the subject, *Der Scheintod*, the narrator of *Der Schuß auf die Kanzel* remarks that '*Schilten* könnte direkt in den Hufeland münden' (SK 105). The same could surely be said of numerous other works by Burger. Graveyards, mortuaries, early deaths, murders, fatal illnesses and a recurrent toying with the possibility of prematurely ending one's own life leave their maudlin stamp on most of his fiction. Burger's dissertation[3] was tellingly on the work of another suicide, Paul Celan, and from its writing onwards, as the *Tractatus*, above all, bears witness, his interest has been as much in real suicides as in fictive ones.

It would be intellectually satisfying, in the light of Burger's remark about our 'Todes-Analphabetentum', to be able to equate these concerns with some large-scale endeavour at 'Todes-Aufklärung'. But the host of *momento mori* markers which Burger puts down in his novels, poems and short stories are less unified in function and mood than this would suggest. At times, death is contemplated with serenity and even longed for, as in the case of the *Tractatus*. On other occasions, human mortality can be invoked in states ranging from abject despair to simulated self-pity. The preoccupation with bodily decay and the nightmare of 'Scheintod' are usually the products of a state of angst, yet sometimes it is an anguish decked out with such scintillating rhetorical effects that one has the impression that Burger is all set to laugh his way to the coffin. On some occasions, the voice is unmistakably personal, elsewhere quasi-philosophical. But we are dealing with more than just a range of psychological registers and a matter of character portrayal. A sense of topographical gloom and pervasive 'Todesverfallenheit' is also a frequent feature of the author's concern with the Swiss landscape, with its eerie mountain passes, protective glaciers, gloomy valleys and remote communities. (Tellingly, the few brief happy months with Flavia Soguel recorded in *Die Künstliche Mutter* are spent in Zurich, not in one of Burger's usual depressing rural settings.) With reference to *Die Künstliche Mutter*, Burger speaks of his need 'die Schöllkopfsche Psychosomatik und Depression zu lokalisieren, in Landschaftszwänge umzuwandeln' (AV 78), a process which has its equivalent in *Schilten* and in much of the other work that was to follow. Indeed, one can detect in almost every chapter of *Schilten* the extent to which a key mentor (and fellow suicide), the Austrian Thomas Bernhard, has left his imprint on Burger's handling of the Swiss environment.

In *Schilten*, the work which established Burger as an up-and-coming writer, the village schoolmaster Armin Schildknecht – the name in fact turns out to be a *nom de plume* – is, with the help of his pupils, engaged in writing a manically detailed and intensely solipsistic 'Schulbericht zuhanden der Inspektorenkonferenz' (the work's subtitle). This long document is intended to explain and even justify the abnormal 'Schiltener Lehr- und Lernverhältnisse' he has singlehandedly introduced and which eventually become his downfall. Burger was later to describe his 'original', the first in a whole line of grotesque eccentrics that people his prose, in generic terms as 'einen verkrachten Wissenschaftler in der Manier eines auf Aberwissen spezialisierten Polyhistors' (AV 19), a description that would not be that far off the mark if applied to Burger himself, for the author's work surely belongs to the widespread contemporary fashion for 'Neue Subjektivität' rather than any over-disguised, indirect form of 'Erlebnisdichtung'.

The 'Gräberperspektive' of Schildknecht's isolated school, standing next to the village cemetery, encourages – as well as symbolises – the 'komplizierte Verfilzung von Friedhof- und Schulbetrieb' (S 8f.) we are to hear so much about as the novel unfolds. Through the demented schoolmaster's meticulous yet meandering report we are gradually initiated into a strange world in which the school doubles (*faute de mieux*, yet in splendid conso-nance with its pedagogue's warped purposes) as a mortuary and somewhere where he can live in solitude, 'totenwächterhaft' (S 48), among the tools and bric-à-brac of the mortician's and the gravedigger's trades. Thanks to the hold of this strange environ-ment, and more specifically as a result of Schildknecht's mental aberrations, all pretence at conformity to the statutory Swiss school curriculum has been abandoned, and the pupils of this rustic 'Einförderklasse' have been progressively reduced (raised?) to the status of 'Friedhof-Eleven' (S 79). Under Schildknecht's tutelage, 'Heimatkunde' has given way to an all-consuming 'Friedhofkunde' (S 134); 'im Grunde genommen', as the teacher is the first to admit, his lessons have become no more than 'eine Kontrafaktur zur Arbeit des Totengräbers' (S 271). The extent to which Schildknecht has succeeded in perverting the established school system can be gauged from the following proud declaration: 'Zwei Dinge . . . verlange ich von meinen Schülern am Ende ihrer Schulzeit: daß sie ein Verschollenheitsverfahren einleiten und einem Scheintoten Erste Hilfe darbieten können' (S 242). Certainly, we have en-countered much ghoulish interest in the idea of people disappearing without trace, and it and the phenomenon of 'Scheintod' become *idées fixes* both during the course of this manic 'Schulbericht' and in various subsequent pieces of fiction, especially *Der Schuß auf die Kanzel*. Nevertheless, the reader would not have been surprised if the minimum competences demanded of leaving pupils had been the ability to dig an aesthetically pleasing grave, demonstrate detailed knowledge of the stages of a corpse's decomposition or of embalming and burial rituals peculiar to the Aargau canton. For, throughout, attention has been lovingly lavished on a whole host of burial practices: the measuring out and excavation of graves, the exhumations necessary for the recycling of hallowed ground, the ringing of the death-knell, the customary burial-alignment of coffins, the inscriptions on gravestones, and even prurient details concerning taxidermy and the preparation of the deceased for interment.

The narrating schoolteacher's 'eigenwillige Methoden', as the 'Nachwort des Inspektors' calls them (S 304), constitute a one-man crusade against not only his pupils' 'Todes-Analphabetentum' but also, surely, our own. For although we witness a situation where the deranged Schildknecht finds himself progressively deserted by his few remaining charges on account of his idiosyncratic methods, and is eventually relieved of his post and consigned to psychiatric care (according to *Der Schuß auf die Kanzel*, he will go on to commit suicide), his ideas can be seen, in the last analysis, as little more than a mild caricature of those of his own author. A juxta-position of *Schilten* with the *Kirchberger Idyllen*, *Der Schuß auf die Kanzel* and the *Tractatus logico-suicidalis* would soon show how much of Burger there actually already is in Schildknecht. If one can detect a difference, then it is perhaps in a respect that Burger was to highlight in his Frankfurt lecture on this novel: 'Schildknechts großer Irrtum . . . liegt in der Annahme, man könne dem Tod den Stachel nehmen, wenn man ihn in den Unterricht integriere und verbalisiere' (AV 37). Burger himself could never have maintained that pitch of naivety – or, at least, not for long. But the novel's gradual transition from polemical satire on a teaching profession that had scarred Burger for life to the status of a positively con-ceived, encyclopaedic 'Todesbuch' (AV 37) means that we are dealing with more than just an example of schizophrenic obsession. In its undoubted act of revenge against the teaching establishment,[4] *Schilten* evokes a counter-reality dearer to Burger's heart than is revealed in his later dismissive remarks about the narrator's de-ranged 'didaktische Systematisierung des Unsystematisierbaren' (AV 49).

'Der Friedhof ist in die Landschaft eingebettet', the schoolmaster proudly remarks at one point (S 142). So too, of course, are the village school and the protagonist himself; and it is, as Werner Erne's 'Materialienband' *Schauplatz als Motiv* demonstrates, a closely observed, largely real landscape.[5] *Schilten*'s source village and the Schiltwald are to be found in the Aargau; Burger has based his fictive school on a tangibly three-dimensional real region and established a whole series of connections between its parochialism and Schildknecht's eccentricities. (Burger was later to refer to 'die Dämonie des Ortes, die Landschafts- und Architekturzwänge . . . die hermetische Welt von Schilten', AV 29). The all-too-familiar ritual caveat at the beginning of *Die Künstliche Mutter* – to the effect that 'Alle Personen und Örtlichkeiten dieses Romans sind frei erfunden, selbst dort, wo Namen aus der realen Topographie übernommen wurden' – remains programmatic for the novels *Schilten* and *Brunsleben* and for most of the short stories and poems set in Switzerland, but it does not prevent the reader from detecting a whole range of highly complex refractions between Burger's fictional *Mater Helvetica* and his actual native country. Neverthe-less, Burger was always tickled at the credulity of many of his readers, when it came to his subtle amalgams of fact and fiction. Thus, much to his amusement, Schildknecht's spoof observations on the linguistic peculiarities of the local dialect – 'eine Oberschilt-taler Spezialität, die sonst nirgends in der schweizerischen Sprach-geographie bezeugt ist, nämlich die konjunktivisch gemeinten Substantiv-Umlaute . . . "de Töd" für einen eventuell eintreten-den Tod' (S 185) – resulted in Burger being inundated with requests from professional linguists for further details.[6]

But, of course, despite the mock-Swiss elements in *Schilten* and the pronounced use of regional dialect in *Brunsleben*, it is not for such linguistic local colour, be it overtly spoof or largely authentic, that Burger's language is primarily remembered, but for its riotous artificiality, its rich neologisms and sheer vigour. He is, to use the words of Ambros Umberer, a 'Solözismen-Radebrecher' of the first order (SK 71). Yet there is more to this feature of Burger's work than mere surface verbal bravura.

To take a simple example: the schoolboyishly suggestive list of guests at a 'Sittlichkeitskongreß' – 'aus Frankreich habe Kardinal Archevec c'est mon tour teilgenommen und aus San Remo Conte Onanini, der Chinese Hymen Peng sei ebenso vertreten gewesen wie Verena Immerschwanger aus dem Schanfigg, Schweden habe seine Exzellenz Gunnar Tripperstroem entsandt und der Spanische Hof den Grande Laß-sie-ran-cho-denn-sie-will-ja' etc. (KM 61) – is in a manner superficially reminiscent of the guests named after trees in the 'Cyclops' chapter of Joyce's *Ulysses*. Nevertheless, there is usually no more than a deceptive veneer of jolliness to such verbal antics, in Burger's case. For as Elsbeth Pulver rightly stresses, in the best analysis of Burger's style outside the author's own indis-pensable 'Frankfurter Poetik-Vorlesung': 'Das Gewebe von Wort-witz und Wortspiel, von humoristischen und kuriosen Einfällen ist so dicht und so bunt, daß die Verzweiflung, die sich dahinter versteckt, leicht übersehen wird.'[7] Certainly, this interplay between flamboyant surface and a strong undercurrent of inescapable pessimism is a crucial feature of works like 'Diabelli, Prestidigitateur' and *Die Künstliche Mutter*. What one can detect in such instances is a connection between the sombre themes touched on so far (deprivation, emotional isolation, a fixation with death) and something that may at first appear to be an innocent rejoicing in the German language's resources for inventiveness. Sometimes, Burger's language successfully masks the underlying pain, sometimes it acts as little more than frenetic compensation, but seldom is it verbal play for its own sake.

Having introduced the (for Burger) painful central subject of 'innere Verstümmelung' (D 76) by reference to his own emotionally deprived early years, the illusionist Diabelli admits 'daß [er] im Kaschieren besser geübt ist als im Entschleiern'. Both this bald professional admission and what he goes on to say about his style are as much Burger speaking *pro domo* as the confidences of the story's ostensible subject: 'Der Vortrag des Täuschungskünstlers ist ein wahres Feuerwerk von Anaphern, Oxymora, Tautologien, Euphemismen, rhetorischen Fragen und Paraphrasen; Winkelparliererei und metonymischer Mummenschanz. Eine Mauldiarrhöe sondergleichen' (D 81). In the performer's 'Hang zu Superlativen, zu Apodikta . . . die Vorliebe für die Präfixe ultra-, super-, hyper- etcetera' we see a surface rendered deliberately dazzling in order to mask deepseated anxieties (no wonder so much interest is shown by the narrator in theatrical Houdini's courtship of death for most of his career.) As far as such linguistic virtuosity and its ability to deceive are concerned, 'jeder ist sein eigener Prestigeprestidigitateur' (D 82f.); but, in the case of this frenetic work, the resultant display is on the whole more a product of existential angst than the literary equivalent of the illusionist's performance.

As the reader knows to his or her delight, Burger has always revelled in the richness of specialist vocabularies: the patois of the magicians' circle, Swiss argot, the technical terminology of the wintersports world or the cigar industry, medical or psychiatric jargon, the in-language of model railway buffs or the vocabulary of the Swiss public transport system, not to mention the idiolects of his own two main fields, architecture and Germanistik. But as his work progressed, what began as a series of bravura performances – Diabelli's initiation of the reader into the mumbo-jumbo of the magician's art or Schildknecht's savouring of the language of the necropolis – gradually assumed a more desperately manic quality. Thus, when Wolfram Schöllkopf, 'Doktor Infaustus', as he likes to call himself, reports his sacking at the beginning of *Die Künstliche Mutter*, he emits a veritable smokescreen of rhetoric to hide the clearly painful link between this unloving *Alma Mater* and his childhood sufferings at the hands of his real mother: 'Was war das für eine Schreckensmutter, diese Alma Mater Helvetica, von nähren konnte weder im pekuniären noch im übertragenen Sinn die Rede sein, eher von akademischem Liebesentzug; ein Privatdozent war ja genauso wehrlos wie ein blaugeschrieener Säugling, der vergeblich nach der monumentalen Kuppelbrust verlangte' (KM 14). As we move disconcertingly between manneristic allegorising images of the campus buildings as embodiments of the University-Mother's mammary endowments, and parallels between various unloving mother figures (the hero's actual mother, the ETU, the Swiss Motherland, the subterranean 'mother earth' of the Artificial Mother cure, and even the Mother Church, castigated in the person of the Virgin Mary for not doing more to prevent the events of the crucifixion), we sense a deeply scarred man, frantically 'camping it up' by making an elaborate verbal performance out of his emotionally deprived and ultimately suicidal predicament. It is an act that can be viewed as part indulgent self-pity and part an attempt at defusing the anguish through verbal play. Or, looking at it another way, one could say that the narrator is both the baby crying until it is blue in the face and also the dazzlingly precocious Germanist able to watch and wittily subject the infant's problem to a whole battery of literary analogies and rhetorical effects.

A comparable strategem can be observed when Schöllkopf prepares to unburden his sexual problems on the reader: 'Mir gab . . . kein Gott, zu sagen, wie ich leide, ich gehöre als Chronischkranker und Malefizenz zu jenem Teil der Menschheit, der in seiner Qual verstummt' (KM 141). In actual fact, far from maintaining a respectful silence, he gleefully decants his sufferings into ornate image after ornate image, yet doing so with contrived verbal gusto, not just introspectively, as he tries to communicate the cause of the depression which eventually leads to his treatment in the latterday 'Zauberberg' that is the setting for the main part of the novel.

Here is the way he indicates that his problems, requiring treatment at the hands of 'die Künstliche Mutter', largely stem from the way he was maltreated by his real mother: 'mich, das Phänomen, das die Plauder-Psychotechniker als maternelle Deprivation umschreiben. . . . Das Schlimme ist, Verheerende, daß ich mich an

keine einzige Zärtlichkeit erinnere. . . . Es bräuchte Tausende von
Miss Worlds, diesen Schaden zu reparieren!' (KM 138). The problem is that the Miss Worlds he thinks he needs to conjure up to
compensate for these early experiences can be no more than the
products of mere verbal ideation. Hardly surprisingly, then, his
literary forays into the erotic tend to be symptoms of, rather than
panaceas for, his emotional state, and in fact drive him more
irresistibly to the brink of suicide rather than offering any release:

> Dem bei Mädchen mehr vermuteten als diagnostizierten Penisneid
> müßte Wolframs Penisschmach gegenübergestellt werden. . . . dieses
> beginnende Würmzeitalter meiner Lumbalvergletscherung gipfelte im
> Eid am Krankenbett [meiner] Mutter, nie mit einer Frau zu schlafen, es
> sei denn mit der Nupturientin in der unbefleckten Hochzeitsnacht.
> (KM 147)

When he talks of the painful memories of Flavia Soguel, the one
person who might have rescued him from his predicament,
Schöllkopf again takes sorry refuge in an elaborate linguistic defence mechanism. Memories are artificially kept at arm's length
through a form of self-consciously applied multiple intertextuality:
she is introduced as 'die erste Blondfrau, an der ich nicht gescheitert
war als Tonio Kröger-Spezialist' (KM 32). Flavia is also so frequently compared with Ingeborg Bachmann that Schöllkopf finds
himself steering an uncomfortable path between trying to reduce
her to the status of a literary memory and taking on board the role
of being Max Frisch's double in a problematic relationship. All this
is part of a general attempt at anaesthetising painful experiences
through a process of *Literarisierung*: 'Hero und Leander, Philemon
und Baucis, Romeo und Julia in der Altstadt: in Flavias Gegenwart
wurde die Literatur wahr, Mulieribus poetarum opus est, ars
amandi, nicht ars moriendi' (KM 28). Or, to take another example,
the self-lacerating diagnosis of his predicament after Flavia's death:
'Hinter der Inge Holm-Projektion steht der kühle Vamp der
fünfziger und frühen sechziger Jahre, das Babydoll-Gesicht
Marilyn Monroes, die chirurgische Maske einer Kim Novak. Tat-
sache ist, daß Sie sich an all diesen Frauen zutode erkältet
hätten, . . . denn Ruhm und Glamour, Pelze und Colliers, Wasser-
stoffsuperoxyd und Mannequinbeine, das sind zu Schranken aufge-
baute Äußerlichkeiten. Sie haben sich verliebt in das Prinzip der
Uneinnehmbarkeit' (KM 193).
    It is this stubborn love for the unattainable which finds its
frustrated expression in paroxysms of verbal excitement about

what Schöllkopf has been deprived of by his mother's destruct-
ively powerful hold over him: a mixture of the maternal and the
libidinous:

> 20th Century-Fox, o Glamour, Glanz und Gloria: Wäre das etwa zuviel
> verlangt gewesen, notfalls aus einer der unzähligen Kebsehen des
> Schwedischen Eisbergs hervorgegangen zu sein oder die Jugend als
> Adoptivkind Ingrid Bergmans verbracht zu haben, ständig auf Reisen,
> in Palace-Hotels: Mutterliebe aus dem Koffer? Dafür wäre aus diesen
> Koffern und Hutschachteln und Beautycases gequollen, wessen ich ein
> Leben lang entbehrte: rauschende Toiletten aus Crêpe-de-Chine, anis-
> gelbe Seiden-Satin-Negligé-Phantasien, Lachs- und Champagnertöne,
> Parfumflacons und Perlencolliers, Pelzmäntel und goldgefaßte Lippen-
> stifte: die Accessoires der Weltweiblichkeit und Schönheit, das heidni-
> sche Zubehör der Venus. (KM 136)

As these illustrations indicate, Schöllkopf's condition can only find
an outlet in a series of compensatory verbal forms, but the outlet
offers no real solution, something more radical than that will
eventually be required. Elsewhere, we find him repeatedly trying
in vain to sublimate: e.g. in his lascivious poring over the visual
language of lingerie in women's underwear advertisements (apolo-
getically presented as his attempt 'eine Grammatik des Weiblichen
anzulegen', KM 183); in his grandiose metaphor of the Collected
Works of his Suffering ('alles Schöllkopfsche Erstausgaben, in
Leiden gebunden, sozusagen eine historisch-psychosomatisch-
kritische Edition der Mamamnese, Papamnese und Katamnese',
KM 190); and, over and over again, in his frantic desire to see
painful experiences through the spectacles of comparative literature. Take, for example, the way in which his Faustian (therapeutic) journey to 'The Mothers' is presented in a strange amalgam
of winter sports and literary imagery: 'Mephisto trat als Spielleiter
an die Rampe in seinem schwarzen, inseitig scharlachrot
gefütterten Radmantel und sprach; Especially for you, Mister
Schöllkopf, the Downhill to the United Kingdom of the mother-
in-laws' (KM 205).

After the hyperbole and sometimes even shrillness of such effects, Burger's final phase was to take him in two fresh directions:
first, in the attempt, in much of *Brunsleben*, to counteract the
mother-fixation and depression of most of the previous fiction by
a tranquil recollection of the early years of Hermann Arbogast
Brenner, man-of-leisure and self-indulgent cigar connoisseur, a
work which, though incomplete, was clearly intended to become

Burger's *A la recherche du temps perdu*, *Der Stechlin* and *Buddenbrooks* all rolled into one, until, unfortunately, it collapses in its later chapters into morbid introspection and suicidal despair, this time largely unrelieved by the verbal wit of the earlier fiction. And second, in a mock-Wittgensteinian treatise on the subject of suicide: suicide as a philosophical concept, the contemplation of suicide as a way of life, the thoughts of suicides in history and suicide as a literary topic. The resultant chain of aphorisms and literary excerpts can be profitably read as a *post mortem* on so many of Burger's earlier works and as an *ante mortem* to what little was left of the author's own life.

The book in question, *Tractatus logico-suicidalis*, is presented as a systematic contribution to the two related disciplines of 'Totologie' ('die Lehre und Philosophie von der totalen Vorherrschaft des Todes über das Leben') and 'Suizidologie' ('die Selbstmord-Wissenschaft', T 19[8]). In 1,046 entries, the reader is offered a series of aphorisms, notes, excerpts from other sources and *obiter dicta* on the subject of death and 'Selbsttötung'. Invented quotations exist alongside extracts from genuine writings. Thus, we have the fictive entry:

> **81** Der Tod ist nicht nur das Ende des Lebens, er ist auch das Heilmittel gegen das Leben. Nirgends ist man so gut aufgehoben wie in einem Sarg. (Mahnteuffel, *Totologie und Ontologie*)

and, in another vein:

> **202** Heinrich Heine sagt: 'Gut ist der Schlaf, der Tod ist besser - freilich / Das beste wäre, nie geboren zu sein.'

In an effective mixture of tongue-in-cheek academicism and deadly earnest, Burger, himself by now on the verge of suicide, devotes much space to speculations about what someone's death does to those who are left behind. We are offered, in addition, a veritable *Who's Who* of the great suicides of the past ('Jeder Selbstmörder wird in letzter Sekunde in die Familie all derer aufgenommen, die "es schon getan" haben'; No. 677). The subject of suicide is looked at from many angles and treated in many diverse moods. At one stage, it is seen as the most sensible personal step to take, given the ecological state of the world and its likely 'Omnizid' (No. 243) in the foreseeable future. Elsewhere, it is viewed more historically:

> **807** Im Genie-Kult des 18. und 19. Jahrhunderts war der frühe Tod der

natürliche Preis für außerordentliche Fähigkeiten. Es scheint, als habe der Tod besonders Mühe, diesem Treiben der gefährdeten Elite lang zuzuschauen.

The suicide is often seen as someone heroically pointing the way to others: 'Er setzt auf die Lehrbarkeit seiner Tat' (No. 630). 'Das mutige Beispiel, das er gibt, ist so epochal, daß man sich fragen muß, weshalb nicht jeder publik gewordene Suizid eine Selbstmordwelle auslöst' (No. 244); 'das Suizidal-Opus' is only complete 'wenn dem Helden nachgestorben wird' (No. 246). Indeed, Burger supplies the reader with much meticulously presented information about the relative merits of various methods of terminating one's life. Yet at the same time, other entries stress the essentially personal nature of the *Tractatus*. For example, No. 932: 'Der *Tractatus logico-suicidalis* ist die einmalige Begründung eines einmaligen Suizids.' No wonder Burger's readers were at a loss as to how to react to it, when the work appeared![9] But for all its enigmas, this treatise remains more than just a literary curiosity, given a further anecdotal twist by the author's suicide a year after it appeared. It is both the most detailed commentary on Burger's entire 'suizidographisches Werk' and a richly ingenious exploration of an important aspect of life: its ending.

At one point in the *Tractatus*, Thomas Bernhard is hailed as the ultimate *poeta doctus suicidalis* (No. 121). And no doubt with this work Burger set out to create, for his part, a mock-philosophical counterpart to Bernhard's work. In doing so, he also supplied the reader with a systematic justification for his own imminent suicide and something of an epitaph for much of his previous writing.

Needless to say, Burger was well aware, toying with the subject as he had for so long, of the impact and repercussions which both the *Tractatus* and his companion act of suicide would have. 'Genau so, mit zerbrochener Kopfsäge sezieren und obduzieren die Hinterbliebenen ihren Selbstmörder, schneiden ihn auf und nähen die Cavitäten wieder zusammen, wenn nichts mehr von ihm übrigbleibt als das zum Alibi umfunktionierte Motiv' (No. 657). But Burger was evidently unwilling to let those left behind – us, his readers – have the last distorting word. In a series of entries in the *Tractatus* devoted to the subject of Kleist's suicide, he seems to come closest to preparing for the reception of his own future act, especially in the following one:

650 Auf Kleists Grabstein müßte stehen: 'Und er hat recht.'

No doubt Burger would have wanted this to be his own epitaph, if he had not in a sense been writing it for the past two or more decades – encoded in his fiction, his poetry and even in his literary essays. So instead, he eventually made it into the inscription on the gravestone of Armin Schildknecht, the narrator of his first novel *Schilten*.[10]

With the late story *Der Schuß auf die Kanzel* of 1988, where we hear about this gravestone, we come to a revealing moment in the author's development, when Burger not only returns to one of his earliest creations but also, ominously, appears to bring him back from the limbo to which he had been previously consigned merely in order to seal his fate, irrevocably this time, with a suicide. At one stage in this strange footnote to his best-known and arguably finest novel, Burger has Peter Stirner (alias the 'Armin Schildknecht' of *Schilten*) imagine in vivid terms what the death which his author now has in store for him (and for himself, it might be added) will be like: 'Dann plötzlich bist du im schwarzen, konisch nach unten verlaufenden Raum mit der Exit-Falltür, bist aus der Schöpfung ausgestoßen, der Logik des Lebens entfremdet, der Todeslogik verfallen, die da heißt: de nihilo nihil, wie in der Magie, der Zauberer und der Tod' (SK 111). But then, hard on this, comes the compensating thought that 'nihil' is hardly the right word. Rather than creating nothing out of and about the vacuum of depression and death, such suffering can also be productive; and in Burger's case as well as that of this particular protagonist it clearly was: 'Das Kranksein ist mit dem Schreiben gekoppelt.' And, as his achievement with *Schilten* comes to Schildknecht's mind, we are informed: 'Je unheilbarer das Leiden, desto reiner die Form, wir müssen vollständig unten durch, dann oben hinaus.' The first part of this path is taken by most of Burger's characters, for they all seem to go through the caverns of depression and pace the graveyards of despair evoked in *Schilten* and *Die Künstliche Mutter*. But only some manage to find their way up and out ('oben hinaus'). It might be argued that the Schildknecht of *Schilten* had in a sense managed to write his way 'oben hinaus', only to find himself pushed back down again by the author of *Der Schuß auf die Kanzel*. Similarly, a Burger who had thematised suicide so often without committing the act itself, must have been thought by many to be 'oben hinaus', even after the appearance of the *Tractatus* and *Der Schuß auf die Kanzel*. But reality caught up with fiction in the end. Schildknecht's earlier association of the phrase 'de nihilo nihil' with 'Magie' and 'der Zauberer' is instructive, in this respect. For the particular form of magic that figures large in Burger's work, from

John J. White

Diabelli to *Brunsleben*, is the art of the escapologist, of Houdini and his lesser followers. Such a performance is invariably a matter of dicing with death; it is the art of one evading what will come in the end, a highly theatrical presentation of the 'mir galt es diesmal noch nicht' of the *Kirchberger Idyllen*. And yet, as both Houdini and Burger demonstrate in their different but related ways, the performance – whether one merely goes 'unten durch' or eventually comes 'oben hinaus' – resides in more than the audience's knowledge of the risks undergone and this time survived: it lies in the sheer panache and professionalism with which the artist's existential need to take such risks is staged. And in that, Burger was surely Houdini's literary equal.

Notes

1. References to Burger's work are as follows: S = *Schilten. Schulbericht zuhanden der Inspektorenkonferenz*, Zurich and Munich, 1976; page references to later edition, Frankfurt am Main, 1979; D = *Diabelli. Erzählungen*, Frankfurt am Main, 1979; KI = *Kirchberger Idyllen*, Frankfurt am Main, 1980; KM = *Die Künstliche Mutter*, Frankfurt am Main, 1982, page references to 1986 edition; AV = *Die allmähliche Verfertigung der Idee beim Schreiben. Frankfurter Poetik-Vorlesung*, Frankfurt am Main, 1986; AS = *Als Autor auf der Stör*, Frankfurt am Main, 1987; SK = *Der Schuß auf die Kanzel. Eine Erzählung*, Zurich, 1988; T = *Tractatus logico-suicidalis. Über die Selbsttötung*, Frankfurt am Main, 1988; B = *Brenner, Erster Teil: Brunsleben*, Frankfurt am Main, 1989.
2. Ambros Umberer, the narrator of this story, is already in another guise known to the reader: as the 'Stefan Wigger' of *Schilten*.
3. Published as *Paul Celan. Auf der Suche nach der verlorenen Sprache*, Frankfurt am Main, Zurich and Munich, 1974.
4. On this central issue in much of Burger's fiction, see Gerda Zeltner's survey of his writings in *Das Ich ohne Gewähr. Gegenwartsautoren aus der Schweiz*, Zurich and Frankfurt am Main, 1980, pp. 173-97. In 'Wovon soll der Lehrer leben?' (AS 56-65), Burger relates *Schilten* to his unhappy years as a victim of the school system (what is referred to in *Die Künstliche Mutter* as his 'Kinder-KZ' time, cf. the 'Brief an die Mutter' section, especially, KM 145 and also similar remarks in B 303); however, in the Frankfurt lecture, he also draws a number of illuminating parallels between the schoolteacher and the writer.
5. *Schauplatz als Motiv. Materialien zu Hermann Burgers Roman 'Schilten'*, Zurich and Munich, 1979.
6. 'Sie glauben nicht', Burger was later to tell his Frankfurt audience, 'wie viele Linguisten mich allen Ernstes auf diese völlig aus der Luft gegriffene Kuriosität angesprochen haben' (AV 11). For details of this inventive linguistic dimension to Burger's 'schleifende Schnitte zwischen dem Realen und dem Irrealen', see AV 10ff.
7. 'Hermann Burger', in Heinz Ludwig Arnold (ed.): *Kritisches Lexikon zur deutschsprachigen Gegenwartsliteratur*, vol. 2, Munich, 1978, pp. 8f.

8. T 19; future references to entries in the *Tractatus* will cite them by number, rather than page. The further discipline mentioned – 'Suizidographie . . . die Darstellung eines Lebens, die sich auf die Kausalketten beschränkt, die letztlich zur Selbstauslöschung führen' (ibid.) – furnishes an apt description of Burger's entire literary *œuvre*.

9. No doubt the author of the *Tractatus*' blurb-text voiced the puzzlement of many readers on the work's appearance: 'Dieser Traktat ist Literatur eben dadurch, daß der Autor das Allgemeine aus dem Besonderen zu entwickeln versteht. Das Besondere, Individuelle: das ist Hermann Burgers persönliche Betroffenheit und die Faszination, über den Freitod zu berichten und ihn nicht zu suchen wie Kleist, Trakl und viele andere. . . . Dieses radikale Buch über die Selbsttötung wird als Negativutopie zu einem vehementen Plädoyer für das Leben und für die Kunst.'

10. For details of this figure's suicide by poisoning and his funeral, see SK 174ff. In this later work, the culmination of the anti-Church attack running through much of Burger's fiction, the narrator claims that *Schilten* can also be read as a 'shot at the pulpit' (SK 121).

13
Gertrud Leutenegger:
A Feminist Synthesis
Elizabeth Boa

Gertrud Leutenegger's *Nineve* (1977) is built round the symbol of a whale's corpse which reaches land-locked Switzerland on its last stop as a spectacle of popular entertainment. The whale's network of veins and arteries becomes a metaphor for the social relations through which we live our lives, but where a zoologist might construct a model of the whole system, the novelist can only partially illuminate the myriad links between the subjective experience and society. Drawing connections which remain partial is both the structural principle and the central theme of Leutenegger's work. In her first novel, *Vorabend* (1975), the narrator spends the evening before a demonstration walking the network of streets which it will follow, past windows covered with blinds which prompt her to reflect on hidden connections between subjective experience and collective action. Like the criss-crossing streets, the novel offers not a linear narrative but a frayed network of unfinished stories. In the symbolic novel, *Gouverneur* (1981), the narrator constructs a mountain to stand opposed to the Governor's domain on the high plateau, but connections link the two realms and the novel ends on an unresolved confrontation. *Kontinent* (1985), set in a Swiss village with flashbacks to a visit to China, juxtaposes continents. Here the motif of connections appears in the labyrinthine water system underlying the village and in the narrator's montage of concrete music without linear melody. Finally, *Meduse* (1988) draws on symbols from the sea and mountains, but the two realms are linked in this novella, which interweaves a descent into the psyche with an elegiac lament for a dying culture and which, like the novels, makes no claim to total vision.

The novels mix present-tense stories with retrospection; only *Meduse* is narrated in the preterite, but it too interleaves different times. Temporal oscillation, lack of narrative closure and first-person narration produce the sense of a subject in flux, but not a retreat into subjectivity. An external world of mountains, valleys and villages is palpably evoked, but not a tourist-board Switzerland: the mountain landscapes are juxtaposed with Zurich or Berlin; the wild pastoral and the village idyll are invaded by multifarious intrusions of modernity, juxtaposing *Fasnacht* ritual and factory, primordial rock and aluminium works; multiple connections link Switzerland with Italy and Germany; in *Kontinent* the lines stretch between continents. But consciousness is not just a reflection of such historical and geographical arteries: the intricate veinwork of subjective experience remains irreducible to linear historical narrative or to the sociological construct. An implied reader of *Vorabend* accuses the narrator of lacking a concept, an accusation she accepts: 'Ich habe nicht einmal einen fixen Gedanken. Um jeden fixen Gedanken gerinnt die Welt' (V 17).[1] The open forms convey communal culture and individual subjectivity in flux, cultural adulteration but also cultural exchange, the ills of modernity but also the passing of old oppressions.

Gertrud Leutenegger was born in 1948 and grew up in Schwyz. After a spell of theatre work following the publication of *Vorabend*, she has lived as a writer and travelled extensively. In 1978 she was awarded the Ingeborg Bachmann Prize and in 1979 the Meersburg Droste Prize. Primarily a novelist, she has also published two works intermediate between prose, drama and lyric, *Lebewohl, Gute Reise* (1980) and *Komm ins Schiff* (1983), and a volume of sketches and stories, *Das verlorene Monument* (1985). Metaphors, dream sequences and mythical motifs lend poetic resonance to her more naturalistic works; in the more surreal works fragments of contemporary life intrude into the symbolic landscapes. Thus her work recalls the poetic realism of the age of Droste while, like Bachmann, uncovering connections between the psychic and the political.

Vorabend

Das Radikale in den Nuancen aufsuchen (V 88)

Set in 1975, *Vorabend* probes below the collective surface to uncover subjective experiences which may spur individuals to unite in social protest. The project combats right-wing denial of social identity, but also left-wing suppression of experience which does not fit privileged analytical categories; for the descent into the Chinese boxes of subjectivity may uncover what separates as much as what unites, but unity bought by suppressing division cannot last, and the novel is a challenge to create a community lasting longer than the day of a demonstration. *Vorabend* belongs, then, with the 1970s literature of subjectivity, but it seeks an extension, not a denial, of politics.

The difficulty of finding a communal voice comes out in shifting personal pronouns. While the narrator writes mainly as 'I' or as an impersonal 'one', she sometimes speaks in dialogue with a familiar 'du' and occasionally as 'we'. But there is also that hectoring voice, a formal 'Sie', demanding a novel tailored to the fixed ideas of a political faction or a psychological school. *Vorabend* does address issues of the 1970s which might satisfy the voice: the exploitation of foreign workers; the Zurich housing crisis; tensions in the educational system; alienation at work. Repressed miseries lie below the prosperous surface of patrician architecture, banks, shopping precincts and Alpine kitsch. Switzerland is 'soou cliiiiiin', the English exclaim; even the Emmental cow pats are delightful (V 174). Set against clean Switzerland is the image of stagnant water broken by sulphurous bubbles, evoking communal tensions but also individual memories, which may either inhibit or spur on to action. The streets grow longer as the narrator, named once as Gertrud, follows memories centring on her relations with Ce, a woman friend, and with two men, both with the initial Te. The memories seem to have no connection with politics, but their very strangeness as disconnected fragments makes them 'zum tiefen unablässigen Stachel' (V 127). A recurring structure of feeling, associated also with gender, is identification with, yet estrangement from others. The narrator imagines asking a man why he is demonstrating (V 127); the novel explores why a woman should want to protest, who the others are through whom she might find a social self, but also why she has difficulty reaching the demonstration.

In the third street, the narrator remembers the scream of an injured Italian worker and envisages the miserable barracks where the foreign workers live. But empathy turns to fear: her crimson blouse must be a provocation to these men, separated from wives and families, looking down from prison-like windows at blond Swiss women. In fact the men only call out 'ciaòbella', but the narrator sees herself through their imagined gaze not as a subject and their potential ally, but as an object shaped by a triple difference of sex, class and culture, signalled in the colours of a red blouse and blond hair. Later, such self-division is linked to gender when the narrator deviates from the planned route to walk through an archway, whose red underside is now covered with advertisements for pornographic films. It reminds the narrator of another archway, in the garden behind her school, which led to a pavillion where the statue of a woman stood gazing at her with a face full of absence. The unknown womanhood awaiting the child in the future is a womanhood also of the past, written in stone, and is somehow connected with the pornographic advertisements. The narrator first finds feminine identity in looking at her friend Ce in her nightdress, but the knowing grin of another girl divides her from Ce: femininity is shaped both through difference from the other gender and separation from what is alike. Women see themselves through the imagined gaze of men as objects for men in a culture of compulsory heterosexuality. Pornography is the ultimate denial of women as subjects who might speak in community with one another or with men. In the last street, the narrator visits Ce, whose wardrobe, empty of dresses, is full of black jeans and pullovers. Ce recalls a shopping trip where she tried on a brilliant red sweater, yet left with another black purchase. Thus modern woman, seeking to escape thraldom as object of lust and afraid to seem provocative in red, signals a sad black denial of sexuality.

Relations with men are just as problematic. The narrator knows Zurich-Te, old enough to be her father, and Paris-Te, two years younger than her. Paris-Te's blue-green pullover acts for her as a colour-signal of love for a young brother, though she has no brother. The prelapsarian interlude mixes arcadian images of butterflies with the abandon of disco dancing, today's Dionysian rites. But the idyll is broken by Paris-Te's demand for total commitment, a desire the narrator recognises as an emotional mechanism which turns eros into mutual oppression. She feels constrained, too, to tell young Te about old Te. And so the woman stands between two men. As she refuses to be a mother–lover to young Te, so old Te refuses the role of father–lover. But the threat of subjection remains. Near the end, the narrator remembers visiting Zurich-Te in the role of handmaiden, to type for him, and a decisive moment arrives: should she stay or leave? The dark chess figures in the psyche might play through the strategies of domination and servility. Both refuse the game, but as she runs towards the demonstration, she is afraid she has lingered too long, seduced by regressive desire to shelter with Te.[2]

In Freudian terms, separation from Ce repeats separation from the Mother, followed by conflicting desires for the Father and the Son. But the narrator runs from the emotional machinery of the Oedipal triangle towards the carnivalesque demonstration where she may rediscover the radical potential in the nuances of relationships, those moments of free play signalled in the aroma of omelettes, the flutter of butterflies on the skin, or Ce's green eyes. Such motifs recall 1960s faith in the radical Freudians who preached sexual liberation. But the novel speaks also with the feminist voice of the more sceptical 1970s. If the narrator reaches the demonstration, she will be spurred by the memory of Brigitte, a mentally retarded woman with a subnormal son, the outcome of a rape by a drunken soldier. Brigitte wears red, the signal of female sexuality. She desires and enjoys intensely but with no understanding of coitus or feeling for the soldier. As sexuality unsubordinated to maternal instinct or emotion, Brigitte could seem like a female throwback to the monsters of animal vitality imagined by Georg Heym or the young Brecht. But Brigitte is nonetheless abused and the brutal coitus results in a child. Brigitte's Expressionist analogues conveyed an aggressive cult of male sexuality; a more recent analogue, Beppi in Franz Xaver Kroetz's *Stallerhof* (1972), serves a rhetoric sympathetic to women, but Kroetz finally makes an icon of motherhood. In Brigitte the narrator finds herself as a sexual subject who in turn will speak for Brigitte in protesting against the stereotypes of victim, sex object, handmaiden or mother. A contrasting type is virginal Virginia. Doubly an old maid as feudal servant and spinster, Virginia seems to have little in common with the modern young woman who can take a variety of jobs or of lovers. Yet the narrator sees Virginia as an ancestress whose image is 'ein unabläßiger Stachel' (IV 127; 165). Virginia brings hope as well as anger, for the nuances of her narrow life had a chastening dignity. The young Swiss woman's sense of descent from the Italian old maid suggests that women can find connections across history and culture. But although the patriarchy which divided women of the household from women beyond the margins has gone, women who today demonstrate in public alongside men must still fight to find a social voice independent of men.

Nineve

Eine Vermischung der Welten (N 128)

Virginia is the first of several older women who link epochs and cultures. In *Nineve*, generation, gender, nationality and class cross: in Berlin young Fabrizio, Swiss but of Italian descent, meets elderly aristocratic Frau Golzowand, and a nameless urban waif; in Sils, during a stay in the communal house attached to the Nietzsche Museum, the Swiss narrator meets an elderly German Jewish intellectual, Dr Bernstein, and young Italian Tina. (Nietzsche and Sils are never named, but clues abound.) Through this grid of characters *Nineve* explores the mixing of worlds. As a novel of *Vergangenheitsbewältigung*, it shows that the past exists not just in museums but mixes with the present through memories which uncover class, ethnic and gender tensions, though on gender *Nineve* is reconciliatory: the present and the childhood story both begin with the narrator and Fabrizio coming together. As children, they first meet during Carnival when Fabrizio protects the frightened girl from the 'Dorfgouverneure', the village bully-boys (N 18). They next meet when, out roller-skating, she misinterprets Fabrizio's greeting as an attack, then recognises the gesture of friendship. When Fabrizio takes her to meet his mother, who works in the local textile factory, his brothers and sisters at first reject the girl from the Swiss community, who despise the Italian factory-children, but the mother accepts her into the family. The memories uncover proto-fascist tendencies as children imitate adult patterns of aggressive masculinity, snobbery and xenophobia. But that the frightened girl and the Italian factory-child make common cause is a sign of hope for a politics to oppose class and ethnic oppression, while the mother's double burden of wage and domestic labour signals the need for feminist politics too.

The village with its *Fasnacht* rituals and textile factory introduces the theme of tradition and modernity. Modernity brings cultural loss, but regret for old customs can turn into a reactionary cult of an illusory folk past, illusory because until recently Switzerland had to export where it now imports labour. In Sils the locals depend on tourism, yet sign petitions against foreign invasion. One landlord does point out that foreigners are needed to serve the tourists, but his appeal to economic value, not human worth, only further upsets Italian Tina. As she starts up in protest, tomato ketchup spills down her white dress, then spatters over the sky-blue walls in the commune, dripping red over the ideal of an international creative community. A local boy calls the German Jew 'Friedhofs-gras' (N 142), and on a mountain walk the narrator fails to communicate with Bernstein: his eyes directed downwards into the past, he has not even seen the Lej de la Tscheppa, the destination of the walk. The sky-blue walls and the Lej de la Tscheppa are utopian symbols, but the narrator must recognise that the past may be too terrible to come to terms with and present conflicts reach even into the high mountains. Modernity, recently arrived in the Alps where

Nietzsche once fled from the masses and the flies in the market, came earlier to Berlin. Berlin seems a different world from the utopian commune in the Engadin, but sinister affinities link the dark underworld and the luminous mountains, and Berlin has its utopian moments too. The mountain walk has its counterpart in Fabrizio's meeting in the underground with a girl who urges the provincial youth to identify with the urban masses. Fabrizio does join with immigrants and young people in communes in protesting against property development. But his most intense feeling is for his blind landlady, whose family once owned the whole house, but who now lives in a small flat. Fabrizio admires Frau Golzowand's courage in protesting along with the others, but what draws him most is a double vision of a life marked by public history but also of an unknowable personal depth. In this, Frau Golzowand is like the portrait of her ancestress, one side of the face brightly lit, the other in deep shadow. The friendship between the Italian factory-child and the blind aristocrat could seem a sentimental denial of social divisions, like the ending of Fritz Lang's *Metropolis*. But just as the narrator fails to redeem Bernstein from the past and descends from her high mountain, so Fabrizio is no folk-hero and leaves the metropolis with nothing resolved: Frau Golzowand, who has survived so much, must still confront the present threat.

The stories set in Schwyz, Graubünden and Berlin are accompanied by essayistic commentaries, prompted by aspects of the whale as a threatened species, tradition and modernity, urban and rural life, social divisions and community, the masses and the nuances of individuals. A central speculation concerns apocalypse and utopia. As consuming Leviathan and rotting corpse, the whale suggests the end of history: the fascist regimes perhaps signalled an apocalypse already upon us, for Nineveh was a doomed city, and the song about the Lord from Nineveh come to carry off the youngest daughter evokes an archetypal rape of the feminine, presaging nuclear destruction and the rape of the planet. But Jehovah saved Jonah from the belly of the whale and spared Nineveh. The portrait of Frau Golzowand's ancestress is dated 1789, the year of the deluge, which presaged the Terror but also the overthrow of feudalism; likewise the fascist era was a nadir from which we can rise again. Conversely, utopia is not a cosmic happy ending but a potential within history, realised in moments of mutuality enabling a politics of cooperation. Hidden in the entrails of the whale is the sweet-smelling ambergris, the sign of hope.

Gouverneur

Einen unermeßlichen Garten für meine Liebe wollte ich anpflanzen, aber ein Unbekannter hat darin Wohnung genommen. (G 121)

After the reconciliatory *Nineve*, sexual antagonism returns massively in *Gouverneur*, where the narrator wants to build a mountain with hanging gardens to symbolise life in opposition to the mausoleum at the centre of the Governor's domain on the high plateau. The narrator and the Governor seek allies among various groups: a troupe of German actors; inspectors overseeing the garden project; country folk; city friends; and two women in thrall to the Governor, the whore and the woman in red. Given the profusion of episodes and symbols, I can only sketch a reading in the context of feminist debate. Following Simone de Beauvoir, many feminists argue that under patriarchy the feminine is always the negative of the masculine: woman is the Other, is that which man is not.[3] Thus woman is a utopian metaphor for man's aspirations towards what he is not yet, but her negativity is also the foil confirming man's humanity, hence the contradictory images of women in patriarchal discourse. As the title designating rulers of ancient cities such as Nineveh or Babylon, 'Governor' evokes a patriarchy stretching from Biblical times through to the 'Dorfgouverneure' in *Nineve*, although the new Governor's demand for untrammelled sexual freedom indicates a shift from father-power rooted in tribe or family to the modern battle of the sexes. The masculine principle still holds the high ground, but as the mountain rises above the plateau, a patriarchal culture of war, hierarchy and exploitation should cede to life-nurturing love and harmony with nature. This kind of feminism poses two problems. Firstly, how do the terms masculine and feminine relate to actual men and women? If we are born female or male but are socialised into femininity and masculinity, then feminism should promote the feminine in both sexes or androgyny. Thus the narrator finds male and female allies amongst the theatre troupe, including a gay transvestite. But some allies merely pay lip service and desert, conveying the strength of gender conditioning and the lure of sexual difference. A second difficulty is that the definitions are drawn from patriarchal discourse. The *male* overseers of the garden suggest that the cult of femininity may merely fix women in the roles men have always assigned them: the project may express not the narrator's autonomy as a woman, but her subjection to femininity as defined by the hidden patriarch dwelling in her garden. In competing with the Governor who built the gardens of Babylon, she may merely perpetuate the symbolism also of the Song of Songs: woman's body as a pleasure garden for man.

Radical feminists promote not sexual convergence but woman-power based in the body. This move produces a third dilemma: how to translate the meaning of the body into woman-power? The statue of a naked woman to preside over the gardens and the narrator's pleasure in the menstrual flow suggest woman's body as the site of pleasure and fertility. But the discursive alienation of the body in stone or writing simply reproduces the patriarchal meanings: the statue, like the statue in *Vorabend*, is the perennial object of phallic power. The statue carved by patriarchy is perhaps mutilated, however, lacking not the phallus but the harpy's claw. Accordingly the radical feminists proclaim the return of clawed matriarchal deities. But matriarchy as absolute antagonism between female and male is self-contradictory: claws grasping a dead boy-child cannot symbolise life-giving fertility but merely transfer death-dealing power from male to female. Finally, the narrator banishes all statues, which ominously recall the statues of Nebuchadnezzar, the power-mad Governor of Babylon, and helped by the landlady, one of Leutenegger's older women, she burns a model of the Governor's domain. Miniaturisation to a carboard cut-out demystifies the patriarchal discourse which constantly infiltrates feminist discourse and may presage a descent from the discursive plain down to practical politics in the city. But the novel closes up on the plateau as the narrator confronts the Governor, and the discursive conflict remains in her vision of the agave rising through her body, for Agave, the mother of Pentheus, joined the Maenads in rending her son asunder, a symbol of woman-power perhaps, but also of the deadly cult of the male deity, Dionysus.

Gouverneur explores the theory that the origins of patriarchy lie in the dominant symbolic order, as in Lacan's punning claim that the female sex cannot be symbolised because the female genitals have the character of an absence.[4] But the putative alternative symbolic order merely confirms the dominance of the phallic prime signifier, signalled in the title and in the closing word: 'Gouverneur'. Can anything be rescued from this seemingly vicious circle? Only by way of negation of patriarchal claims to control the female body and psyche and of closed symbolic systems, whether monolithic patriarchy or a mirror-image matriarchy. This is in line with *Vorabend* and *Nineve*, which eschew the totalising metaphoric vision for a metonymic montage. But the profusion of hermetic symbolism is a paradoxical way to attack closed symbolic systems, and *Gouverneur* risks coagulating around the *idées fixes* of a feminism over-influenced by neo-Freudian theory.[5]

Lebewohl, Gute Reise is in similar vein. Adapting the Gilgamesh epic, preserved in Nineveh, it evokes the overthrow of sexual complementarity: patriarchy initiates antagonism between the sexes and between humanity and nature as Enkidu, alienated from his monkey origins, joins the culture-hero and war-lord in desecrating the rites of the goddess, turning the phallus into a weapon against the temple-hetaera and establishing hierarchy and racial antagonism, symbolised in the division of the monkeys into higher and lower orders. Further episodes follow which interleave the world-historical defeat of the female sex with references to National Socialism, nuclear weapons, hubristic medical science and the ecological crisis, and like *Gouverneur* the text closes on an unresolved confrontation. *Lebewohl, Gute Reise* anticipates Christa Wolf's *Kassandra* (1983): both attack patriarchy as the fundamental cultural evil but risk ahistorical overstretching of the concept, tendencies to a degree obviated by the *Kassandra* essays and the elements of travesty in Leutenegger's text.[6]

Kontinent

Jeden Morgen schwillt auf irgendeinem Kontinent die Sintflut an. (K 44)

Kontinent returns to a more focused realism though beginning in a Kafkaesque manner: a stranger called to perform a mysterious task arrives in a village; the men driving the removal van seem farcical yet threatening; two buildings, the Canal House and the Observatory, are obscurely significant; nameless villagers tell stories out of sequence about a predecessor, which seem grotesquely surreal; unsignalled flash-backs disconcert. Gradually, however, estrangement gives way to understanding both at the level of the character confronting a community and of the reader confronting a text. The European village, initially so exotic it might be in another continent, acquires a history, and the reader disentangles four stories: the story of the narrator's present life; the story of her visit to China; the story of her predecessor; the story of the Peking Monkey Opera. The first story uncovers the history of a village economy now based on an aluminium works and monoculture of the vine. The narrator has come to make a record of concrete music to celebrate the 75th anniversary of the works. She hopes to produce music that will transfuse all the ravished elements of nature to become one with the inner pulse of the world (K 38), and so records sounds of machinery and helicopter spraying as well as of wind and water. The project is fraught with paradox: the music recording the rape of nature has been commissioned by the rapist; the natural sounds are recorded by a machine and will be mixed electronically by the works engineers; the innermost pulse will provide background music to make the workers work better; the music is eventually played at the village festival, moved to coincide with the celebration of the works which has poisoned the village environment. When the villagers invite the narrator to move from the Canal House, on the outskirts, to the Observatory, on high ground overlooking the village, she requests that it be repainted blue rather than the obtrusive red her predecessor had chosen. The musical passage from rape to universal harmony, the combined festival and the choice of blue might seem to signal a conservative and collusive artistic stance. But such a reading conflicts with the horrifying documentation of industrial injuries and pollution; enforced monoculture and consequent loss of trees and shrubs leading to landslides which sweep away whole villages; the effects of helicopter spraying on people and wildlife; the agony of a bat entangled in plastic netting; the bribery and threats which keep the villagers quiet, and their collusion under duress.

The documentation, the move to the blue Observatory and the electronic music, not traditional accordion music, played the evening *before* the works anniversary, together convey a statement by an artist–observer confronting the ills of modernity. The precise documentation directly addresses the Swiss State, industry and people. As fictionalised documentary, it generalises a real case first raised in a newspaper article reprinted in *Das verlorene Monument* – a two-pronged attack comparable to Wolf's *Kassandra* and its essays. The move to the Observatory marks a shift from being a works employee to solidarity with the villagers: artists may depend on state or industrial patronage but their work can still protest in the name of the people. To attack environmental damage need not mean reactionary rejection of the modern world: electronic music can be as expressive as the accordion, which, after all, is a machine. The choice of traditional blue to harmonise with sky and landscape is not reactionary – the grinding poverty before the advent of the works is made clear – but a rejection of an élitest programmatic modernism. As in *Nineve*, blue is also the utopian colour, and along with the music it signals not collusion but refusal of crippling despair – the continent can be saved from the poisonous deluge.

If it is to be saved, then the politics of protest must win over the people. The danger of isolation is dramatised in the predecessor, who insisted on painting the Observatory red but despaired when her collaboration with the Water Inspector in opposing the villagers' collusion in their own exploitation failed. This story explores how green politics must steer a way between radical marginality and populism which can turn into conservative reaction – like the unholy alliance between the ideologues of *Blut und Boden* and industrialists during the Third Reich. *Kontinent* embodies this dilemma in the contrast, which also has feminist implications, between the predecessor's relations with the Water Inspector and the narrator's with the 'Verwalterin', a title ambiguous between administering and holding in trust. The Water Inspector administered the network of canals and underground passages built up over centuries to regulate the water supply: exploitation of natural resources, the always evolving prerequisite of human culture, need not be a rape of nature. But from being a critic of environmental damage, the Inspector becomes a lackey of the works when he feels his status as village leader threatened by the young woman who tries to work with him as a partner, not a handmaiden. His transmogrification into a rapacious clown, dressed up for Carnival as the Emperor of China, is also provoked by fear of waning sexual potency, a reaction which casts a shadow over his earlier stance: the lust for sexual power shares a deep psychological basis with the lust for material and social power, lusts which patriarchy fostered in men and which changing relations between the sexes may provoke into hysterical reaction. Such lust is a perversion of human creativity and sexual vitality which, like the fear of death, are instincts in both sexes. The story is counterpointed with the Monkey Opera: the Inspector dresses up as the Emperor but is really the Monkey who, for all his hubristic vitality, must submit to the Emperor of the Dead, though sometime he may rise again. Human instinct is always expressed through cultural forms, and a significant measure of a culture is how it shapes sex and integrates death as well as how it deploys its technological capacity, the central themes in this story, which culminates in the death of the Water Inspector. The conflict between the predecessor and the Inspector is contrasted with the friendship between the narrator and an older woman. The 'Verwalterin', a title emblematic of conservation, experiments in ecologically friendly viniculture and refuses sharp distinctions between flowers and weeds: had the white-thorns not been weeded out, the landslides would not have happened. Once again, cross-generational relations between women are a sign of hope.

An unresolved mystery is what became of the predecessor, who went off on a journey. Her *alter ego* has returned from a journey to

China where she came to love a Chinese man and to value Chinese sociability. The Chinese and European stories stand in complex counterpoint: at a Party Congress in Peking the old men on the platform speak of the need to modernise and to pluck out weeds that flowers may grow, an ominous metaphor when juxtaposed with the European story; the old men in China once led a revolution and the old man in Europe fought for conservation, but both cling to power in alliance with industry; the old men in China regulate the rivers of people who, under the stress of modernisation, may overflow in a flood which only brutal repression can control; in his last frenzy the old man in Europe, regulator of groundwaters, lashed a whip across the nape of a young boy; the narrator remembers the delicate nape of her Chinese lover's neck and though they had to part, the memory of love in China is crucial in her journey towards community in Europe, a community the predecessor failed to achieve as she failed to find love. *Kontinent* combines protest against a local scandal with a global reflection – of remarkable prescience in the Chinese case – on the different problems of modernisation within different political systems. Like the earlier novels, it reflects too on the relation between subjective experience and collective action. The stories of the narrator and her predecessor show that the subjective and the political are finally inseparable: personal alienation inhibits communal politics; men tyrannical in their personal relations cannot be trusted politically. As a feminist text, it avoids monolithic abstraction. On green issues, it promotes conservation but not conservatism and values the local and provincial with no trace of a cult of *Heimat*.[7] In combining realist precision, thematic range and symbolic resonance, *Kontinent* is Leutenegger's most impressive work to date.

Meduse

Zu einem bestimmten Zeitpunkt meines Lebens sah ich aus dem Meer eine Meduse auftauchen, groß wie ein Kinderkopf, rosa marmoriert, mit Fangfäden, die tief ins Wasser hinabhingen. (M 7)

The opening sentence contains the whole of *Meduse* in embryo. The temporal phrase pinpoints a moment in the past when the medusa released memories of a day in the still earlier past, when the narrator and her lover Fabrizio, on holiday in the village of Rovina (literally ruin) in the Italian Alps, set off to climb to a wood. Here they spend the night beside the ruined *nevera*, the ice-house where the milk was once stored before being winched down the mountain, the only means of moving goods to and from a village inaccessible to motor transport. In contrast to the novels, the present is here a blank: two past moments both open backwards into memories, metaphorically evoked in the tentacles hanging deep into the sea, which metamorphose into Rovina and the mountains as a world upside-down in the watery medium of memory; conversely, up on the mountain, the *nevera* sinks well-like down into the past. Within the narrative of the one day, analepses to the past mix with prolepses to what will happen in the immediate future: Fabrizio's uncle and his sister Giuditta, the last of the villagers, will fall mortally ill; the narrator will break with Fabrizio, despite their perfect – too perfect – love, to move into a new future. But all we see of that future is the one, already past moment, and the text closes with an image of the narrator's hair dripping rain and her mouth filling with water as the medusa floats away into the sea. The narrating 'I' and the epic preterite are the only sign that she was not engulfed, but is now writing an elegy for a phase of her own life and for a dead village.

While tomorrow's fresh fields and pastures new remain empty of realist content, the future is evoked symbolically at the turning point of the novella, truly 'eine unerhörte, sich ereignete Begebenheit',[8] when the narrator has a vision of a child in the *nevera*, anticipated in the medusa as a pink-veined, embryonic child's head. The medusa and the child are interlinked symbols of multiple resonance. The medusa, embryonic and womb-like, drifting translucent in its amniotic sea, evokes a life-phase before individuation. It is also vulva-like: its moist surface, mouth and fringe of tentacles suggest all-pervasive sensation from a centre to extremities. But the mouth and stinging tentacles evoke also engulfment and pain. The medusa's ambiguity parallels the ambiguity of the adolescent love between childhood friends, which acts as the bridge to adult sexuality and as a birth passage to a new life-phase. Yet the ecstasy of pulsing blood, the loss of separate identity and the fading away of the outer world are potentially regressive. This quasi-sibling love is parallelled in the literal incest between Giuditta and the uncle, who from birth have lived in conflict-ridden symbiosis with one another in the village which is now dying as they will soon die. The miraculous child in the *nevera* is at once dead and alive. It is a phantasm of the child Giuditta never had; Giuditta's last illness is a tumour growing inside her, an embryo of death. If the pattern of enclosure without future is not to be repeated, the narrator must break with Fabrizio. The live child flowing into her embodies herself as a child and her present birth through love. In each phase, the earlier self is not denied but carried through – the archaic deposit of the mother–child dyad remains in the psyche. But birth is also separation, and the child embodies a future self separate from Fabrizio, though their love will remain in the timeless psyche to be reborn in memory.

The psychic is more seamlessly blended with the social than in any other of Leutenegger's works. The manner is reminiscent of the novella of poetic realism, recalling the uncanny in Droste-Hülshoff's work, or Stifter's *Der Hochwald*, with *Jugendstil* echoes in the watery medusa. Initially, the village grows from the tentacles – like Undine's underwater world, it is a sensual realm without guilt or death. The lovers' joy is transfused by the idyllic atmosphere of the village as they make love in meadows and up above the church cupola where the bells ring out their ecstasy. They float in a fluid of love which imbues everything. But their love also cuts them off. Guilt creeps in as they set off up the mountain, forgetting to let the uncle know they are leaving. They arrive, like Hansel and Gretel, in a threatening wood where the ruined *nevera* metaphorically evokes a dark history below the idyllic surface, of hatred for the people from across the border, stoked by recent memories of the destruction of forests during the war against the partisans; Giuditta's tumour is perhaps caused by lingering poisons from that time. Unlike many of the villagers, Giuditta always sought reconciliation with the world beyond the village and the borders. She treasures traditions, but recognises too that the *nevera* now belongs in the past, like the village itself which will find no new life when she and her brother die. The narrator's break with Fabrizio is also an act she commits on behalf of Giuditta. The child enters her as the daughter Giuditta might have had, and she moves on to new life beyond the shrinking village and sibling love.

In psychoanalytic theory, the uncanny is the manifestation of what is at once intimate but hidden, *heimlich* in both senses; it is the return of the repressed. The medusa's head as petrifying image of the female genitalia is an archetypal manifestation of the repressed. In *Meduse*, however, the jellyfish loses its uncanny quality as the narrator examines it, probes it with her sandal, notes its fragility, and finally throws away the sandal: out of its watery medium, the poor medusa would dry out and die. The metaphoric density of *Meduse* is a literary medium, in contrast to the dry language of theory, through which the narrator celebrates the sign of female desire for oneness with the beloved, represented through the narrator, and for motherhood, represented through Giuditta, who pressed the moist polenta as a surrogate child to her breast. Both desires echo archaic oneness before separation from the mother. *Meduse* might be labelled post-feminist in celebrating desires which for many feminists represent a regressive femininity. But the child makes manifest another desire, long repressed and suppressed in women, the desire for autonomy: *Meduse* conveys the difficult birth of independence achieved without repressive denial of romantic and maternal feeling. It attempts to reconcile feminism with femininity and so perhaps to move beyond the squinting double focus which Sigrid Weigel attributes to women's writing.[9] But the elegiac mode, the circular return to the sea of memory, the lack of a represented world beyond the village, the backward-looking preterite, the masterly deployment of metaphor, make *Meduse* Leutenegger's most formally unified but also most closed and least socially critical work, except perhaps for *Komm ins Schiff*, which shares watery images, and blurs the boundaries between dream and reality more radically than *Meduse*. Such a form, and the narrator's comment on the hidden order of the psyche which no intellectual achievements can counterbalance (M 58), might seem to make *Meduse* a programmatically irrationalist work. Yet there is enlightenment too in the de-demonisation of the uncanny, in the refusal to solve conflicts of desire through repression of desire, and in the intrusion of history into idyll. And there is protest against stunted lives: Giuditta, sexually fulfilled but childless, is a variation on Virginia in *Vorabend*, who knew neither sexual nor maternal fulfilment, and within the text, on the Virgin of the Seven Swords mourning a dead child conceived without sexual joy.

Postmodernism and Feminism

To conclude, I want to situate Leutenegger's work in two contexts, the postmodernist debate and arguments within feminism, not with a view to labelling her work, but to highlighting its links with current cultural debate. Leutenegger's scepticism of historicism, be it narratives of inevitable progress or doom, has affinities with Lyotard's 'postmodern condition'.[10] Her stress on cultural difference, on what divides as much as what unites, goes against both the Enlightenment vision of universal emancipation of the people and the Marxist theory of an international proletariat as historical agent. Her work can also be read as a critique of Lyotard's third grand narrative, the rationalist tradition, which, as *Kontinent* suggests, posits supposedly universal norms of reason justifying the power of élites such as the old men in Peking or the technocrats of Western capitalism. So defined, the 'postmodern' and the feminist impulse in Leutenegger's work are closely related: 'the people' in the Enlightenment vision excluded women, Marxism left sexual and reproductive relations as side issues, and the rationalist tradition defined woman as nature and stigmatised as irrational needs and desires which disturbed the social consensus. Aesthetically, Leutenegger's work conveys not a wholesale rejection of modernism but a rejection only of the totalising claims of a single style: it values the vernacular without philistine parochialism. Architectural postmodernism double-codes modernism with a vernacular or classical style:[11] *Nineve* double-codes the metropolitan and the provincial; *Kontinent* combines modernist techniques reminiscent of Kafka with the Swiss village tale; *Meduse* revives the classical novella to express contemporary feminist sensibility. Such double-coding, and the juxtaposing of local narratives which resist reduction to a totalising master narrative, nonetheless preserve the pleasure of narrative story telling with which Leutenegger's more radical texts break. In its mixing of dream and reality and its rhythmic pulse, *Komm ins Schiff* appropriates a *symboliste* modernism as advocated by French theorists such as Kristeva.[12] *Gouverneur*, by contrast, with its psychedelic imagery, episodic excess and cartoon-like figures, presents a pastiche of the adventure story in a radical anti-narrative reminiscent of popular forms such as rock videos or comic strips.[13] The pastiche of myth interleaved with a song of the 1930s and fragmented images of ruined postindustrial landscapes in *Lebewohl, Gute Reise* might be compared with Robert Wilson's postmodernist production of Heiner Müller's *Hamletmaschine*, which interleaved pastiche of Greek myth and *Hamlet*, and dethroned the heroes of Marxism to the obsessive accompaniment of a phrase from the song, 'Bring on the Clowns'.

'Postmodernism' is a less misleading label than 'critical irrationality', as proposed by one critic, for Leutenegger's work does not promote irrationality but contests definitions of reason designed to stigmatise as irrational anything which conflicts with the efficient exercise of power.[14] But the term 'postmodern' contains its own historicism in proclaiming the end of an epoch, sometimes even of history, and the grand simplicity of Lyotard's Marxist narrative is remote from the actual conflict-ridden history of left-wing politics.[15] The prophets of postmodernism are not alone in rejecting linear historical narrative with a single heroic collectivity as protagonist. This has been the central claim of socialist feminism, first in contesting Marxist stress on relations of production to the neglect of reproduction and then in refusing to replace a male proletariat with an equally abstract female collectivity.[16] Leutenegger's work conveys the variety of women's experience at different times and places and sets psychological explorations of dreams, desires and fantasies in social contexts. In that sense it interestingly bridges the division between socialist feminism and feminism influenced by psychoanalytic theory. As Cora Kaplan notes, socialist feminists tend to foreground the socioeconomic and to see romantic longings or fantasies as regressive, whereas critics deploying psychoanalytic theory value such psychic expression as subversive of the dominant culture; Leutenegger's novels explore female subjectivity as a site where, to quote Kaplan, 'the opposing forces of femininity and feminism clash', but they also gesture beyond such an opposition.[17] *Vorabend*, for example, conveys how femininity may inhibit political activism, but rather than demanding the repression of 'irrational' desires which conflict with the instrumental reason of a left-wing male consensus, it seeks a double path of a new kind of politics and the self-transformation of women though solidarity in difference. The New Woman cannot be represented because there is no single model and the meaning of desire is context-dependent: the longing for love may be at once regressive, utopian and activating; it may inhibit autonomy now, yet point towards the transcendence of the conflict between autonomy and love and arouse anger that there should be such conflict. In this respect, Leutenegger's work belongs in the same tradition as Bachmann's *Todesarten* cycle or Wolf's *Nachdenken über Christa T.*[18] Likewise, the meaning of maternal feeling may be at once regressive, utopian and activating. *Meduse* appeared within a year of Toni Morrison's *Beloved* (1987). Both texts are ghost stories centring on the miraculous appearance of a child. In both, the child is the uncanny emanation of past social oppression and of the repressed in the psyche. In both, a dark past and repressed desires threaten to engulf the subject in self-consuming depression. In *Beloved*, though the ghost is finally laid to rest, the memories remain as a spur to political identification with black struggle; in *Meduse* the child is a utopian sign of non-repressive self-transformation. The comparison, also of the differences, between these texts reflecting on the history of American slavery and on the slow death of an Alpine village culture cannot be developed here. But the intertextual echoes between two works of such disparate provenance, going back to nineteenth-century writing by women such as the Brontes or Droste-Hülshoff and beyond that to folk tales and legends, suggest that respect for cultural difference need not herald the collapse of feminism into 'post-feminism', but expands the possibilities of dialogue between women far more than could the vain pursuit of monolithic unity. Such is the feminism Leutenegger's works express.

Notes

1. References are as follows: V = *Vorabend*, Frankfurt am Main, 1975; page references to paperback edition, Frankfurt am Main, 1980; N = *Nineve*, Frankfurt am Main, 1977; page references to paperback edition, Frankfurt am Main, 1981; G = *Gouverneur*, Frankfurt am Main, 1981; page references to paperback edition, Frankfurt am Main, 1986; K = *Kontinent*, Frankfurt am Main, 1985; M = *Meduse*, Frankfurt am Main, 1988. Other texts referred to are *Lebewohl, Gute Reise. Ein dramatisches Poem*, Frankfurt am Main, 1980; *Komm ins Schiff*, Frankfurt am Main, 1983; *Das verlorene Monument*, Frankfurt am Main, 1985.
2. Cf. Manfred Jürgensen, *Deutsche Frauenliteratur der Gegenwart*, Bern, 1963, pp. 242–4, for a more positive view of the love affairs.
3. Simone de Beauvoir, *The Second Sex*, Harmondsworth, 1983.
4. Jacques Lacan, *Le Séminaire. Livre III: Les Psychoses*, texte établi par Jacques-Alain Miller, Paris, 1981, pp. 198–9.
5. Cf. Manfred Jürgensen, *Women, Writers, Women Writers – An Alternative History of German Literature*, Queensland, 1984, p. 19, for a more positive evaluation.
6. Dorothe Schuscheng, *Arbeit am Mythos Frau. Weiblichkeit und Autonomie in der literarischen Mythenrezeption Ingeborg Bachmanns, Christa Wolfs und Gertrud Leuteneggers*, Frankfurt am Main, 1987, offers a critical but sympathetic reading.
7. See Malcolm Pender, 'Themes in the German-Swiss Novel of the Eighties: Beat Sterchi's *Blösch* and Gertrud Leutenegger's *Kontinent*' on *Kontinent* and the genre of the *Dorfgeschichte*, in Arthur Williams, Stuart Parkes, Roland Smith (eds), *Literature on the Threshold. The German Novel in the 1980s*, Oxford, 1990, pp. 153–68.
8. Johann Peter Eckermann, *Gespräche mit Goethe*, ed. H. H. Houben, Wiesbaden, 1959, p. 171. Leutenegger does not specify a genre.
9. Sigrid Weigel, 'Der schielende Blick', in Inge Stephan and Sigrid Weigel, *Die verborgene Frau. Sechs Beiträge zu einer feministischen Schreibpraxis*, Berlin, 1983, pp. 83–137.
10. Jean-François Lyotard, *The Postmodern Condition. A Report on Knowledge*, Manchester, 1986.
11. See Charles Jencks, *The Language of Post-Modern Architecture*, London, 1977; *Post-Modern Classicism: The New Synthesis*, London, 1980.
12. *The Kristeva Reader*, ed. Toril Moi, Oxford, 1986, p. 97.
13. See E. Ann Kaplan, 'Feminism/Oedipus/Postmodernism: The Case of MTV' in *Postmodernism and its Discontents: Theories and Practices*, ed. E. Ann Kaplan, London, 1988, pp. 30–44, on postmodernism and popular forms.
14. Peter von Matt, 'Kritischer Patriotismus' in *Entwicklungstendenzen der deutschsprachigen Literatur der Schweiz in den sechziger und siebziger Jahren*, ed. Klaus Pezold, Leipzig, 1984, p. 47.
15. See Warren Montag, 'What is at Stake in the Debate on Postmodernism?' in Kaplan (ed.), *Postmodernism and its Discontents*, pp. 88–103, for a critique of Lyotard and of the whole concept.

16. See Patricia Waugh, *Feminine Fictions. Revisiting the Postmodern*, London and New York, 1989, pp. 1–33, on affinities and differences between feminism and postmodernism.

17. Cora Kaplan, *Sea Changes: Culture and Feminism*, London, 1986, p. 154.

18. See Elizabeth Boa, 'Women Writing about Women Writing and Ingeborg Bachmann's *Malina*' in *New Ways in Germanistik*, edited by Richard Sheppard, London, 1990, pp. 128–44.

V

Continuity and Change

14
The Fourth Generation after Frisch and Dürrenmatt
Malcolm Pender

In his very successful book, *Gebrochenes Eis. Aufzeichnungen* (1980), Lukas Hartmann (b. 1944) seeks to account for the malaise which he saw afflicting his generation. In order to describe how the social framework of normative expectations has become existentially inadequate, he has recourse to the traditional image of the Swiss house which has now lost its comforting stability: 'Durch dieses solide Lebensgebäude, erbaut aus vorgefertigten, von Schule, Kirche und Wirtschaft empfohlenen Teilen, zog sich plötzlich ein Riß, der Angst und Verzweiflung hereindringen ließ.'[1] In the book he presents his social background and upbringing in narrative sections which are interspersed with transcripts of tape-recorded conversations with his parents. By this painful and often embarrassing process, Hartmann wishes to lay bare the attitudes which have been transmitted to him, and he conducts his enquiry with the aim of working towards 'neue Formen des Zusammenlebens' (GE 28). Hartmann's rejection of the values of a conventional Swiss experience represents the first step towards personal emancipation, as reflected in the title, *Gebrochenes Eis*. This title also has symbolic significance at the start of a decade which witnesses the emergence of writers who, born at the end of the 1940s and at the beginning of the 1950s and starting to publish at the end of the 1970s and the beginning of the 1980s, constitute a fourth generation since the advent of Frisch and Dürrenmatt.[2]

Both the perception that the Swiss house was inadequate and the conviction that more viable forms of social living must be evolved figured also at about this time in the work of the generation born before the Second World War. In Hansjörg Schneider's novel *Lieber Leo* (1980), for example, the first-person narrator symbolically refuses to inherit the house which his father has worked all his life to buy. O. F. Walter's *Die Verwilderung* (1977) examines the practical and emotional difficulties of establishing a commune and, significantly, posits as the most likely outcome of the experiment a violent confrontation with the intolerance generated by existing social structures. On the other hand, two years after the appearance of *Die Verwilderung*, a member of the fourth generation, Rolf Niederhauser (b. 1951), published a cautiously optimistic account, based on an actual experiment, of how a commune might just possibly survive, *Das Ende der bloßen Vermutung*. Yet the disturbances which began in Zurich in the summer of 1980 and the hostile reaction of the authorities and of large sections of the population seemed, while not entirely undermining Niederhauser's account, to confirm in reality the much darker prognostication contained in Walter's novel. Furthermore, the narrative by Reto Hänny (b. 1947) of the events leading up to these disturbances and of his own unexpected experience of police methods, *Zürich, Anfang September* (1981), reinforced the widespread belief that there was intransigent resistance to change in Swiss society. Significantly, Hänny invokes the image of a frozen landscape, which was very much part of the verbal currency of the time, in the third section of his book, entitled 'Freiheit für Grönland – schmelzt das Packeis', arguing for movement in the body politic as Hartmann had in the case of the individual. But if, at this time, there are similarities of theme between older and younger writers, perspective and tone differentiate the members of the fourth generation.

In the first place, a more widespread and more sharply heightened perception of an endangered planet and of the cost in human terms of the structures and prosperity of modern society promotes the further development of literary themes which stress, not the historical or political peculiarities of Switzerland, but the manner in which she too reflects general aspects of modern civilisation. The claim by Silvio Blatter (b. 1946) – a more established writer in the sense that he started publishing in the early 1970s – has in this respect representative status: 'Die Schweiz als Staat ist für mich kein Thema. Die Schweiz als Lebensraum schon.'[3] Thus, if it is true that, within the framework of German culture, the writer in German-speaking Switzerland still finds himself part of 'an intricate network of cultural antagonisms and conflicting identities involving divided cultural loyalties',[4] the intensity of the pressures which this formerly generated has now slackened for younger writers, partly as a result of this greater global awareness, partly as a result of greater mobility which often permits prolonged residence abroad, and partly as a result of the increased status accorded German-speaking Switzerland within the broader context of German culture.

Secondly, the tone of the new writing is more radical. This

derives both from the impingement of huge, intractable problems on specific areas and individual groups, and also from the feeling that the structure of Swiss society, especially after the events of 1980, is ill-suited to cope with these problems. This perception accounts for the impatience manifested, for example in Rolf Niederhauser's sarcastic remark: 'Der Mensch hat sich schon immer verändert. Warum sollte das vorbei sein, ausgerechnet hier und heute?';[5] and Lukas Hartmann, looking back on what he now considers to be his humiliating and degrading experience as a recruit in the army, an institution central to Swiss society, proclaims programmatically his determined revolt: 'Keine Versöhnlichkeit!' (GE 194). The radical nature of much of the writing of the fourth generation constitutes a response to this call without necessarily sharing Hartmann's intensity.

Thirdly, the new writers of the 1980s bring to a culmination developments which, set in train originally in the 1950s with the publication of Frisch's *Stiller*, had gathered momentum in the 1960s and 1970s. Forms have become more open and, above all, traditional designations such as 'Dorfroman' and 'Heimatroman' can now only be used in contemporary German-Swiss literature 'wenn sie ihre eigene Sprengung miteinbeziehen'.[6] *Blösch* (1983), the highly successful novel by Beat Sterchi (b. 1949), which is set partly in the Swiss countryside and partly in an abattoir in the city, provides one of the best examples of the force and power generated by this opposition between form and content to describe the decline of what it appears to be affirming. *Blösch* subverts its form by depicting Switzerland from the perspective of the Spanish 'Fremdarbeiter' as a grotesque landscape, where the traditional craft and husbandry of the farmer is reduced through mechanisation to the drudgery of the unskilled factory worker, and 'Heimat' is everywhere ruthlessly exploited by profit-oriented economic forces.

The continuity of development into the 1980s can be seen in the work of other figures of this fourth generation. The depiction of the workplace in the 1970s in books by Silvio Blatter, Emil Zopfi and Urs Karpf acquires an altogether more radical dimension in the early writing of Franz Böni (b. 1952). Here the degradation inflicted on the lives of those who service mechanical processes in the modern economy manifests itself in mental and emotional isolation. Marcel Konrad (b. 1954) goes behind the dark and sombre picture of the countryside which was presented to the outside observer in, for example, E. Y. Meyer's *In Trubschachen* (1973), to show from the inside the constraints and pressures which stand so starkly at odds with the traditional idyll. The themes of death and terminal illness, which first featured sensationally in Fritz Zorn's *Mars* (1977), are taken up in the stories of Thomas Hürlimann (b. 1950), in which individual death is linked to manifestations of change and decay in the social fabric. The relationship between personal identity and the values of the individual's environment which so exercised the eponymous hero of *Stiller* is examined, for example, by Hansjörg Schertenleib (b. 1957) and Dante Andrea Franzetti (b. 1959). The rediscovery in the 1960s of the work of Robert Walser highlighted the possibilities of parody and linguistic play as a reaction to the severe fragmentation of the world. These possibilities were developed in the 1970s by authors such as Jürg Laederach and Felix Philipp Ingold, and continue in the 1980s in the novels of Matthias Zschokke (b. 1954). And Martin Dean (b. 1955) carries forward in two major novels the search initiated by Gertrud Leutenegger in the 1970s for a balance between emotion and the rational inheritance of the Enlightenment. A more detailed discussion of these authors provides an overview of some aspects of the new writing.

The sense of personal dislocation in Hartmann's *Gebrochenes Eis* is shown by Franz Böni to be the central experience of an entire section of the population, namely, the modern proletariat, which sells its largely unskilled labour indiscriminately to the factory or to agriculture or which travels the inhospitable countryside hawking goods. The demands made on the workers exhaust them both physically and mentally so that there is no question of organised protest. Indeed, those individuals who do rebel or who seek fairer treatment from superiors and officials, who are concerned merely that the system function with maximum efficiency, are also regarded with hostility by their fellow workers for jeopardising their livelihood. At every turn, social institutions and processes conflict with the natural rhythms of life; at every turn, these institutions and processes ruthlessly enforce conformity to their dictates. The lack of real human contact is seen again in the mean and makeshift habitations which, far from providing a base for replenishment of energy, simply offer the opportunity to unleash frustration and aggression. Deprived in this way of necessary emotional succour, the characters become increasingly isolated and their eccentricities are described without a trace of warmth or sympathy. 'Heimat' has become a labyrinthine network of restriction and deprivation.

This dispiriting world, first introduced in the volume of stories *Ein Wanderer im Alpenregen* (1979), achieves its fullest expression in the two novels *Schlatt* (1979) and *Die Wanderarbeiter* (1981). *Schlatt* is the designation for the bleakest of the models of Switzerland constructed since 1945 – Andorra, Güllen, Jammers, Schilten, Ruch (Reto Hänny) and Barbarswila (Gerold Späth) have been some of the others – and is part of the 'Archipel Schweiz'[7] which features in Böni's writing. Here, the anonymous dictatorship which determines the nature and availability of work holds sway; here, the workers are 'Fremdarbeiter' in their own country, like the young Swiss apprentice in *Blösch*. *Schlatt* contains a brilliantly sustained depiction of the subjection of human beings to mechanical processes which require unremitting attention. In a variant of the theme of return, a *topos* in German-Swiss literature since *Martin Salander*, the hero of *Schlatt* returns home after working for six years as a loader, not abroad, but in another part of Switzerland, to discover that he, needing warmth and understanding after his experience, can no longer reintegrate into his former community, the nature of whose members is as cold and forbidding as its natural surroundings. In *Die Wanderarbeiter*, the inner barrenness has its external counterpart in the ceaseless movement from workplace to workplace, a change each time to what remains basically the same. It occurs to Arthur, one of the two protagonists, that he and his companion Karl are in a position to point out that all workplaces are bad in the same way, and that this awareness might provide the impulse for common action, 'doch wer glaube schon dem Worte eines Wanderarbeiters'.[8] Insight and knowledge gained by experience cannot be communicated and the vicious circle of exploitation and waste will never be broken.

The trilogy, *Die Alpen* (1983), *Alle Züge fahren nach Salem* (1984) and *Wie die Zeit vergeht* (1988), centres round the autobiographical figure Nowak, casual worker and artist, and presents, from the margins of society, a picture of Switzerland in the 1970s and early 1980s. On the one hand, white-collar society is ruled by the most rigid and inflexible norms, breach of which results in expulsion. On the other hand, a constantly changing army of the dispossessed and needy are cynically exploited in the unpoliced darker areas of industry and commerce, often in danger of life and limb, with their health always at risk. Nowak moves between these two sections of the one society, constantly seeking not to be duped and to avoid the sanctions of the more powerful. As in Böni's earlier work, there is no human solidarity: 'Weshalb unternimmt einer einsame Wanderungen in unwegsame Schluchten? – Um den Menschen zu entgehen.'[9] In *Die Residenz* (1988), a novel which forms a thematic compendium of previous work, the same lack of contact is still a central feature. Yet, if Böni's work deals almost exclusively with human failure and waste, the dynamism of his presentation sustains his material. In a short essay 'Der Dichter', written in 1978 but not published until 1983, Böni takes issue with those who complain: 'Schade, daß er [der Dichter] nicht über die Liebe schreibt. Diese Toren: Auch wenn er über Irrenhäuser schrieb, so schrieb er in Wirklichkeit nie etwas anderes als über die Liebe.'[10]

The first novel published by Marcel Konrad, *Stoppelfelder* (1983), has similarities of theme, not only with the work of his country-man Franz Böni, but also with that of other writers in what is called the 'Oberdeutsch' area: with the early plays of Franz Xaver Kroetz and the prose of Herbert Achternbusch in Bavaria and the writing in Austria of Klaus Hoffer, Franz Innerhofer and Josef Winkler. These works form part of what has been termed critical 'Heimat-literatur' and present certain broad common features: the sheer physical drudgery of work, the exploitation of atavistic fears, an immutably hierarchical social order oblivious to human needs. *Stoppelfelder*, for example, presents in its first-person narrator a very powerful picture of an individual at the mercy of his physical and mental nature in a rural community which suppresses discussion and inquiry. The gradual emergence in the narrator's mind of a fantasy world, a counter-reality in which the sexual urge is free from sin and disease and in which subjugation is transformed into its opposite, is depicted as the inevitable consequence of the domi-nant social ethos. For the violence which the system employs to obtain its ends, here symbolised by the aggressive, drunken father, also becomes a means of escape from systematic repression: the rape and murder committed by the narrator, for example, or the murder of the father by his wife and her lover are understood by the perpetrators as acts of liberation. The half-perceived links in the mind of the narrator between individual behaviour and social ethos never progress to the point of articulation which might lead to analysis and change. Thus, as in the world of Franz Böni, individ-uals are unable to exert pressure for change on social structures.

If, in *Stoppelfelder*, the damage inflicted by society is not chal-lenged by the victims, the central figure in *Erzählzeit. Ein Zustand* (1984) goes so far as to justify his maltreatment. An elderly man recounts his upbringing and the values which were inculcated into him, and the manner in which he sought to embody these values in the conduct of his later life. As his tale develops, however, it becomes clear that he has had virtually no control over the events in his life and that he is presenting as a success in terms of these values a life which to the external observer, the reader, has been charac-terised by limitation and waste. The deleterious effects of a harsh and repressive upbringing are a continuation in the work of the

fourth generation of a theme which featured earlier. Rosalia Wenger's 'Erlebnisbericht' *Rosalia G – Ein Leben* (1978), for example,
was followed by Mariella Mehr (b. 1947), who draws on her own
childhood as a gypsy foundling in the composition of *steinzeit*
(1981), and by Alain Claude Sulzer (b. 1953), who shows in *Das
Erwachsenengerüst* (1983) how a child is moulded into patterns of
behaviour which have been prepared for him in advance.

Death, as treated by Thomas Hürlimann in his two best-known
prose works, the short story *Die Tessinerin* (1981) and the novella
Das Gartenhaus (1989), is not the result of violence but of natural
causes, and in each case the theme has a wider framework of
reference. Both tales highlight the lack of control exercised by the
individual over death: in *Die Tessinerin* disease implacably destroys
the body of the schoolmaster's wife; in *Das Gartenhaus* the mental
processes of the colonel gradually detach themselves from the
normative patterns of the everyday world. Both tales depict the end
of a world, in an individual sense, and also in relation to the
environment of the dying person. The death of the teacher's wife is
parallelled by the closure of the school in the tiny village in Canton
Schwyz, a symbolic break with the past caused by the inexorable
movement of population from the countryside to the conurbations
as the economy becomes increasingly centralised. The death of the
colonel is linked to the redundancy of the *bürgerlich* world in which
he played a significant role. The villa in which he lives is falling into
disrepair; the park in which the villa stands is gradually being
reclaimed by vegetation; beyond stands the menacing building of
the factory; and the family feasts and rituals, attended by a lack-
lustre younger generation, have become empty and meaningless.
Yet the most potent symbol of an age that has passed, even before
the death of the colonel, is, in the summer house, the model
railway which belonged to the son who died as a teenager. For the
model, contemplated sadly by the old man and his wife, symbolises
a vision of Switzerland as it was once perceived. Both tales, despite
their concern with death and wider connotations of decay, point to
continuity: in the village, the place left at the 'Stammtisch' by the
teacher is taken by the Turkish doctor who tended his wife; the old
colonel, as his own vitality ebbs, responds to the life force of the cat
he finds at the grave of his son. Both *Die Tessinerin* and *Das
Gartenhaus*, while treating of death, also deal with the responsibility
of the survivors towards life.

The model railway in *Das Gartenhaus* points to the fact that a
once vibrant history has been reduced to a dead plaything. From
a different perspective, Dante Andrea Franzetti and Hansjörg

Schertenleib, who reached maturity in the 1970s, take up the theme figured so prominently in that decade in E. Y. Meyer's major novel *Die Rückfahrt* (1977): a relationship to the past is an essential constituent of personal identity. Like Meyer, Franzetti sees the matter in terms of the cultural impoverishment of the technological age: 'So perfekt und reibungslos wie unsere Moderne vernichtet keine Kultur die Spuren eigener und fremder Vergangenheit.'[11] In this situation, the individual, deprived of a historical dimension in the present, must seek to establish his own connections. Franzetti does this in *Der Großvater* (1985) through the invented figure of an Italian grandfather who came to Zurich to work on the extension of the main railway station. The writer tells this character that he wishes to recreate the past through the medium of his craft: 'So will ich versuchen, mich schreibend Erlebnissen und Gedanken zu nähern, die du gehabt haben könntest' (DG 54). In doing so, he also evokes other characters, whose lives were determined by forces such as war, economic crisis, fascism and changes in manufacture and consumption – the great army of the forgotten who provide the workforce for a culture which uproots and disperses. If *Der Großvater* describes the impact of modern life on traditional local cultures, *Cosimo und Hamlet* (1987) portrays a later situation where the cultural insecurity of the two brothers of Italian parentage growing up in the Zurich of the 1970s becomes a metaphor for the manner in which the multifarious influences of modern society disorientate the individual and can also foster the creation of an artificial relationship to the past through appeals to chauvinism.

If it can be said of Franzetti that he is initially concerned with a temporal dimension of the relationship to the past, Hansjörg Schertenleib addresses himself more to a geographical aspect. In his first novel, *Die Ferienlandschaft* (1983), the first-person narrator returns to the home of his Austrian relations, where he spent the holidays of his childhood. As with Franzetti's narrator on his return to the fictitious Italian village of Limoli, the narrator in Schertenleib's novel both has a claim to belong and yet has the status of an outsider, which provides a double perspective.[12] He experiences a strong emotional response to the sturdy framework of life which he observes in rural Austria: 'Mein Neid auf die festen, scheinbar unzerbrechlichen Verhältnisse hier, auf das aus Brauchtum, Tradition und Heimatliebe gekittete Gefüge'; yet, simultaneously, he suspects that the price paid for living within this framework is that the individual becomes 'gefangen' and 'genügsam' (DF 58). The comportment and plans of his cousin Rudi, who appears to identify fully with his environment, increase rather than dispel his doubts.

Nonetheless, he recognises the strength and legitimacy within himself of 'dieses Verlangen nach Heimat' (DF 86), and the structure of the novel reflects the narrator's attempts to come to terms with this in a manner which he can accept: the narrative juxtaposes the memories of Austria from childhood and youth with the observations of the adult and the synthesis towards which the narrator is striving takes the form of five regularly spaced 'Entwürfe', each entitled 'Gegenheimat'. In the third 'Entwurf', a statement halfway between a question and an answer points towards the direction in which a solution might lie: 'Kann man in der Heitmatlosigkeit Heimat finden' (DF 122). The move towards a break with traditional concepts of 'Heimat' is completed when the narrator declares at the close: 'Doch, auch in Worten, in der Sprache kann man ein Zuhause finden' (DF 150).

Schertenleib seeks to construct, through writing, a 'Gegenheimat', as Franzetti tries, also through writing, to establish links to the past which are free of the clichés which are exploited by *bürgerlich* society for political purposes. Arguably, Schertenleib perceives fewer difficulties than Franzetti in trying to redefine concepts which relate to existential needs but the current definitions of which are at best meaningless and at worst damaging. Certainly, in Schertenleib's second novel *Die Geschwister* (1988), the manner in which the characters of the brother and sister are utilised to highlight the outmoded nature of existing social values, verges at times on the simplistic. Franzetti's *Cosimo und Hamlet*, on the other hand, gives a very clear indication of the price which still must be paid for flouting perceived norms: at the close, the two brothers have become socially marginalised, the artistically talented one as box-office attendant for a group of travelling players, the mathematically talented one learning Latin by means of a computer. What the characters of Schertenleib and Franzetti have in common, however, is that they have absolutely no sense of loss or regret for the vaunted and normative lifestyles which they reject, and this is perhaps indicative of another tone in the 1980s.

If Schertenleib and Franzetti seek to create with their writing a framework which will develop and support personal identity, for Matthias Zschokke disintegration and disharmony are such all-pervading features of modern life that the only possible response is play – in the case of the writer, play with language. In three books, *Max* (1982), *Prinz Hans* (1984) and *ErSieEs* (1986), for example, satire, parody and word association are harnessed in dynamic fashion to create fleeting cohesion in a world where reality is irretrievably fragmented. Yet the creation of cohesion through written language is in itself part of the general futility since our age is characterised by an inability which it imagines was endemic to the preceding dark ages: 'Unser Analphabetentum ist total und unerschütterlich. . . . Wir haben lesen gelernt, um lesen zu können, nicht um zu lesen . . . Wir sind freiwillige Analphabeten.'[13] Zschokke's mockery, linked to the work of his colleagues such as E. Y. Meyer and Franzetti, who see us cut off from the lessons of the past through our arrogance, also pillories our inability to read the signs of the way in which the world is going.

It is appropriate that *Max* should have won the Robert Walser Prize in 1982 since it has several parallels with Walser's *'Raüber'-Roman* (written 1925, first published 1972): the mock discussion with the reader about the development of the narrative, the feigned indecision about the role and function of the hero, the ironic use of form to show its dissolution. But whereas Walser closes his novel with an apparent reconciliation between his hero and society (an ending which is in fact as subversive as the hero's overt social opposition), Zschokke has Max killed in a car accident at the end of the book – Max has fulfilled his function of showing the impossibility of establishing meaningful identity. The sex of another central figure, Ersieës de Glych in *ErSieEs*, is variable and so adds one more element to the many variables in Frisch's *Mein Name sei Gantenbein* twenty years before, but the surname of Zschokke's figure also indicates that the attempt to find a permanent role always fails. The world of Zschokke, pullulating with bizarre figures and events and sustained by a marvellous inventiveness, seems a far cry from the dour, harsh world of Franz Böni, but arguably they both portray, in very different ways, figures on the margins of society who are engaged in establishing strategies of survival which involve compliance with a normality which they reject; ultimately, of course, the life-destroying contradiction cannot be maintained, and where this is made explicitly clear in Böni's work, it is implicitly so in Zschokke's. It has been claimed that Swiss literature is a literature rich in clowns who adopt an ironical stance towards themselves and who, by exposing their own inner dreams and needs to mockery, reveal the conditions which govern the lives of others; and that in this respect Zschokke is a very Swiss writer.[14] Certainly, he has in common with Robert Walser a dark awareness of the limitations of play.

Links to the more immediate past are apparent in the work of Martin R. Dean. Whereas an important strand in post-1945 German-Swiss literature was perceived, and perceived itself, as being iconoclastic – the most potent image of this is Anatol Stiller's destruction of his clay figures – the 1970s experienced a certain change of attitude towards the untrammelled application of rationality to human affairs. Gertrud Leutenegger, whose date of birth (1948) relates her to the fourth generation but who began publishing in the mid-1970s, pleads for a restoration of the elements of myth and emotion which will complement and enhance, but not call in question, the element of rationality.[15] Dean's first novel, *Die verborgenen Gärten* (1982), continues this redirection of emphasis, and also, by incorporating the image of the labyrinth present in German-Swiss writing since the early prose of Dürrenmatt,[16] fuses and reworks two different traditions.

Die verborgenen Gärten deals with the conflicting directions of forces central to human life, the circular motion of organic nature and the linear progression of rationality. The experience of this conflict is depicted in the figure of the student Manuel Kornell. The millionaire Brosamer, whose life is governed by the application of rationality and who, significantly, is suffering from amnesia which ruptures his link to time and nature, employs Manfred to act for a year as supervisor of his estate in Provence, the centrepiece of which is an overgrown garden equipped with a maze. As in a similar philosophical *Entwicklungsroman* of the 1970s, E. Y. Meyer's *Die Rückfahrt*, there is virtually no plot; the dynamism of the book is generated, as in the earlier novel, by its discourse.[17] Manuel struggles, on the one hand, against the blandishments of Brosamer to embrace a rationality which seeks to control and wield power and, on the other hand, against the attraction towards unadulterated physical sensation exerted by the sun-drenched luxuriant vegetation. Manuel seeks to retain his identity by keeping a written record which both takes cognisance of, and utilises, the two forces. He must establish his past in relation to the eternal rhythm of nature: 'Nur die genaue, schonungslose Erinnerung bietet Gewähr dafür, daß das unablässige Kreisen der Zeit aus der Bahn zu bringen ist. Schreiben ist Erinnerung'; and he must ensure his future in relation to the timeless dimension of rationality symbolised by Brosamer: 'Ich schreibe einerseits, um ihn [Brosamer] noch besser zu verstehen, andrerseits aber schreibe ich gegen ihn an, schreibe mich aus seinem Schatten heraus, mir zu, in die Zukunft.'[18] Thus the novel charts the emergence of Manuel towards a balance in which identity becomes possible, towards a modern form of Keats's 'negative capability', the ability to accept 'uncertainties, mysteries, doubts, without any irritable reaching after fact and reason'.[19]

Fact and reason are again central concerns in Dean's second

novel, *Der Mann ohne Licht* (1988). The title is a reference to Thomas Edison, the inventor of, amongst other things, the electric light bulb, a consequence, both literally and figuratively, of the Enlightenment and in this respect symbolic of the perversion which the legacy of the Enlightenment has undergone, both in the sense that human ingenuity is harnessed solely to commercial exploitation ('Das Glühlicht erzeugt eine längere Konsumzeit'[20]), and in the sense that ratiocination sets itself reductive aims (the ambition of the inventor of the lightbulb was to move towards 'der totalen Ersetzung des Menschen', ML 199).

In the first place, it is not only the technologist who is the apostle of reason in *Der Mann ohne Licht*. The writer Eugen Loder, interviewed shortly before his death by the central character in the novel, the thirty-year-old journalist Mario Dill, is an embittered opponent of all that he considers to be irrational. Whereas Loder rejects the notion of linear progress, which is for him embodied above all in the figure of Edison, whose life and attitudes have attracted his attention in the last years of his life as a betrayal of the spirit of the Enlightenment, he is equally contemptuous of what he regards as the illogical attitudes of his Swiss countrymen to their place in history and in the world. His diatribes, conducted in the name of reason, are structured by the novel in such a fashion that they acquire more than a little of the unreason which they are attacking. The enlightened writer with a certain missionary zeal is presented, not unsympathetically, as being slightly ridiculous.

Secondly, Dean's novel appears to be much less concerned with questions of moral rightness and wrongness. If *Die verborgenen Gärten* has conceded the fascination for Manuel of the figure of Brosamer, *Der Mann ohne Licht* shows that the tendency to develop rationality unchecked is a central drive in human nature. Insull, Edison's secretary who represents the reflective, as opposed to the active, principle of rationality, and on whose diaries Loder had been working prior to his death, brings the novel to a close with an entry which underlines the similarity of behaviour generated by the two principles: 'Aber wenn es dunkel ist, werde ich aufstehen und mich für die Nacht frischmachen. Ich werde die Lampe anzünden und das weiße Blatt Papier wird hell aufleuchten. Ich werde weiterschreiben, wie er [Edison] da drüben im Labor immerzu weiterarbeitet' (ML 216). It is a dispassionate statement which does not adopt a moral stance.

A contrast to this world of rationality presented in the interview with Loder in Switzerland and the consultation of the remains of his *Nachlaß* there – symbolically nearly destroyed by fire – is provided in the visit made by Dill to Provence, where 'neue Formen des Zusammenlebens' are being tried out. Some, such as in the old *château* where each room is being converted in accordance with the wishes of one individual, have little prospect of a viable future; others, such as the attempts undertaken by the Swiss sisters Marthe and Mon, have better chances. This symbolic landscape without signposts offers a challenge which increasingly attracts the observer Dill. Just as in the work of Franzetti and Schertenleib there is no sense of loss at failure to adopt socially approved lifestyles, so in *Der Mann ohne Licht* there is no desire to return to the old, more adequately mapped territory but, at the same time, there is no full commitment to the new. The sense of an unproblematic break with outmoded forms is nowhere clearer than in the coolly detached manner in which the hero, 'ein postmoderner Parzifal', passes in review the attitudes of both the contemporary and the older generations, to the extent that *Der Mann ohne Licht* can be regarded as 'an epitaph . . . for the entire literary period that began after the war'.[21] The sense of emancipation which emanates from the novel derives from its full awareness of intellectual and emotional choice.

It is perhaps fitting to close this brief review of continuity and change in the writing of the fourth generation with *Der Mann ohne Licht*, since the novel also points to an altering perception of the writer – the gently mocking presentation places the zealously committed figure of Loder firmly in the past. Hugo Loetscher once warned intellectuals and writers that they must not adopt postures as if they were beyond the influence of society,[22] and the implication of this is that writers mirror their society. Thus Dean and his colleagues portray change, not all of it yet visible, which is taking place, glacier-like, in the highly conservative society of Switzerland. Some public indications are manifest at the beginning of the 1990s: changing attitudes to institutions, such as the army, the altering nature of 'Vielsprachigkeit' with the increase in dialect and the dominance of English, concern at the impact on Switzerland of the wider political changes in Europe. The role of the writer alters with social change. A few months before his death in 1974, Karl Schmid, who had done so much to chart the course of writing in German-speaking Switzerland, foresaw the necessity of the writer creating in the technological world of the future 'eine Gegenwelt' containing the three elements of 'Schwerkraft', 'Schatten' and 'Trauer':

> Bei Schwerkraft darf an alles gedacht werden, was an Existenz und Herkunft erinnert. Im Schatten liegt und birgt sich, was der wissen-

schaftliche Verstand nicht sieht, nicht zuletzt der unverwechselbare Mikrokosmos der Person. Und Trauer stehe hier, ohne jede Dramatik, für jenes schwermütige Wissen um die Unplanbarkeit und Endlichkeit der menschlichen Existenz und Kultur.[23]

The literary themes discussed above in relation to the fourth generation go a considerable way towards fulfilling these conditions.

Notes

1. Lukas Hartmann, *Gebrochenes Eis. Aufzeichnungen*, Zurich, 1980, p. 26 (subsequently GE in the text).

2. Compare Elsbeth Pulver, 'Gegenwartsliteratur der deutschen Schweiz. Ein Überblick', in Gürsel Aytaç, Viktoria Rehberg and Sara Sayin (eds), *Dokumentation der Beiträge des II. Izmirer Colloquiums*, Izmir, 1987, pp. 3–14 (p. 7); and Heinz Schafroth, 'Zehn Einfälle im Zusammenhang mit der Schweizer Gegenwartsliteratur', in H. L. Arnold (ed.), *Bestandsaufnahme. Gegenwartsliteratur Bundesrepublik Deutschland, Deutsche Demokratische Republik, Österreich, Schweiz*, Munich, 1988, pp. 257–66 (p. 260).

3. Silvio Blatter, 'Zwischen Alphorn und Computer. Als Erzähler in der Schweiz', in Wilhelm Solms (ed.), *Geschichten aus einem ereignislosen Land*, Marburg, 1989, pp. 69–84 (p. 83).

4. Michael Böhler, 'Swiss Literary Culture since 1945: Productive Antagonisms and Conflicting Identities', *German Quarterly*, vol. 62, 1989, pp. 293–307 (p. 295).

5. Rolf Niederhauser, *Das Ende der bloßen Vermutung*, Darmstadt and Neuwied, 1979, p. 199.

6. Schafroth, 'Zehn Einfälle', p. 264.

7. Helmut Schödel, 'Drei Tage vor dem Krieg der Tramps', *Die Zeit*, 5 October 1984.

8. Franz Böni, *Die Wanderarbeiter*, Zurich and Frankfurt am Main, 1981, p. 38.

9. Franz Böni, *Alle Züge fahren nach Salem*, Frankfurt am Main, 1984, p. 99.

10. Franz Böni, 'Der Dichter', in *Die Fronfastenkinder. Aufsätze 1966–1985*, Frankfurt am Main, 1985, pp. 12–13 (p. 13).

11. Dante Andrea Franzetti, *Der Großvater*, Zurich, 1985 (subsequently DG in the text); page references to later edition, Munich and Zurich, 1987, here p. 9.

12. 'Die Schweizer sind wieder da, hatten die Nachbarskinder damals gerufen. Die Fremden!', Hansjörg Schertenleib, *Die Ferienlandschaft*, Zurich and Cologne, 1983, (subsequently DF in the text); page references to later edition, Frankfurt am Main, 1986, here p. 125; see also Franzetti: '"Arrivano gli svizzeri", schrien die Kinder in Limoli, als wir . . . vor dem Haus unserer Großeltern hielten', *Der Großvater*, p. 63.

13. Matthias Zschokke, *Max*, Munich, 1982, pp. 66–7.

14. Christoph Neidhart, 'Elefanten und ein Clown, der rot wird', *Die Weltwoche*, 22 May 1986.

15. See Peter von Matt, 'Kritischer Patriotismus. Formen und Zielrichtungen der Auseinandersetzung mit der Schweiz bei den Schriftstellern der sechziger und siebziger Jahre', in Klaus Pezold (ed.), *Entwicklungstendenzen der deutschsprachigen*

Literatur der Schweiz in den sechziger und siebziger Jahren, Leipzig, 1984, pp. 41–9; see also the essay by Elizabeth Boa in this volume.

16. See Anton Krättli, 'Labyrinthen und Höhlen. Beobachtungen an der deutschschweizerischen Gegenwartsliteratur', *Neue Rundschau*, vol. 95, 1984, pp. 71–87.

17. See Jürgen Manthey, 'Nietzsches Geist und Berner Geist oder: Die Geburt der autobiographischen Literatur als nationelles Ereignis – E. Y. Meyers "Die Rückfart", Zarathustra und der Schweizerroman', in Herbert Heckmann (ed.), *Literatur aus dem Leben*, Munich, 1984, pp. 39–57.

18. Martin R. Dean, *Die verborgenen Gärten*, Munich and Vienna, 1982; page references to later edition, Munich, 1985, pp. 63–4 and p. 207.

19. *The Letters of John Keats*, ed. H. Buxton Forman, London 1895, p. 57 (28 December 1817).

20. Martin R. Dean, *Der Mann ohne Licht*, Munich and Vienna, 1988, p. 179 (subsequently ML in the text).

21. Anton Krättli, 'Das eigene Leben suchen. Zu Martin R. Deans "Der Mann ohne Licht"', *Schweizer Monatshefte*, vol. 68, 1988, pp. 669–73 (p. 672); Böhler, 'Swiss Literary Culture', p. 294.

22. Hugo Loetscher, 'Der Auftritt des Engagements', in Dieter Bachmann (ed.), *Fortschreiben, 98 Autoren der deutschen Schweiz*, Zurich, 1977, pp. 294–8 (p. 298).

23. Karl Schmid, 'Funktionswandel der Dichtung in der Zukunftsgesellschaft', in Karl Schmid, *Fortschritt und Dauer. Aufsätze und Reden III*, Zurich and Munich, 1975, pp. 113–31 (pp. 130–1).

Afterword

The post-1945 literature of German-speaking Switzerland discussed in this book was written in a framework unique in the
German-speaking countries of Europe. For only in Switzerland had
pre-war sociopolitical structures, and the ideology which underpinned them, remained intact. This continuity helped to keep alive
a perception, strongly fostered during the period of 'geistige Landesverteidigung', of the writer as supporter and promoter of a
traditional notion of Swiss identity. At the same time the very
neutrality that had guaranteed this continuity enabled a writer like
Max Frisch to question the basis of such identity. For him, the
collapse of German culture under Nazism brought in its train a
radical examination of the common principles which related his
country intimately to the larger culture beyond its borders. And it
was Frisch, more than any other author, who successfully challenged such a reductive view of the writer by encouraging a critical
exploration of the permanent dialectic between German culture and
Swiss politics within which the writer in German-speaking Switzerland functions.

This change in the role of the writer can now be seen to have
anticipated the necessity to rethink political attitudes brought about
by recent events in central and eastern Europe. The history of the
relationship between writer and society in Switzerland since 1945
has thus not been a comfortable one. A conservative society,
bolstered by steady and occasionally spectacular economic progress, has not proved particularly benign towards its critics, who in
their turn have often reacted to the condescension of their fellow
countrymen with an acute hypersensitivity which is peculiarly
Swiss. However, the emancipation of the writer from the oppressive obligation to affirm his roots has helped to create a literature
free from parochialism and has enabled the writer in German-
speaking Switzerland to create works which have made their mark
in the wider world of German culture.

The essays in this book have sought first of all to indicate the
pioneering role played by Max Frisch and Friedrich Dürrenmatt in
this liberating process, and to place the work of their successors in
the context they helped to define. The generational approach helps

to identify similarities of attitude and theme; for example, due to circumstances of birth and experience, the older writers are much more exercised by particular aspects of Switzerland – whether at a visceral level as with Peter Bichsel or at an ironic distance as in the case of Hugo Loetscher – whereas the younger writers treat such features more as convenient paradigms for restrictions which the concrete reality of any advanced industrialised society places on the individual. Nevertheless, the essays on individual writers demonstrate that common themes and formal experiments do act as links between the generations. On the other hand, their very diversity precludes neat generalisations that could establish their work as specifically 'German-Swiss'. It is clear that the discussion of whether a Swiss national literature can be said to exist at all belongs to a specific historical period which tried to create an artificial, and fundamentally defensive, synthesis. Gottfried Keller's famous statement of 1880 that the Swiss writer belonged primarily to the wider culture of his particular language remains an essential part of the dialectic today.

A second aim of this book has been to identify and discuss the wider relevance of the authors selected. For the impact of these writers outside Switzerland depends on them producing work whose validity can be appreciated elsewhere. Many of their themes appear to fulfil this requirement in that they deal with the generalised problems of Western culture: a critique of the fundamental philosophy of an increasingly technological age; the precarious relationship between the individual and society; the transmission of societal values within the family unit; the difficult and complex role of women in a patriarchal society; the emotional alienation, both at a private and public level, which modern forms of living inflict – all these themes inevitably strike echoes beyond Switzerland herself. Indeed, the central unifying concern of all our authors is the defence of the individual against the insidiously depersonalising pressures of the modern age. Rejection of such forms of bondage in their work is matched by persistently imaginative attempts to suggest strategies of emancipation.

Notes on Contributors

Elizabeth Boa: Senior Lecturer in German, University of Nottingham. Her main publications are (with J. H. Reid) *Critical Strategies. German Fiction in the Twentieth Century* (1972) and *The Sexual Circus. Wedekind's Theatre of Subversion* (1987). She is currently working on a feminist study of Franz Kafka.

Michael Butler: Professor of Modern German Literature, University of Birmingham. Publications include *The Novels of Max Frisch* (1975), *The Plays of Max Frisch* (1985), *Frisch: 'Andorra'* (1985), an anthology (with Ilsabe Arnold-Dielewicz) *Englische Lyrik der Gegenwart. Gedichte ab 1945* (1981) and numerous articles on modern German literature.

Clive H. Church: Reader in European Studies, University of Kent. Publications include *Revolution and Red Tape* (1981), *Europe in 1830* (1983), edited volumes on *Aspects of Switzerland: Sources and Reflections* (1986) and *Approaching the Channel Tunnel* (1987), as well as numerous articles on the European Community, the European Free Trade Association, and French and Swiss history and politics.

Ian Hilton: Senior Lecturer in German, University College of North Wales, Bangor. Former Editor of *Modern Languages*, author of *Peter Weiss: A Search for Affinities* (1972), *Peter Huchel: Plough a Lonely Furrow* (1986) and *Peter Weiss: 'Marat/Sade'* (1990), and various articles in the field of modern German literature.

Malcolm Pender: Reader in German Studies, University of Strathclyde. His principal research interest is in the modern literature of German-speaking Switzerland, and his publications include *Max Frisch: His Work and its Swiss Background* (1979), *The Creative Imagination and Society: Aspects of the German-Swiss 'Künstlerroman' in the Twentieth Century* (1985) and *Max Frisch: 'Biedermann und die Brandstifter'* (1988).

Hans Seelig: Free-lance writer and lecturer, formerly Senior Lecturer in German, Middlesex Polytechnic. Publications include

'Neue Wege'. German short stories since 1945 (2nd edition, 1973) and various articles on contemporary German literature.

Ronald Speirs: Reader in German, University of Birmingham. He is the author of *Brecht's Early Plays* (1982), *Bertolt Brecht* (1986) and *Thomas Mann: 'Mario und der Zauberer'* (1990). He is currently working on a study of Franz Kafka.

Mary E. Stewart: Lecturer in German, Cambridge University and Director of Studies in Modern Languages, Robinson College. Main research interests are in late nineteenth- and twentieth-century narrative fiction (especially Max Frisch and Uwe Johnson). Numerous articles on nineteenth-century and post-1945 German literature.

H. Morgan Waidson: Emeritus Professor of German, University College of Swansea. He has written extensively on German and German-Swiss literature. His books include *Jeremias Gotthelf* (1953). His *Anthology of Modern Swiss Literature* appeared in 1984.

John J. White: Reader in German, King's College, London. His publications include *Mythology in the Modern Novel. A Study of Prefigurative Techniques* (1971), *Literary Futurism. Aspects of the First Avant-garde* (1988) and edited volumes on Stramm, Kafka, Musil and Grass. His research interests lie in modern drama and fiction, and the avant-garde.

Wilfried van der Will: Professor of Modern German Studies, University of Birmingham. His publications include *Pikaro heute* (1967), (with R. H. Thomas) *The German Novel and the Affluent Society*, (with R. Burns) *Arbeiterkulturbewegung in der Weimarer Republik* (1982), (with R. Burns) *Protest and Democracy in West Germany. Extra-Parliamentary Opposition and the Democratic Agenda* (1988) and (with B. Taylor) *The Nazification of Art* (1990).

Select Bibliography

The bibliography of secondary literature has been restricted to books and articles published since 1980. János Szabó, *Erzieher und Verweigerer. Zur deutschsprachigen Gegenwartsprosa der Schweiz*, Würzburg, 1989, pp. 145–85, contains a useful bibliography of the post-1945 period. Detailed up-to-date information on secondary literature and on authors can be found in the periodic publication, *Bibliographie zur deutschsprachigen Schweizerliteratur*, Schweizerische Landesbibliothek, Bern 1975ff.

The bibliography of primary literature contains the main works of the authors discussed. Useful survey articles on the twelve main writers featured, as well as on some of the younger writers, are available in *Kritisches Lexikon zur deutschsprachigen Gegenwartsliteratur*, ed. Heinz Ludwig Arnold, Munich, 1978ff. Further relevant information can be found in the annual volumes of *Germanistik* and *The Year's Work in Modern Languages*.

I   Secondary Literature

Aytaç, Gürsel, Rehberg, Viktoria, Sayin, Sara (eds), *Dokumentation der Beiträge des II. Izmirer Colloquiums über 'Die Schweizer Literatur der Gegenwart'*, Izmir, 1987

Böhler, Michael 'Swiss Literary Culture since 1945: Productive Antagonisms and Conflicting Identities', *German Quarterly*, vol. 62, 1989, pp. 293–307

Burger, Hermann, 'Schweizer Literatur nach 1968', in *Als Autor auf der Stör*, Frankfurt am Main, 1987, pp. 219–42

Burkhard, Marianne, 'Diskurs in der Enge. Ein Beitrag zur Phänomenologie der Schweizer Literatur', in Albrecht Schöne (ed.), *Akten des VII. Internationalen Germanisten-Kongresses Göttingen 1985*, Tübingen, 1986, vol. 10, pp. 52–62

——, Acker, Robert (eds), *Zur Frage der Eigenständigkeit der Schweizer Literatur seit 1970*, Amsterdam, 1987

Evans, Tamara, '"Ja, so schön war es noch nie." Zum Heimatbegriff in der Schweizer Gegenwartsliteratur', in H. W. Seliger (ed.), *Der Begriff "Heimat" in der deutschen Gegenwartsliteratur*, Munich, 1988, pp. 97–107

Flood, John (ed.), *Modern Swiss Literature – Unity and Diversity*, London, 1985

Grotzer, Peter (ed.), *Aspekte der Verweigerung in der neueren Literatur aus der Schweiz*, Zurich, 1988

Gsteiger, Manfred, 'Nationales Selbstverständnis in den Literaturen der Schweiz', *Schweizer Monatshefte*, vol. 66, 1986, pp. 499–507

Krättli, Anton, 'Labyrinthen und Höhlen. Beobachtungen an der deutschschweizerischen Gegenwartsliteratur', *Neue Rundschau*, vol. 95, 1984, pp. 71–87

Lerch, Fredi (ed.), *Vorschlag zur Unversöhnlichkeit. Realismusdebatte Winter 1983/84*, Zurich, 1984

Löffler, Heiner (ed.), *Das Deutsch der Schweizer: Zur Sprach- und Literatursituation der Schweiz*, Aarau and Frankfurt am Main, 1986

Manthey, Jürgen, 'Nietzsches Geist und Berner Geist oder: Die Geburt der autobiographischen Literatur als nationelles Ereignis – E. Y. Meyers "Die Rückfahrt", Zarathustra und der Schweizerroman', in Herbert Heckmann (ed.), *Literatur aus dem Leben. Autobiographische Tendenzen der deutschsprachigen Gegenwartsliteratur. Beobachtungen, Erfahrungen, Belege*, Munich, 1984, pp. 39–57

Pezold, Klaus (ed.), *Entwicklungstendenzen der deutschsprachigen Literatur der Schweiz in den sechziger und siebziger Jahren*, Leipzig, 1984

——, 'Die deutschsprachige Literatur der Schweiz in den 70er und frühen 80er Jahren', *Zeitschrift für Germanistik*, vol. 8, 1987, pp. 402–14

Pulver, Elsbeth, 'Die deutschsprachige Literatur der Schweiz seit 1945', in Manfred Gsteiger (ed.), *Die zeitgenössische Literatur der Schweiz*, in *Kindlers Literaturgeschichte der Gegenwart. Autoren – Werke – Themen*, Aktualisierte Ausgabe, Frankfurt am Main, 1980, vol. 7, pp. 137–484

—— (ed.), *Zwischenzeilen. Schriftstellerinnen der deutschen Schweiz*, Zurich and Bern, 1985

——, 'Von einem nächtlichen Fassadenkletterer, von Ambrosio, dem Spanier, und der neuen Lindauerin. Der Fremde als literarische Figur in der deutschschweizerischen Gegenwartsliteratur', in Heinz Ludwig Arnold (ed.), *Bestandsaufnahme. Gegenwartsliteratur Bundesrepublik Deutschland, Deutsche Demokratische Republik, Österreich, Schweiz*, Munich, 1988, pp. 267–81

Schafroth, Heinz, 'Zehn Einfälle im Zusammenhang mit der Schweizer Gegenwartsliteratur', in H. L. Arnold, *Bestandsaufnahme* (see Pulver, 'Vor einem nächtlichen Fassadenkletterer'), pp. 257–66

Schmid-Bortenschlager, Sigrid, 'A – CH: Literatur(en) in Österreich und in der Schweiz. (K)ein Vergleich', in Kurt Bartsch, Dietmar Goltschnigg, Gerhard Melzer (eds), *Für und wider eine österreichische Literatur*, Königstein/Ts, 1982, pp. 116–29

Schulz, Klaus-Dieter, '"Die Zerstörung der Idylle hat begonnen." Zu einigen Entwicklungstendenzen in der deutschsprachigen Prosaliteratur der Schweiz in den sechziger Jahren', *Weimarer Beiträge*, vol. 30, 1984, pp. 1276–95

Siegrist, Christoph, 'Gefährdung und Behauptung. Überlegungen zur Kontinuität der Schweizer Literatur im 20. Jahrhundert', in Albrecht Schöne (ed.), *Akten des VII. Internationalen Germanisten-Kongresses Göt-*

tingen 1985, Tübingen, 1986, vol. 10, pp. 63–71

——, 'Nationalliterarische Aspekte bei Schweizer Autoren', in Ludwig Fischer (ed.), *Literatur in der Bundesrepublik Deutschland bis 1967*, Munich, 1986, pp. 651–71

Solms, Wilhelm (ed.), *Geschichten aus einem ereignislosen Land. Schweizer Literaturtage in Marburg*, Marburg, 1989

Szabó, János, *Erzieher und Verweigerer. Zur deutschsprachigen Gegenwartsprosa der Schweiz*, Würzburg, 1989

Waidson, H. M. (ed.), *Anthology of Modern Swiss Literature*, London, 1984

Zeltner, Gerda, *Das Ich ohne Gewähr. Gegenwartsautoren aus der Schweiz*, Zurich and Frankfurt am Main, 1980

——, *Vom Schweizer Hüsli zur Arche Noah. Betrachtungen zu einem Kapitel Schweizer Literatur*, Wiesbaden, 1984

II   Primary Literature

Peter Bichsel (b. 1935)

Eigentlich möchte Frau Blum den Milchmann kennenlernen. 21 Geschichten, Olten and Freiburg, 1964

Die Jahreszeiten, Darmstadt and Neuwied, 1967

Kindergeschichten, Darmstadt and Neuwied, 1969

Des Schweizers Schweiz, Zurich, 1969

Stockwerke. Prosa, Stuttgart, 1974

Geschichten zur falschen Zeit, Darmstadt and Neuwied, 1979

Der Leser. Das Erzählen. Frankfurter Poetik-Vorlesungen, Darmstadt and Neuwied, 1982

Der Busant, Darmstadt and Neuwied, 1985

Irgendwo anderswo, Darmstadt and Neuwied, 1986

Schulmeistereien, Darmstadt and Neuwied, 1987

Im Gegenteil. Kolumnen 1986–1990, Darmstadt and Neuwied, 1990

Franz Böni (b. 1952)

Ein Wanderer im Alpenregen. Erzählungen, Frankfurt am Main, 1979

Schlatt. Roman, Frankfurt am Main, 1979

Die Wanderarbeiter. Roman, Frankfurt am Main, 1981

Die Alpen, Frankfurt am Main, 1983

Alle Züge fahren nach Salem, Frankfurt am Main, 1984

Die Fronfastenkinder. Aufsätze 1966–1985, Frankfurt am Main, 1985

Wie die Zeit vergeht, Zurich, 1988

Die Residenz. Roman, Zurich, 1988

Select Bibliography

Herman Burger (1942–1989)

Rauchsignale. Gedichte, Zurich, 1967
Bork. Prosastücke, Zurich and Stuttgart, 1970
Schilten. Schulbericht zuhanden der Inspektorenkonferenz, Zurich and Munich, 1976
Diabelli. Erzählungen, Frankfurt am Main, 1979
Kirchberger Idyllen, Frankfurt am Main, 1980
Die Künstliche Mutter. Roman, Frankfurt am Main, 1982
Ein Mann aus Wörtern [essays], Frankfurt am Main, 1983
Blankenburg. Erzählungen, Frankfurt am Main, 1986
Die allmähliche Verfertigung der Idee beim Schreiben. Frankfurter Poetik-Vorlesung, Frankfurt am Main, 1986
Als Autor auf der Stör [essays], Frankfurt am Main, 1987
Der Schuß auf die Kanzel. Eine Erzählung, Zurich, 1988
Tractatus logico-suicidalis. Über die Selbsttötung, Frankfurt am Main, 1988
Brenner, vol. 1: *Brunsleben*, Frankfurt am Main, 1989

Martin R. Dean (b. 1955)

Die verborgenen Gärten. Roman, Munich and Vienna, 1982
Die gefiederte Frau. Fünf Variationen über die Liebe, Munich and Vienna, 1984
Der Mann ohne Licht. Roman, Munich and Vienna, 1988
Ausser mir, Munich and Vienna, 1990

Friedrich Dürrenmatt (1921–1990)

Werkausgabe in dreißig Bänden, Zurich, 1980
Stoffe I-III, Zurich, 1981 (revised edition under the title *Labyrinth. Stoffe I-III*, Zurich, 1990)
Achterloo. Eine Komödie in zwei Akten, Zurich, 1983
Justiz. Roman, Zurich, 1985
Minotaurus. Eine Ballade, Zurich, 1985
Der Auftrag oder Vom Beobachten des Beobachters der Beobachter. Novelle in vierundzwanzig Sätzen, Zurich, 1986
(with Charlotte Kerr) *Rollenspiele. Protokoll einer fiktiven Inszenierung und Achterloo III*, Zurich, 1986
Die Welt als Labyrinth. Ein Gespräch mit Franz Kreuzer, Zurich, 1986
Durcheinandertal. Roman, Zurich, 1989
Turmbau. Stoffe IV-IX, Zurich, 1990

Dante Andrea Franzetti (b. 1959)

Der Großvater. Erzählung, Zurich, 1985
Cosimo und Hamlet. Roman, Zurich, 1987

Die Versammlung der Engel im Hotel Excelsior. Roman, Zurich, 1990

Max Frisch (b. 1911–1991)

Gesammelte Werke in zeitlicher Folge, ed. Hans Mayer, 7 vols, Frankfurt am Main, 1976–86
'Am Ende der Aufklärung steht das Goldene Kalb', *Die Weltwoche*, 15 May 1986 (= 'Solothurner Rede')
Schweiz ohne Armee? Ein Palaver, Zurich, 1989
Schweiz als Heimat? Versuche über 50 Jahre, ed. Walter Obschlager, Frankfurt am Main, 1990

Christoph Geiser (b. 1949)

Zimmer mit Frühstück. Erzählung, Basle, 1975
Grünsee. Roman, Zurich and Cologne, 1978
Brachland. Roman, Zurich and Cologne, 1980
Wüstenfahrt. Roman, Zurich, 1984
Das geheime Fieber. Roman, Zurich, 1987

Thomas Hürlimann (b. 1950)

Die Tessinerin. Geschichten, Zurich, 1981
Das Gartenhaus. Novelle, Zurich, 1989

Marcel Konrad (b. 1954)

Stoppelfelder. Roman, Zurich, 1983
Erzählzeit. Ein Zustand, Zurich, 1984
In meinem Rücken hängt das Vatertier – vor meinen Füßen liegt das Muttertier. Roman, Zurich, 1988

Gertrud Leutenegger (b. 1948)

Vorabend. Roman, Frankfurt am Main, 1975
Nineve. Roman, Frankfurt am Main, 1977
Lebewohl, Gute Reise. Ein dramatisches Poem, Frankfurt am Main, 1980
Gouverneur. Roman, Frankfurt am Main, 1981
Komm ins Schiff. Dramatisches Poem, Frankfurt am Main, 1983
Kontinent. Roman, Frankfurt am Main, 1985
Das verlorene Monument [essays], Frankfurt am Main, 1985
Meduse, Frankfurt am Main, 1988

Select Bibliography

Hugo Loetscher (b. 1929)

Abwässer. Ein Gutachten, Zurich, 1963
Die Kranzflechterin, Zurich, 1964
Noah. Roman einer Konjunktur, Zurich, 1967
Der Immune, Darmstadt and Neuwied, 1975; revised edition, Zurich, 1985
Wunderwelt. Eine brasilianische Begegnung, Darmstadt and Neuwied, 1979
Herbst in der großen Orange, Zurich, 1982
Der Waschküchenschlüssel und andere Helvetica, Zurich, 1983
Die Papiere des Immunen, Zurich, 1986
Vom Erzählen erzählen. Münchner Poetikvorlesungen, Zurich, 1988
Die Fliege und die Suppe und 33 andere Tiere in 33 anderen Situationen, Zurich, 1989

Kurt Marti (b. 1921)

republikanische gedichte, St. Gallen, 1959
Dorfgeschichten, Gütersloh, 1960; new and expanded edition, Darmstadt and Neuwied, 1983
gedichte am rand, Teufen, 1963; new and revised edition as:
geduld und revolte – die gedichte am rand, Stuttgart, 1984
rosa loui – vierzg gedicht ir bärner umgangsschprach, Darmstadt and Neuwied, 1967
leichenreden, Darmstadt and Neuwied, 1969
Abratzky oder Die kleine Brockhütte. Lexikon in einem Band, Darmstadt and Neuwied, 1971
heil-vetia, Basle, 1971; new and revised edition as:
Heil-Vetia. Poetischer Diskurs, Basle, 1981
undereinisch – gedicht ir bärner umgangsschprach, Darmstadt and Neuwied, 1973
Zum Beispiel Bern 1972. Ein politisches Tagebuch, Darmstadt and Neuwied, 1973
Die Riesin. Ein Bericht, Darmstadt and Neuwied, 1975
abendland. gedichte, Darmstadt and Neuwied, 1980
Bürgerliche Geschichten, Darmstadt and Neuwied, 1981
Zärtlichkeit und Schmerz. Notizen, Darmstadt and Neuwied, 1981
Schon wieder heute. Ausgewählte Gedichte 1959–1980, Darmstadt and Neuwied, 1982
wo chiemte mer hi? gedicht und schtückli ir bärner umgangsschprach, Münsingen, 1984 (includes *rosa loui* and *undereinisch*)
Ruhe und Ordnung. Aufzeichnungen, Abschweifungen 1980–1983, Darmstadt and Neuwied, 1984
Tagebuch mit Bäumen, Darmstadt and Neuwied, 1985
Nachtgeschichten, Darmstadt and Neuwied, 1987
Mein barfüßig Lob. Gedichte, Darmstadt and Neuwied, 1987

Der Gottesplanet. Aufsätze und Predigten, Darmstadt and Neuwied, 1988
Der Vorsprung Leben. Ausgewählte Gedichte 1959–1987, Frankfurt am Main, 1989
Wen meinte der Mann? Gedichte und Prosatexte [anthology], Stuttgart, 1990
Högerland. Ein Fußgängerbuch, Frankfurt am Main, 1990

E. Y. Meyer (b. 1946)

Ein Reisender in Sachen Umsturz. Erzählungen, Frankfurt am Main, 1972; revised edition, Frankfurt am Main, 1983.
In Trubschachen. Roman, Frankfurt am Main, 1973
Eine entfernte Ähnlichkeit. Erzählungen, Frankfurt am Main, 1975
Die Rückfahrt. Roman, Frankfurt am Main, 1977
Die Hälfte der Erfahrung. Essays und Reden, Frankfurt am Main, 1980
Plädoyer – Für die Erhaltung der Vielfalt der Natur beziehungsweise für deren Verteidigung gegen die ihr drohende Vernichtung durch die Einfalt des Menschen, Frankfurt am Main, 1982
Sunday morning. Theaterstück. Berndeutsch, Bern, 1984
Sunday morning. Theaterstück. Hochdeutsche Fassung, Kreuzlingen and Bern, 1987
'"Das Naturversöhnungsprojekt". Aus dem Roman *Das Naturtheater*', *Schweizer Monatshefte*, vol. 67, 1987, pp. 831–4
'Die Fahrt durch das Land der Nekrophilen' (excerpt from *Das Naturtheater*), *Der Bund*, Bern, 11 April 1987
'"Reservat im Schloß". Aus dem Romanmanuskript *Das Naturtheater*', *Neue Zürcher Zeitung*, 21/22 February 1987
'Das Naturtheater', *drehpunkt*, no. 71/2, 1988, pp. 149–55.

Adolf Muschg (b. 1934)

Im Sommer des Hasen. Roman, Zurich, 1965
Gegenzauber. Roman, Zurich, 1967
Fremdkörper. Erzählungen, Zurich, 1968
Mitgespielt. Roman, Zurich, 1969
Liebesgeschichten, Frankfurt am Main, 1972
Albissers Grund. Roman, Frankfurt am Main, 1974
Entfernte Bekannte. Erzählungen, Frankfurt am Main, 1976
Gottfried Keller. Ein literarisches Porträt, Munich, 1977
Besuch in der Schweiz. Erzählungen, Stuttgart, 1978
Baiyun oder Die Freundschaftsgesellschaft. Roman, Frankfurt am Main, 1980
Literatur als Therapie? Ein Exkurs über das Heilsame und das Unheilbare. Frankfurter Vorlesungen, Frankfurt am Main, 1981
Leib und Leben. Erzählungen, Frankfurt am Main, 1982
Das Licht und der Schlüssel. Erziehungsroman eines Vampirs, Frankfurt am Main, 1984

Select Bibliography

Goethe als Emigrant. Auf der Suche nach dem Grünen bei einem alten Dichter, Frankfurt am Main, 1986
Der Turmhahn und andere Liebesgeschichten, Frankfurt am Main, 1987
Die Schweiz am Ende – am Ende die Schweiz. Erinnerungen an mein Land vor 1991. Frankfurt am Main, 1990

Hansjörg Schertenleib (b. 1957)

Grip. Drei Erzählungen, Zurich and Cologne, 1982
Die Ferienlandschaft. Roman, Zurich and Cologne, 1983
Die Prozession der Männer. Erzählung, Cologne, 1985
Die Geschwister. Roman, Cologne, 1988

Margrit Schriber (b. 1939)

Aussicht gerahmt. Roman, Frauenfeld, 1976
Ausser Saison. Erzählungen, Frauenfeld, 1977
Kartenhaus. Roman, Frauenfeld, 1978
Ein Platz am Seitenpodest. Hörspiel in: *manuskript. Zeitschrift für Literatur*, vol. 18, 1978, 16–25
Vogel flieg! Roman, Frauenfeld, 1980
Luftwurzeln. Erzählungen, Frauenfeld, 1981
Muschelgarten. Roman, Zurich, 1984
Tresorschatten. Roman, Zurich, 1987
AugenWeiden. Roman, Zurich, 1990

O. F. Walter (b. 1928)

Der Stumme. Roman, Munich, 1959
Herr Tourel. Roman, Munich, 1962
Die ersten Unruhen. Ein Konzept, Reinbek bei Hamburg, 1972
Die Verwilderung. Roman, Reinbek bei Hamburg, 1977
Wie wird Beton zu Gras. Fast eine Liebesgeschichte, Reinbek bei Hamburg, 1979
Das Staunen der Schlafwandler am Ende der Nacht. Roman, Reinbek bei Hamburg, 1983
Zeit des Fasans. Roman, Reinbek bei Hamburg, 1988
Gegenwort. Aufsätze, Reden, Begegnungen, Zurich, 1988

Matthias Zschokke (b. 1954)

Max. Roman, Munich, 1982
Prinz Hans, Munich, 1984
ErSieEs, Munich, 1986

Index

Note: For additional guidance, the works of contemporary German-Swiss writers are listed with dates in chronological order of appearance.

Achleitner, Friedrich, 126
Achternbusch, Herbert, 230
Adorno, Theodor, 119
Aristotle, 153
Arnold, Heinz Ludwig, 43
Artmann, H. C., 126

Bach, Johann Sebastian, 34
Bachmann, Guido
  Gilgamesch-Trilogie (1966–1982), 169
Bachmann, Ingeborg, 134, 195, 203
  Todesarten, 219
Bacon, Francis, 168
Ball, Hugo, 152
Barth, Karl, 14
Baur, Margrit, 33
Beck, Julian, 125
Beckett, Samuel, 152
Bernhard, Thomas, 146, 148, 151, 189, 198
  Das Kalkwerk, 148
  Verstörung, 148
  Watten, 148
de Beauvoir, Simone, 209
Beutler, Maja, 28
  Fuß fassen (1980), 33
Bichsel, Peter, 3, 35, 44, 45, **74–92**, 240, 246
  Frau Blum (1964), 28, 29, 74–8, 86, 124
  Die Jahreszeiten (1967), 28, 36, 78–85, 88, 90
  Des Schweizers Schweiz (1969), 27
  Kindergeschichten (1969), 86–7, 90
  Geschichten zur falschen Zeit (1979), 90
  Der Busant (1985), 87–9
Blake, William, 134
Blatter, Silvio, 2, 226, 227

Schaltfehler (1972), 34
Genormte Tage, verschüttete Zeit (1976), 34
Böll, Heinrich, 107, 132
  Ansichten eines Clowns, 97
  Frankfurter Vorlesungen, 132
  Gruppenbild mit Dame, 132
Böni, Franz, 28, 34, 227, **228–30**, 230, 234, 246
  Ein Wanderer im Alpenregen (1979), 228
  Schlatt (1979), 34, 228
  Die Wanderarbeiter (1981), 34, 228
  Die Alpen (1983), 34, 35, 229
  Alle Züge fahren nach Salem (1984), 229
  Wie die Zeit vergeht (1988), 229
  Die Residenz (1988), 229
Bonjour, Edgar, 14
Bosch, Hieronymous, 55
Bräker, Ulrich, 49
Brecht, Bertolt, 121, 206
  Das Leben des Galilei, 42, 104
  Der gute Mensch von Sezuan, 42
  Mutter Courage, 42
Brontë sisters, 219
Buber, Martin, 152
Büchner, Georg, 52, 53
  Woyzeck, 53
Burger, Hermann, 4, 28, 34, 35, 45, **184–201**, 247
  Rauchsignale (1967), 184
  Die Leser auf der Stör (1970), 26
  Schilten (1976), 28, 29, 32, 185, 186, 188, 189–93, 199
  Diabelli (1979), 185, 200
  Kirchberger Idyllen (1980), 185, 191, 200
  Die Künstliche Mutter (1962), 185,

186–7, 192, 193, 194–6, 199
Blankenburg (1986), 185
Der Schuß auf die Kanzel (1988), 187,
  188, 190, 191, 199
Tractatus logico-suicidalis (1988), 184,
  189, 191, 197–9
Brunsleben (1989), 184, 187, 192,
  196, 200
Burkart, Erika, 2
Burkhard, Marianne, 171, 174
Burren, Ernst, 128

Camus, Albert, 86, 146
  La Peste, 158
Caravaggio, Michelangelo da, 166,
  167, 168
Celan, Paul, 51, 134, 189
Churchill, Winston, 9, 148
Cincera, Ernst, 129
Courtier, Sidney H., 152
Cromwell, Oliver, 152

von Dach, Margrit, 36
  Geschichten vom Fräulein (1982), 33
Dean, Martin R., 34, 35, 228, **234–7**,
  247
  Die verborgenen Gärten (1982), 235,
  236
  Der Mann ohne Licht (1988), 235–7
Delors, Jacques, 21
Diderot, Denis, 49
Diggelmann, Walter Matthias, 2, 26, 28
  Die Hinterlassenschaft (1965), 29, 70
  Schatten (1979), 33
Droste-Hülshoff, Annette von, 203,
  216, 219
Dürrenmatt, Friedrich, 1, 3, 4, 25, 28,
  30, **41–56** passim, 106, 109, 116,
  119, 235, 240, 247
  Es steht geschrieben (1947), 43
  Der Richter und sein Henker (1952),
  28
  Die Stadt. Prosa I–IV (1952), 28, 34,
  51
  Der Verdacht (1953), 28
  Ein Engel kommt nach Babylon (1953),
  51
  Der Besuch der alten Dame (1956), 42,
  51
  Die Physiker (1962), 25, 42, 44, 51
  Der Meteor (1965), 45, 51
  Die Wiedertäufer (1966), 45
  'Zur Dramaturgie der Schweiz'
  (1968/70), 41

Play Strindberg (1969), 45
Monstervortrag über Gerechtigkeit und
  Recht (1969), 50, 109
Porträt eines Planeten (1970), 45
Der Mitmacher (1972), 45
Zusammenhänge. Essay über Israel
  (1976), 45
Der Mitmacher. Ein Komplex (1976),
  50
Stoffe I–III (1981), 34, 51
Achterloo (1983), 52, 53
Justiz (1985), 34, 53–4
Minotaurus (1985), 53
Die Welt als Labyrinth (1986), 52
Rollenspiele (1986), 53
Der Auftrag (1986), 34, 54
Durcheinandertal (1989), 34, 55
Turmbau. Stoffe IV–IX (1990), 51–2
Duttweiler, Gottlieb, 13

Edison, Thomas, 236
Edward VIII, 148
Eggimann, Ernst, 128
Einstein, Albert, 152
Eluard, Paul, 134
Enzensberger, Hans Magnus, 59
Erne, Werner, 191

Farner, Konrad, 107
Federspiel, Jürg, 2
  Orangen und Tode (1961), 29
Flaubert, Gustave
  Bouvard et Pécuchet, 129
Fontane, Theodor
  Der Stechlin, 197
Franklin, Benjamin, 52
Franzetti, Dante Andrea, 25, 228,
  231–2, 233, 237, 247–8
  Der Großvater (1985), 232
  Cosimo und Hamlet (1967), 31, 232,
  233
Freud, Sigmund, 150
  Das Unbehagen in der Kultur, 95
Frisch, Max, 1, 3, 4, 14, 20, 25, 28,
  30, **41–56** passim, 70, 106, 109, 125,
  134, 176, 195, 225, 240, 248
  Jürg Reinhart (1934), 42
  Blätter aus dem Brotsack (1940), 48
  Tagebuch 1946–1949 (1950), 27, 28,
  45, 46
  Stiller (1954), 25, 27–8, 28, 43, 43–4,
  47, 59, 227, 228
  Biedermann und die Brandstifter (1958),
  42

Index

Andorra (1961), 42, 45
Mein Name sei Gantenbein (1964), 45, 47, 131, 180, 234
Öffentlichkeit als Partner (1967), 26
Biografie (1967), 45
Wilhelm Tell für die Schule (1971), 30, 46, 48
Tagebuch 1966–1971 (1972), 45, 46
Dienstbüchlein (1974), 29, 30, 48
Montauk (1975), 46–7, 158
Triptychon (1978), 47
Der Mensch erscheint im Holozän (1979), 47, 48, 129
Blaubart (1982), 34, 48
Schweiz ohne Armee? Ein Palaver (1989), 26, 34, 48

Ganz, Raffael
   Orangentraum (1961), 29
de Gaulle, Charles, 26
Geiser, Christoph, 4, 28, 31, **156–70**, 248
   Zimmer mit Frühstück (1975), 156, 157–8, 160, 162, 163
   Grünsee (1978), 31, 36, 156, 158–60, 162, 163, 165
   Brachland (1980), 31, 156, 160–3, 164, 165
   Wüstenfahrt (1984), 156, 153–66
   Das geheime Fieber (1987), 156, 166–8
Glauser, Friedrich, 27
Goethe, Johann Wolfgang von, 93, 101
   Faust II, 142
Gomringer, Eugen, 120, 126
   Konstellationen (1953), 24
Gotthelf, Jeremias, 3, 36, 124, 146
Grass, Günter, 59
   Die Blechtrommel, 97
Greising, Franziska
   Kammerstille (1983), 33
Guggenheim, Kurt
   Alles in allem (1955), 25
Guisan, Henri, 8, 70
Gwerder, Alexander Xaver, 120

Hänny, Reto, 25, 229
   Zürich, Anfang September (1981), 226
Hamsun, Knut, 152
Hartmann, Lukas, 225, 226, 227
   Pestalozzis Berg (1976), 31
   Gebrochenes Eis (1980), 27, 225, 228
Hasler, Eveline, 33
Hegel, Friedrich, 146
Heidegger, Martin, 153

   Sein und Zeit, 146
Heine, Heinrich, 180
Hesse, Hermann, 152
Heym, Georg, 206
Hitler, Adolf, 8, 41, 42, 50, 103
Hockney, David, 168
Hoffer, Klaus, 230
Hofmannsthal, Hugo von, 62, 142
Hohler, Franz, 28
Horace, 152
Houdini, Harry, 193, 200
Hürlimann, Thomas, 228, **231**, 248
   Die Tessinerin (1981), 33, 231
   Das Gartenhaus (1989), 33, 231
Hus, Jan, 52
Hutmacher, Rahel, 35

Imboden, Max, 14
Inglin, Meinrad, 3
   Schweizerspiegel (1938), 25
Ingold, Felix Philipp, 36, 228
Innerhofer, Franz, 230

Jaruzelski, Wojciech, 52
Johansen, Hanna, 35
Joyce, James, 89
   Ulysses, 110, 192
Jünger, Ernst, 152

Kafka, Franz, 148, 150, 151, 152, 153, 218
   Amerika, 154
Kant, Immanuel, 51, 146, 147, 148, 150, 152
   Kritik der reinen Vernunft, 147
Kaplan, Cora, 219
Karpf, Urs, 227
   Der Technokrat (1977), 34
   Die Versteinerung (1981), 34
Kauer, Walther
   Spätholz (1976), 35
Keats, John, 235
Keller, Gottfried, 3, 93, 124, 152, 188, 241
   Der grüne Heinrich, 31
   Martin Salander, 229
   Romeo und Julia auf dem Dorfe, 65
   Zürcher Novellen, 75
Kerr, Charlotte, 52, 53
Kierkegaard, Søren, 43, 51
   Either/Or, 54
Kleist, Heinrich von, 148, 198
   Michael Kohlhaas, 67
Kopp, Elisabeth, 20

Index

Konrad, Marcel, 35, 227, **230–1**, 248
  Stoppelfelder (1983), 230
  Erzählzeit (1984), 36, 230–1
Kreuzer, Franz, 52
Kristeva, Julia, 182, 218
Kroetz, Franz Xaver, 230
  Stallerhof, 206
Kunert, Günter, 59

Laederach, Jürg, 228
  Einfall der Dämmerung (1974), 36
  69 Arten den Blues zu spielen (1984), 36
Lacan, Jacques, 210
La Fontaine, Jean de, 117
Lang, Fritz
  Metropolis, 208
Lenz, Siegfried
  Deutschstunde, 97
Lessing, Gotthold Ephraim
  Nathan der Weise, 50
Leutenegger, Gertrud, 4, **202–21**, 228, 235, 248
  Vorabend (1975), 32, 33, 169, 202, 203, 203–6, 210, 217, 219
  Nineve (1977), 202, 206–8, 209, 210, 212, 218
  Lebewohl, Gute Reise (1980), 203, 211, 218
  Gouverneur (1981), 203, 209–11, 218
  Komm ins Schiff (1983), 203, 217, 218
  Das verlorene Monument (1985), 203, 212
  Kontinent (1985), 35, 202, 203, 211–14, 217, 218
  Meduse (1988), 202, 214–17, 218, 219
Linsmayer, Charles, 27
Loetscher, Hugo, 3, 35, 45, **106–18**, 237, 240, 249
  Abwässer (1963), 109, 110, 111–12, 113
  Die Kranzflechterin (1964), 29, 111, 112–13
  Noah (1967), 113–14
  Der Immune (1975, 1985), 26, 32, 107, 108, 111, 115–16
  Wunderwelt (1979), 114
  Herbst in der großen Orange (1982), 114–15
  Der Waschküchenschlüssel und andere Helvetica (1983, 1988), 108
  Die Papiere des Immunen (1986), 32, 115, 116
  Vom Erzählen erzählen (1988), 106

Die Fliege und die Suppe (1989), 110, 116–17
Lyotard, Jean-François, 218

Mangold, Christoph
  Konzert für Papagei (1969), 36
Mann, Thomas, 149, 150
  Buddenbrooks, 197
  Der Zauberberg, 149–50
Marchi, Otto
  Schweizer Geschichte für Ketzer (1971), 26, 30
  Rückfälle (1978), 31
Marti, Kurt, 3, 14, 62, 111, **119–37**, 249–50
  republikanische gedichte (1959), 120–1, 122
  Dorfgeschichten (1960), 29, 124
  gedichte am rand (1963), 122–3
  Die Schweiz und ihre Schriftsteller (1966), 26
  rosa loui (1967), 126–8
  leichenreden (1969), 122, 123–4, 126
  Abratzky oder Die kleine Brockhütte (1971), 128–9
  heil-vetia (1971), 121–2
  undereinisch (1973), 126, 128
  Zum Beispiel Bern 1972 (1973), 27, 129–30
  Die Riesin (1975), 131–2
  abendland (1980), 132–4, 136
  Bürgerliche Geschichten (1981), 124–5
  Zärtlichkeit und Schmerz (1981), 132
  Ruhe und Ordnung (1984), 125
  Nachtgeschichten (1987), 132, 134
  Mein barfüßig Lob (1987), 134–5, 136
Marx, Karl, 52, 146
Matter, Mani, 128
Mehr, Mariella
  steinzeit (1981), 231
Meienberg, Niklaus, 2, 26
  Die Erschiessung des Ernst S (1974), 29
  Die Welt als Wille und Wahn (1987), 32
Meier, Gerhard, 2, 35
  Der schnurgerade Kanal (1977), 32
  Toteninsel (1979), 28
  Borodino (1982), 28
  Die Ballade vom Schneien (1985), 28
Meier, Helen, 34
Meier, Herbert, 2
Mettler, Clemens
  Glasberg (1968), 36

Index

Meyer, Conrad Ferdinand, 3, 52
Meyer, E. Y., 4, 28, 30, 35, 45,
  141–55, 234, 250
  Ein Reisender in Sachen Umsturz
    (1972), 142, 146
  In Trubschachen (1973), 29, 30, 31,
    32, 143–50, 153, 154, 227
  Eine entfernte Ähnlichkeit (1975), 150
  Die Rückfahrt (1977), 27, 32, 35, 148,
    149, 150–3, 232, 235
  Die Hälfte der Erfahrung (1980), 149
  Plädoyer (1982), 144, 149
  Das Naturtheater (unpublished),
    153–4
Meylan, Elisabeth, 28
Montaigne, Michel de, 65
Morrison, Toni
  Beloved, 219
Mozart, Wolfgang Amadeus
  Die Zauberflöte, 96
Müller, Heiner
  Hamletmaschine, 218
Muschg, Adolf, 2, 3, 26, 28, 35, 44,
  45, **97–105**, 250–1
  Im Sommer des Hasen (1965), 93,
    96–7, 101, 104
  Gegenzauber (1967), 28, 97–8
  Fremdkörper (1968), 102
  Mitgespielt (1969), 98
  Das Kerbelgericht (1969), 100
  Liebesgeschichten (1972), 102–3
  Albissers Grund (1974), 30, 98–100,
    101, 104, 169
  Entfernte Bekannte (1976), 103
  Besuch in der Schweiz (1979), 28
  Literatur als Therapie? (1981), 93–6,
    101, 104
  Das Licht und der Schlüssel (1984),
    100–2, 104
  Der Turmhahn und andere
    Liebesgeschichten (1987), 103
Musil, Robert
  Der Mann ohne Eigenschaften, 103
Mussolini, Benito, 8, 41

Napoleon I (Bonaparte), 52
Neruda, Pablo, 134
Niederhauser, Rolf, 227
  Das Ende der bloßen Vermutung
    (1979), 226
Nietzsche, Friedrich, 90, 143, 152,
  153, 207, 208
  Unzeitgemäße Betrachtungen, 90
Nizon, Paul, 2, 35, 44, 109

Canto (1963), 36
Noll, Peter
  Diktate über Sterben und Tod
    (1984), 33
Novalis (Friedrich von Hardenberg),
  134

Pedretti, Erica, 2
  Valerie oder Das unerzogene Auge
    (1986), 33
Plato, 47, 153, 179
Proust, Marcel
  A la recherche du temps perdu, 197
Pulver, Elsbeth, 81, 192

Rabelais, François, 134
Rakusa, Ilma, 34
Richelieu, Cardinal, 52
Rieser, Ferdinand, 42
Rilke, Rainer Maria, 142
Ritschard, Willy, 74
Robespierre, Maximilien de, 52

Sartre, Jean-Paul, 26
Schaffner, Jakob, 3
Schertenleib, Hansjörg, 228, 231,
  232–3, 237, 251
  Die Ferienlandschaft (1983), 232–3
  Die Geschwister (1988), 233
Schiller, Friedrich, 172
Schlick, Moritz, 146
Schmid, Karl, 24, 237
Schmidli, Werner, 2, 28, 30, 31, 156
  Fundplätze (1974), 31, 169
Schneider, Hansjörg, 2
  Lieber Leo (1980), 31, 169, 225
Schriber, Margrit, 4, 28, **171–83**, 251
  Aussicht gerahmt (1976), 171, 177,
    179
  Ausser Saison (1977), 175
  Kartenhaus (1978), 173, 174, 180
  Ein Platz am Seitenpodest (1978), 175
  Vogel flieg! (1980), 177, 180
  Luftwurzeln (1981), 180
  Muschelgarten (1984), 173, 174, 175,
    176
  Tresorschatten (1987), 173, 174, 176,
    178–9
  AugenWeiden (1990), 182–3
Schwarzenbach, James, 15, 16, 129
Shakespeare, William
  Hamlet, 218
Späth, Gerold, 2, 28, 30, 34, 35, 229
  Commedia (1980), 33

Spitteler, Carl, 24
Staiger, Emil, 25, 44
Stefan, Verena, 182
  Häutungen (1975), 33
Steiner, Jörg, 2
  Strafarbeit (1962), 29
Sterchi, Beat
  Blösch (1983), 27, 28, 34, 35, 227,
  229
Stifter, Adalbert, 148, 152
  Der Hochwald, 216
  Der Nachsommer, 149, 153
Stoker, Bram, 101
Storz, Claudia
  Jessica mit Konstruktionsfehlern (1977),
  33
Stramm, August, 124
Sulzer, Alain Claude
  Das Erwachsenengerüst (1983), 231
Swift, Jonathan, 152
  Gulliver's Travels, 153

Tolstoy, Leo, 146
Trakl, Georg, 134

Unseld, Siegfried, 148

Varlin (Willy Guggenheim), 45, 107
Villard, Arthur, 43
Vogt, Walter, 2, 28

Wälterlin, Oskar, 42
Wagner, Richard, 152
Walesa, Lech, 52
Walser, Martin, 83
Walser, Robert, 3, 26, 30, 148, 228,
  234
  'Räuber'-Roman, 234
Walter, Otto F., 3, 14, 29, 36, 45,
  59–73, 251
  Der Stumme (1959), 25, 29, 59–61,
  72
  Herr Tourel (1962), 61–2, 64, 66, 67,
  72
  Die ersten Unruhen (1972), 30, 63–4,
  65, 66

  Die Verwilderung (1977), 64–6, 68,
  225
  Wie wird Beton zu Gras (1979), 66–7,
  70
  *Das Staunen der Schlafwandler am
  Ende der Nacht* (1983), 32, 67–70
  Gegenwort (1988), 59
  Zeit des Fasans (1988), 31, 59, 68,
  70–2
Wechsler, Daniel
  Ein Haus zu wohnen (1961), 29
Weigel, Sigrid, 217
Wenger, Rosalie
  Rosalia G – Ein Leben (1978), 32,
  231
Widmer, Urs, 2, 28, 30
  Schweizer Geschichten (1975), 28, 35
Wiesner, Heinrich
  Schauplätze (1969), 29
  Notennot (1973), 30
  Der Riese am Tisch (1978), 31
Wille, Ulrich, 32
Wilson, Robert, 218
Wolf, Christa
  Nachdenken über Christa T., 219
  Kassandra, 211, 212
Wyss, Laure
  Frauen-Protokolle aus der Schweiz
  (1974), 32

Yeats, W. B., 120

Ziegler, Jean, 17
Zollinger, Albin, 27
Zopfi, Emil, 227
  Jede Minute kostet 33 Franken (1977),
  34
  Computer für tausendeine Nächte
  (1980), 34
Zorn, Fritz
  Mars (1977), 27, 33, 44, 95, 96, 228
Zschokke, Matthias, 35, 228, **233–4**,
  251
  Max (1982), 36, 233, 234
  Prinz Hans (1984), 233
  ErSieEs (1986), 233, 234